Do-Good Boy

Also by Jerry Bledsoe

The World's Number One, Flat-Out, All-Time Great Stock Car Racing Book (1975)

You Can't Live on Radishes (1976)

Just Folks: Visitin' With Carolina People (1980)

Where's Mark Twain When We Really Need Him (1981)

Carolina Curiosities, Jerry Bledsoe's Outlandish Guide to the Dadblamedest Things to See and Do in North Carolina (1984)

From Whalebone to Hot House: A Journey Along North Carolina's Longest Highway, U.S. 64 (1986)

Bitter Blood: A True Story of Southern Family Pride, Madness, and Multiple Murder (1988)

Country Cured: Reflections from the Heart (1989)

Bare-Bottomed Skier: And Other Unlikely Tales (1990)

North Carolina Curiosities: Jerry Bledsoe's Outlandish Guide to the Dablamedest Things to See and Do in North Carolina (revised second edition) (1990)

Blood Games: A True Account of Family Murder (1991)

Blue Horizons: Faces and Places from a Bicycle Journey Along the Blue Ridge Parkway (1993)

Before He Wakes: A True Story of Money, Marriage, Sex and Murder (1994)

The Angel Doll: A Christmas Story (1996)

Death Sentence: The True Story of Velma Barfield's Life, Crimes, and Execution (1998)

A Gift of Angels: Sequel to the Angel Doll (1999)

Partial to Home: A Memoir of the Heart (with Bob Timberlake, 1999)

Death by Journalism: One Teacher's Fateful Encounter with Political Correctness (2001)

Built on a Rock: A Memoir of Faith, Family and Place (with Jerry D. Neal, 2005)

Fire in The Belly: Building A World-leading High-tech Company From Scratch In Tumultuous Times (with Jerry D. Neal, 2005)

Do-Good Boy: An Unlikely Writer Confronts the '60s and Other Indignities (2018)

Books in which Jerry Bledsoe's work also appears

Kays Gary, Columnist, A Collection of His Writings Compiled by His friends, East Woods Press, 1981

Our Words, Our Ways, Reading and Writing in North Carolina, Sally Buckner, Carolina Academic Press, 1991

Creative Writing Cooking, Recipes from the Authors You Love, Down Home Press, edited by Nancy Gotter Gates, 1994

Pete & Shirley, The Great Tar Heel Novel, edited by David Perkins, Down Home Press, in association with Raleigh News & Observer, 1995

Close to Home, Revelations and Reminiscences by North Carolina Authors, edited by Lee Harrison Child, John F. Blair, Publisher, 1996

An Outer Banks Reader, edited by David Stick, University of North Carolina Press, 1998

No Hiding Place, Uncovering the Legacy of Charlotte-area Writers, edited by Frye Gaillard, Amy Rogers and Robert Inman, Down Home Press in association with Charlotte, Mecklenburg Public Library, 1999

Novello, Ten Years of Great American Writing, edited by Amy Rogers, Robert Inman and Frye Gaillard, Down Home Press in association with Charlotte, Mecklenburg Public Library, 2000

Making Notes, Music of the Carolinas, edited by Ann Wicker, Novello Press, 2008

Sports in the Carolinas, From Death Valley to Tobacco Road, edited by Ed Southern, Novello Press, 2009

Do-Good Boy

*An Unlikely Writer Confronts the '60s
and Other Indignities*

Jerry Bledsoe

Copyright © Jerry Bledsoe
All Rights Reserved. No part of this book may be reproduced or transmitted in any form or by any means, electronic or mechanical, including photocopying, recording, or by any information storage and retrieval system, without permission in writing from the publisher except for the inclusion of brief quotations in a review.

Paperback edition: ISBN 978-0-9983028-5-0
Book and cover design by Angie Dobbs
The text was set in New Century Schoolbook

First Printed Edition January 2019
Scruffy City Press
Austin, TX
https://scruffycitypress.com

1

IF I WASN'T OVERCOME by anxiety I surely would be by sweat. Obviously, this was not a good condition to be in at this moment, but I was trapped. There was nothing I could do about it.

The anxiety was partly due to an overlong northbound Southern Railway freight train that was laboriously blocking my path and threatening to make me late for my appointment, the main source of my anxiety.

The sweat was primarily from a blisteringly hot mid-August morning that would turn into a torturous afternoon, not unusual in North Carolina at this time of year. It already had overwhelmed the deodorant I had caked in my armpits in the hope of making an impression unaffected by body odor. The tattered tan blazer I was wearing with a black Army-issue tie knotted under the collar of my lone long-sleeve white dress shirt clearly wasn't helping the deodorant any.

I kept checking my watch as the clangorous bells, flashing red warning lights and overwhelming rumble of box cars and tankers rattled my brain. The train stretched as far as I could see. My fingers beat impatiently on the steering wheel. If only I had departed ten minutes earlier, I kept telling myself, I wouldn't be in this fix.

My destination, an indistinct row of red-brick buildings, would have been in sight if the train wasn't blocking my view. The back of the buildings faced the railroad tracks about 100 yards away. I only needed to get to the front door, but from the looks of this train that might take half an hour. And my appointment was in five minutes.

I had little doubt that this probably was my last shot at a dream that had begun to foment a few years earlier. That was about a year after I had joined the Army at 18. It was an unexpected dream, surprising in a way because it was so unlikely considering my background, but somehow it stuck and refused to go away despite the overwhelming odds against it.

After barely escaping the Army with an honorable discharge only a year and a half earlier, I had exerted enormous effort in several states to find a newspaper writing job, only to be met by failure. I had decided to make one last desperate attempt by going to a private employment agency that would confiscate my first three weeks' pay if I landed a job.

My assigned counselor knew nothing about the newspaper business but had managed to arrange three interviews on a single day, all the free time my job would allow. Each interview was about 50 miles apart, the first at 10:00, the second at 1:00, third at 4:00. If I blew this, I figured, I likely would spend the rest of my days as a Biff Burger manager, my current position. Tasty though 15-cent, Roto-broiled Biff Burgers with secret sauce and reconstituted onions were, that was not an appealing or promising prospect.

Just as I was about to give in to despair, I thought I spotted a pale hint of caboose red looming far down the track, and miracle of miracles, it turned out to be real. As soon as the tail of the caboose slipped past, I hit the throttle of my recently acquired 1961 black Austin-Healy Sprite convertible (the first non-bug-eyed version of that tiny English sports car), bounced across the railroad tracks as the hands of my watch slipped to 10:00 and took a quick right turn—only to discover that there was no on-street parking near the series of attached, windowless brick buildings that proclaimed themselves to be *The Daily Independent* in big white letters over white double entrance doors.

But just beyond these buildings, in a slight depression fast by the railroad tracks, I discovered an unpaved parking lot lined with scraggly trees offering only spotty shade. I whipped into the lot, kicking up a whirlwind of dust, slid to a halt beside a pickup truck and began the arduous task of unfolding my lanky, six-foot-three frame from this low-slung envelope of a car that not only clearly wasn't designed for the likes of me but also called into grave question my judgment for acquiring it.

Rumpled, sweat-stained, my hair wildly windblown, I snatched up a manila folder containing a meager collection of my published articles and dashed for the entrance.

The middle-aged woman behind the reception counter seemed startled, maybe a little alarmed, by the frantic, scrambled-haired person who had just rushed through the door.

"Can I help you?" she asked, a bit tentatively.

"Uh," I said, trying to settle my brain. "I have an appointment with...."

The name suddenly eluded me, and I had left the paper with the editor's name on it in the car.

"Uh, uh..." I said, panic beginning to stir.

She waited expectantly, but was taking on a look that indicated she had begun to suspect that I was one of those crazies with screwball stories to tell who so regularly were drawn to newspaper offices.

"Wingate!" I nearly cried out with relief. "Wingate. Tom Wingate."

"And your name?" she asked.

"Bledsoe. Uh...Jerry...Jerry."

"Jerry Jerry Bledsoe?" she asked teasingly.

"No, just one Jerry."

"Okay, Just One Jerry," she said with a little smile, "I'll go let him know that you're here."

While she was gone, I wiped the sweat from my brow, patted down my hair, buttoned my jacket to hide a pale mustard stain on my shirt, straightened my tie and made sure my clippings were still in their folder, all the time attempting to calm myself, although I had no grasp of how to accomplish that.

"He can see you now," the woman said when she reappeared around the corner. I followed her into the small newsroom.

Six desks filled the room, only one unoccupied. *The Daily Independent* was an afternoon paper and deadline was looming. Two reporters were tapping intently at old Royal typewriters. Between them, a heavy-set man with a florid face was talking loudly, almost angrily, into a telephone receiver. A short, bushy-haired older man with a wearied look sat across from the three, muttering to himself as he laid out pages and scribbled headlines. A fedora hung on a hat rack behind him.

Tom Wingate, the editor, had no office. He worked in the newsroom, his desk facing the rest of the staff, his back to the composing room wall beyond which impatient typesetters waited. He was marking copy when we entered the room. He was 52, tall, with a slight paunch, his hair thinning. His shirt sleeves were rolled up, collar unbuttoned, tie pulled loose and slightly askew. He stood when he saw us coming, peered over the top of his glasses, and offered his hand as I approached. His eyes were as kind as any I'd ever seen.

"Welcome to Kannapolis," he said. "Have you been here before?"

"Only passing through," I told him. "Usually on Trailways buses when I was in the Army."

"It's an interesting town," he said.

"I'm sorry I'm late. I got held up by a freight train."

"Happens all the time here," he replied, waving off my apology and inviting me to sit in an ancient wooden office chair with a rounded back beside his desk, a chair obviously designed to shorten visits. The scant resume that the employment agency had mailed to him was lying on his desk and he glanced at it.

"So you were in the Army," he said.

I didn't know then that Wingate had been an officer with a tank battalion in World War II, had fought in North Africa and Italy, twice been wounded, was captured and spent a year in prisoner of war camps in Germany and Poland. My Army experience had not been so distinctive.

"Yes, sir. Three years. I joined."

That still was considered an asset in those days and only later would I realize how important an impression it made on Wingate.

"Where did you serve?"

"Well, Fort Jackson for basic; Fort Slocum, New York, for Information School; Fort Rucker, Alabama, where I worked on the post newspaper, *The Army Flier*; then Fort Bragg for psychological warfare training, and finally Okinawa, Taiwan and Japan."

I wanted to appear as if I'd had some experience beneficial to journalism.

"Were you writing overseas?"

"At first just leaflets and reports, but for six months near the end I wrote features for Korean- and Japanese-language magazines in Tokyo. They were supposed to make Koreans and Japanese love America."

"Did you bring clips?"

"I did," I said, handing him the thin folder.

It included articles I had written for a magazine called *Freedom* about John Glenn's first orbital flight, the future of the space program, Secretary of State Dean Rusk's ties to the Korean War, and profiles of Ernest Hemingway, Mark Twain and Robert Frost for a series called "Modern American Authors."

On top was an article from *The Army Flier*. It was about a surgeon at Fort Rucker who had invented new, more precise devices for monitoring and testing the heart and had been assigned to the space program. That article had appeared in *The Montgomery Advertiser*, *The Birmingham News* and *The Ledger-Enquirer* in Columbus, Georgia, three newspapers that regularly received news releases from Fort Rucker's Public Information Office. One of them posted it on the Associated Press wire and it was distributed nationwide. I got no byline but it was my work and I was proud of it. I was 19 when I wrote it.

Wingate shuffled through the short stack of articles but read a large portion of the piece about the heart surgeon.

"That's a good lead," he said.

I thought so too. So much so that I had set it to memory. I could have recited it to him:

"This country's first man into outer space will be only a heartbeat away from an Army Aviation Center physician who has worked closely with the famed astronauts since the project began."

"Let me tell you our problem here," Wingate said. "We need an all-around reporter, somebody who can take obits, write news stories and features. But I also want somebody who can focus on religion. Our coverage of religion is slack. How would you feel about that?"

I was a little taken aback. My experiences in the Army, and friends I'd made who were far more sophisticated than I, had led me not only to question my Methodist upbringing but all religion. Intellectually, I no longer could embrace it. But neither could I deny it. I had become agnostic, a heathen, as one of my religious friends jokingly tagged me. Yet I respected those who held sincere religious beliefs, whatever they may be, although I had little regard for charlatans and dangerous fanatics.

"I could do that," I said.

"When could you start?"

When could I start?

Was he offering me the job?

I must have looked startled because I was, although I tried not to show it.

"Well," I said hesitantly. "I would have to give a two-week notice."

"The sooner the better," he said with a little smile. "But don't you think we need to talk about pay?"

"Well..."

"It's seventy-five a week," he said bluntly. "I suspect you're making more than that."

I was but my salary depended on sales.

"I do," I said, "but I also have to work 60 hours a week, sometimes more."

"If you're accustomed to those kind of hours you'll fit in well here," Wingate said, reaching for a desk calendar.

"I expect you'll need a little time to find a place to live and get settled in," he said, flipping through the calendar.

"I'm sure I will," I said quickly.

"Well, then, why don't we shoot on you starting on Monday, September the seventh? That'll be your desk over there."

I couldn't believe this was happening. It didn't strike me that Wingate may have just been desperate. I was in a daze of wonderment. I had a newspaper job! At a real newspaper! I couldn't wait to get outside. I wanted to shout. It was almost enough to make me a Methodist again.

As soon as I managed to fold myself back into my tight Sprite, I went in search of a telephone booth. Using a handful of nickels and dimes, I called editors in Gastonia and Statesville to let them know that I wouldn't be making my appointments. I had landed a position. Neither seemed troubled by the news.

Then I called Linda, my bride of little more than a month. We had moved into a new apartment only two weeks earlier.

"We're moving," I told her.

"Again?" she said. "Where?"

"Kannapolis."

I had just turned 23 and was about to start a journalism career in one of the country's oddest and quirkiest towns, a life-changing moment that would thrust me into some of the most ghastly scenes of an already turbulent decade and eventually lead me to become a bestselling author, a possibility that neither I nor anybody who had known me likely could have conceived.

2

If the Thomasville High School Class of 1959 had decided to even things out when choosing class superlatives and also pick the opposites, whatever that word may be (inferioratives?), I might have had a chance to get my photo featured in *The Growler*, our yearbook, so named because our school mascot was a bulldog.

I have little doubt that would have been the case if there had been a category for "Least Likely to Become a Writer." I'm sure most of my classmates would have voted me the honor, not to mention my English teachers, all of whom had flunked me or passed me grudgingly with a U (unsatisfactory), in part because I never wrote term papers or book reports.

As it happened, I wasn't allowed to graduate with my class because I had to attend summer school again with the other misfits, all from lower grades. The person in charge of summer school that year was Lee Miller, the biology teacher, a short, dark-haired man whose thick glasses tended to hide the frequent merriment in his eyes. He was known as Bugs & Flowers Miller, because every student at THS was required to attend his 10th grade class and had to collect and classify 50 bugs and 50 wildflowers. I don't recall completing that project, but he passed me anyway and long after high school we became friends.

I can't remember what I was supposed to be studying in that particular summer school session. I think it may have been some required math course that I failed to take, or just failed. It's hard to remember because I wasn't doing any course work at all.

I was instead concentrating on a talent I had fooled myself into thinking I possessed. I had enjoyed drawing for years and thought that art, in some form, might be my future.

The only laudatory recognition I received in high school came because of an art teacher. Without my knowledge, she submitted to some obscure competition a colored pencil drawing of an exotic and unrecognizable species of bird that I had done in class and it received a citation.

A couple of months before the end of my senior year, I went to our local newspaper, *The Thomasville Times*, and talked the editor, Wint Capel, into letting me start an unpaid weekly feature called "T'ville Teen." I would select a person I deemed worthy of recognition, collect a few basic facts and sketch an ink resemblance. My selection process tended to favor pretty girls whose attention I hoped to gain. Unfortunately, my drawings never were as attractive as they were and failed to produce the desired results. I soon lost interest and the feature ended with the school year.

Before summer school started, I sent off for a mail-order course in cartooning that I had seen advertised on a match book cover. "Can you draw this?" it asked above a simple drawing that almost anybody could reproduce. You could send in your drawing for a free evaluation, which I did. I was informed that I had done an exceptional job and clearly had a bright future in cartooning. All I had to do was submit a $15 postal money order to get started. I spent my entire summer school session drawing cartoon-like images that collected increasing praise from my distant, anonymous instructors—along with regular requests for additional money orders.

One day as summer school was waning I was summoned to the office by Bugs & Flowers Miller. I didn't know what to expect but I feared I would be kicked out for doing none of the expected work. He handed me a thick envelope and instructed me to open it. Inside, much to my surprise, was a diploma.

"You better get out of here before we change our minds," he said with a grin.

I got out. Fast.

A new high school had been constructed on the edge of town, and beautiful old Main Street School, which once had housed grades 1-12, and which I had entered in first grade, was about to become a junior high (sadly, it later would be demolished). I proudly hold the honor of being the last person to graduate from that school, the lone member of the Class of '59 ½. It simplifies reunions.

Despite possessing a document confirming that I supposedly was minimally educated, my prospects weren't exactly promising. College was out of question because of my miserable grades, my family's finances and other problems, as well as my lack of interest. I hadn't even considered it. I had a job for the second summer in a row at the Dairy Queen on National Highway beside the Do-Putt-In miniature golf course and across the street from my family's rented house. But the Dairy Queen closed for winter at the end of October and didn't reopen until spring. And I would be out of work with no money.

Thomasville, then a town of about 15,000 in the center of North Carolina near the cities of High Point, Winston-Salem and Greensboro, is called the

Chair City. A huge concrete replica of a Duncan Phyfe chair, one of the styles made in the town's numerous furniture factories in the past, still stands by the mainline railroad tracks in the town square, which actually is rectangular. In 1960 Lyndon Johnson, the vice presidential candidate, campaigning by train, climbed a ladder into that chair to have his picture taken waving his Stetson. It appeared nationally. Furniture factories were the source of most jobs in Thomasville, and some of my former classmates in the required woodworking class already had gone to work in them. I knew instinctively that factory work was not for me. But just what kind of work might be for me remained a haunting mystery.

That winter, I decided to go to Miami. I had relatives there who were willing to harbor me for a short period. My hope was to find a job that would enable me to enroll in art school. It turned out that there was an art school in Miami but the tuition was well beyond my means. The only job offer I got was selling vacuum cleaners door to door. My one-day attempt at that produced zero income. My dad had to send me money for a bus ticket home. Some of my friends derisively called me Do-Good Boy after I returned penniless and without prospects.

I discovered that my buddy, Darrell Hall, who had accompanied me to Miami for the early part of my stay, had decided to join the Navy, in which his older brother was serving. We both were aware that we were facing the draft and that those who weren't in college, or some other school, would be taken much sooner. Joining any of the services meant serving more time but with better duty and training that might provide lucrative civilian jobs later.

I accompanied Darrell to the post office where the military recruiting offices were, but I had no interest in joining the Navy. I couldn't swim, and the one time I'd ventured onto the ocean in a fishing boat I got deathly seasick.

While Darrell was talking to the Navy man, I was whiling away time in the lobby looking at FBI wanted posters. As fate would have it, an Army recruiter came out of his office and approached me. His name was Coon. He wore it on a metal tag. He was a staff sergeant. He asked what I was up to.

"Just waiting on my friend to join the Navy," I told him.

"What do you have in mind for yourself?" he asked.

"Well, I'm hoping to go to art school."

"You know the Army has the best art schools in the world," he said.

"Really?" My surprise was evident in my voice.

"Sure does," he said. "Why don't you come in here and let me give you a couple of tests to see if you're qualified for enlistment."

"I don't do very well on tests," I warned him.

"We'll see," he said.

I breezed right through those suckers. I looked on in awe as he graded them, making dramatic check mark after check mark.

"Perfect," he said, turning his attention back to me. "Not only are you qualified, but I believe you could become an officer."

I was stunned at the news and must have shown it.

He went on to tell me that he'd enlisted some of my classmates who already had finished their training and still were only privates. If I became an officer, returned home on visits and encountered them, they'd have to salute me, he pointed out. I could savor that.

"And, you know, women are really attracted to officers," he noted. "They always get the best looking women."

That sealed it. I was going to become an Army officer artist.

"Have you heard of the buddy plan?" Coon asked.

"No, what's that?"

"If your friend in there decided to go into the Army instead of the Navy, y'all could go on the buddy plan and stay together. What's he interested in?"

"Finance, I think. He talked about going to finance school."

"There's no better finance school anywhere than the Army's," Coon assured me.

He encouraged me to interrupt Darrell's meeting with the Navy recruiter and tell him I needed to speak to him outside. I did.

A few days later we were on a bus heading to the induction station in Charlotte on the buddy plan, our educations and futures assured. After filling out endless forms and enduring grueling written tests, we spent the rest of the day waiting mostly naked in long slow lines to be probed, tapped, drained and have the audio of our innards thoroughly assessed. Darrell sailed right through the physical exams, but I was pulled aside and informed that I had a problem.

I weighed only 139 pounds, and at 6'3" that didn't meet the Army's standard for height and weight. I was going to have to return home and gain some weight before I could enlist. I knew that wasn't going to be easy. When I worked at the Dairy Queen, in the hope of adding weight enough to attract girls, I spooned down a thick chocolate malt and a large hot fudge sundae with bananas, walnuts and whipped cream every day without gaining an ounce. I did grow some specimen pimples though.

Darrell was in a group waiting to be sworn in when I came up to tell him I had failed the physical and they were sending me back home.

"Well, I'm going too," he said. "We're on the buddy plan."

When the Trailways local stopped in front of my house to let us off that night, I noticed an Army sedan in the driveway. Sgt. Coon emerged from it.

"Boys, there's been a big mistake," he told us. "But I've taken care of it. You've got to go back."

He already had prepared vouchers for bus tickets.

If we hadn't done that our lives likely would have taken very different courses, but that possibility didn't occur to me then. We returned. The date was February 29, 1960, Leap Year Day. This time I discovered that my height had shrunk and my weight increased enough to meet the minimum requirements. An overnight miracle had occurred, no thick malts or hot fudge sundaes required.

After we were sworn in and waiting on a bus to haul us off to basic training at Ft. Jackson, near South Carolina's capital, Columbia, I was informed that the major who commanded the induction facility needed to see me. Why me? I wondered. Had the dishonesty edited into my medical records been noticed? Was I about to be discharged after less than an hour in the Army and sent packing again?

No. I was just about to get my second lesson in Army fraud. The major was seated behind his desk, which was strewn with books and documents, including my enlistment papers and the results of the tests I had taken.

"It says here that you signed up for art school," he said.

"Yes, sir," I replied. "I'm really looking forward to it."

"Well, we've been checking but we haven't been able to find an Army art school," he said. "We're going to assign you to Information School at Fort Slocum, New York. We think they may deal with art up there."

I had no idea what Information School entailed, whether I might be interested in it, or capable of it. But it wasn't as if I had a say about it. I was dismissed. The decision had been made. I couldn't have conceived it then, but that quick act by a stranger would allow me to discover abilities unknown and set the direction for the rest of my life.

3

THE CONTRASTS BETWEEN Fort Jackson, where I had suffered through basic training, and Fort Slocum were dramatic.

Fort Jackson was a dreary, dehumanizing place with row upon row of depressingly drab, yellow, World War II-era wooden structures and grim formations of beleaguered, skinned-head trainees in olive-drab fatigues, led by sadistic drill sergeants, marching and running to cadence and shouting forced responses.

Fort Slocum was like a college campus with stately white-columned brick buildings, vast lawns and huge oaks. It was difficult for me to imagine a more beautiful military base when I first set foot on it. It was compact, just 78 acres, because it occupied Davids' Island in the western end of Long Island Sound just offshore from the pleasant, modest-sized city of New Rochelle in Westchester County, one of the wealthiest communities in America.

I had no idea what to expect when I finally reached this fort that had been built during the Civil War. I was nearly exhausted and almost in a daze. Part of my condition was because I never had been to New York City, and my arrival at the Port Authority Bus Terminal earlier that day, after a largely sleepless overnight trip from North Carolina, was overwhelming.

I had caught a train from Grand Central Station, just 16 miles from New Rochelle, and found myself at a small reception center by the docks at the end of Fort Slocum Road where a ferry made regular runs back and forth to the island.

The sergeant who took my orders made a brief presentation to me and a few other newcomers. He provided a rundown of what we could expect. We would be attending five different classes five days a week for eight weeks. If we made it through we would be awarded a 701.1 MOS (military occupational specialty) job ranking, information specialist.

"If you came here thinking you can fool around and just get by, you've got another think coming," he said sternly. "We expect you to work hard, study hard and deliver. Our expectations are high. And if you can't cut it, I can guarantee this: you'll be out of here in a flash and on your way to advanced infantry training."

He seemed to be looking straight at me when he said that, and I took it seriously. For the first time since I was in eighth grade, I intended to be a good student, although quelling my inborn rebelliousness to academic expectations and authority figures would not be easy. I don't think I'd ever been so instantly motivated. I'd already undergone enough infantry training to last a lifetime.

I soon learned that art was not among the subjects we would be studying. Those would be journalism, radio-television, public speaking, public relations, and military, United States and world affairs (MUSWA, it was called, a history course). I had little knowledge of any of these matters but intended to do all I could to master them.

Most of these classes turned out not to be difficult. Often they were interesting, although MUSWA could be a bit dull and sleep inducing. The instructors were a mix of military personnel and civilian employees who previously had worked in the fields they were teaching and seemed to love their subjects.

I was surprised that journalism, which naturally involved writing, something I always dreaded and had gone to great lengths to avoid, turned out to be relatively easy. We were taught the basics of producing news articles and the questions required for that. The five Ws, they were called, accompanied by a provisional H. Who? What? When? Where? Why? Sometimes, How? We also learned about the inverted pyramid: the most important stuff at the top, the least at the bottom. Clarity was emphasized; keep it simple.

This would be the only formal training in journalism I ever received, and thankfully it didn't seem to harm me. Most of the exercise articles were short, the subjects not complicated. I had no problems with them and got passing grades.

The class that caused me the most trouble was public speaking. I was terrified of having to stand in front of others and say something. That fear went all the way back to grammar and Sunday school. In school plays and church pageants I never had speaking roles, and for good reason—nothing would come out. When teachers called on me in class, I got flustered and remained mute until some thoughtful student raised a hand and provided an answer. When oral book reports were required, I was the shy dissenter. I just couldn't do it and sometimes got Fs for it. I dreaded this course.

The sergeant who conducted the classes was a jovial sort who must have had a wall lined with Toastmaster Awards. He gave the impression of being a top graduate of the Dale Carnegie School of Exorbitant Positive Thinking. (A few years later I would get to interview Carnegie and managed to escape unmolested by excessive positivity.) Despite all of his self-confidence, our instructor was conscious of the fear that public speaking provokes for some. He brought it up early in the first class.

This fear could be overcome, he maintained, and we would be able to deal with it. One reason for it, he said, was concern that your mind might suddenly go blank while standing in front of a group of people. This was no cause for worry, he said. It happens to everybody. And there were simple solutions for it. Just pause. Take a sip of water. Glance at your notes, if you have them, and you should. If necessary, take out your handkerchief and softly blow your nose. Your thoughts would come back.

I was more than concerned when the instructor announced that we would be called upon to speak in this first class. Everybody would have to give a three-minute talk about himself (there were no females) so we could learn a little about each other. We would start with the front row. Thank goodness, I was at the back, my usual location in any gathering where choice of seating was allowed, so I hoped I might have a chance to quell my surging panic before my turn came.

One after another, my fellow classmates got up and muttered through boring little details of their lives, none offering any evidence of becoming gifted orators. We did have one exception. An odd little Hispanic guy from Los Angeles began vividly describing his own birth, starting with unpleasant memories of his confinement within the womb. He almost got into a fetal position attempting to imitate his Houdini-like escape, squirming, wriggling and kicking. He got so caught up in it that he went well past his time limit but the instructor didn't interrupt. He finished to the only applause of the day and took a little bow.

"Well, that's a first," the instructor observed. "Next?"

I was next. How could I follow that? Fleeing wasn't an option. I wasn't even sure I could make it to the front of the class without falling on my face. Nonetheless, I got to the podium, turned to my classmates and stood there, silent, as if I were contemplating what to say or do. I noticed that off to one side was a small table with a pitcher of water and a stack of paper cups. Nobody yet had poured any water.

"My name," I said, "is...."

I looked about frantically, stepped over to the table, poured myself a cup of water and returned to the podium.

"...is...uh..."

I took a sip. A few people chuckled. I took another sip.

"...is..."

I finished off the cup, went for another, gulped it down and tossed the empty cup onto the floor. I looked at the instructor and began dramatically searching my pockets for notes that didn't exist.

Ah, but I did have a handkerchief! I whipped it out and blew my nose. Loudly. The class was laughing now. I blew and blew and blew.

"OK, OK," said the instructor, stepping to the front. "We get the point. There's a comedian in every class. But next time you get up here, you better have something to say."

I nodded and headed quickly back to my seat.

"Don't forget to pick up your litter," he called.

Amazingly, I was able to stammer my way through that class in coming weeks, but I never lost the fear that he had assured us could be so easily overcome.

ONE OF THE SUPPOSED highlights of our studies was a bus trip to New York to sit in a session at the United Nations (which turned out to be exceedingly boring) and to tour *The New York Times* (even more boring). I had expected the *Times* newsroom to be a lively place, like newsrooms I'd seen in movies, with ringing phones, clattering typewriters, shouts of "Copy boy!," people hurrying to and fro. Instead it was almost funereal.

A new intern, a fresh college graduate, conducted our tour. He was in awe of the place and seemed to find it difficult to believe that he actually was there. He stopped before closed office doors and spoke in almost reverential terms of the famous people who sat within, presumably engrossed in solemn thought. I'd never heard of any of them and never had seen a copy of *The New York Times* until I saw stacks of them at newsstands soon after my arrival in the city.

If somebody had told me then that the *Times* would one day excerpt my first book, that the book editor would praise another as "powerful and provocative," that yet another of my books would rise almost instantly to the top of the paper's bestseller list, and publisher Arthur Ochs "Punch" Sulzberger would write me a letter lauding a column I had written, I'd have thought that person insane. But all of that would happen.

AS MUCH AS I was learning in my classes, a large part of my education from my two months at Fort Slocum came on the weekends when we were free to get passes and head to the powerful magnet of Manhattan. But when your total pay comes to only $78 a month, there's not much you can afford to do in a place so expensive.

Two spots offered refuge for cash-starved people in the military. One was the USO on 45th Street, just off Times Square. There you could find a comfortable place to rest, free coffee and soft drinks, snacks, newspapers and magazines, TV, card games and other activities. You could get information about all manner of places and events in the city—and sometimes free tickets to Broadway plays and other events.

The other refuge, not only more spacious but offering more possibilities, was not as accessible to the excitement of Times Square. That was the Cardinal Spellman Servicemen's Club on Park Avenue near 58th Street. Cardinal Francis Spellman, Archbishop of New York, was the most powerful cleric in the country, with deep political connections. He also was Vicar of the Armed Forces and spent Christmas abroad with the troops, so it was understandable that he would create a club for service members in his own domain.

The place was always crowded on weekends, mainly because there was a big dance hall on the second floor where bands performed and a free Rockola jukebox played when bands weren't present. Young women from a wide area came to the dances and many romances started there. I attended one of these dances but never had the nerve to approach any young women. Timidity was one reason, another that I didn't know how to dance. As often as not, I came for the big spaghetti suppers and other free food.

THE ONLY CLASSMATE I met at Fort Slocum whose name I remember was Timothy Brownlee. That may be because he was my first black friend, and, as I recall, the only black in our class. Until I joined the Army, I'd never known a black person my age. Segregation was almost unquestioned fact in Thomasville. I have no idea why Brownlee befriended me. He was five years older, a college graduate, one of the smartest people in the class, probably the most sophisticated. After finishing college he had taken a job with Ford in South Africa but had to return when he was drafted.

Brownlee was quiet, soft spoken and didn't say much in class or the barracks. I enjoyed talking with him because he was well informed about many things and almost always interesting.

One weekend, he asked if I'd like to go to Birdland. I had no idea what Birdland was. I thought it must be an exotic aviary.

"What kind of birds do they have there?" I asked.

He laughed. "Well, I guess I'd have to say a great many black birds," he said. "It's a jazz club."

He couldn't believe that the only jazz I'd ever experienced was when Louis "Satchmo" Armstrong appeared on Ed Sullivan's TV show, which he did more than a few times. At that point I'd never heard of saxophonist John Coltrane, who had grown up in High Point, only a few miles from where I grew up, or trumpeter Dizzy Gillespie, who had attended school in Laurinburg, or pianist Thelonious Monk, who was born in Rocky Mount, and whom I later would meet.

This was my first experience in a night club and a smoky one it was for a non-smoker. Brownlee was surprised that not only had I never smoked but I also didn't partake of alcohol. When I was 16 some of my friends had started drinking beer (one of them later died in a car crash as a result; bits of his brain were still in the wreckage when my friends and I went to see it behind the Studebaker place) and they shamed me into trying a taste. I spit it out. Guilt may have had a role in that. When I was baptized by sprinkling at age 11 at First Methodist Church (my pastor was Glenn Lanier, great-great grandson of famed Georgia poet Sidney Lanier), I had signed a vow that I would forever forgo alcohol, and I still was a good Methodist then.

I loved the music (with time it would become my favorite) but I have no idea who I watched perform that night because I'd never heard of any of them.

Brownlee and I made several trips to the city together. One Saturday when we had planned to go with no specific purpose, I went to wake him. He was assigned to a four-man room at the end of our hall. He often slept late on the weekend and this time he was the only one still in the room.

"What time is it?" he said groggily after I shook him awake.

"It's after ten," I said. "You're sleeping the day away."

"I've got to take a shower," he said.

"I'll come back in a little bit," I told him.

When I returned he was dressed except for his shoes. He sat on his bunk to put them on. When he reached for the first one a yellow liquid sloshed onto his hand and the floor. Somebody had pissed in it. He sat there silently looking at it, shaking his head.

I didn't know what to say and didn't say anything. I had no doubt that he had suffered other such indignities.

After a few moments, he got up, carried the shoe to the latrine, emptied what was left in it and thoroughly washed it. He left it to dry on the windowsill near his bunk. He said not a word about the incident that day, or any other.

This was my first direct experience with racial discrimination, and it would have permanent effect.

As our eight weeks at Ft. Slocum wound down, our main concern was where we would land next and what we would be doing. One by one we were called in and handed a package of orders.

My assignment was to Headquarters Company, U.S. Army Aviation Center, Fort Rucker, Alabama. There was no mention of what I would be doing.

Never had I been happier about leaving a place than I was when I escaped Fort Jackson. I left Fort Slocum with more than a tinge of sadness. I was leaving behind new friends that I never would see again. But I also was leaving a school and a huge throbbing nearby city that had pried open my mind and begun to change my perspectives.

This time I was traveling by train. The first leg of my trip was from Penn Station to Washington. From there, I would catch another train to Savannah, where I would arrive in the early morning hours. At 5 a.m. I would take an obscure rail line on a long trek across Georgia to Ozark, Alabama, on Fort Rucker's eastern edge. I only could guess what mind-expanding opportunities might be waiting for me there.

I WAS SURPRISED WHEN I got my first pre-dawn glimpse of the decrepit railway passenger car that would deliver me to Fort Rucker. It was attached directly to an idling diesel locomotive.

"Is this the only car?" I asked the conductor, an elderly black man, who was taking tickets on the platform at the front of the car.

"We'll be picking up some more in a little bit," he said.

"Will there be a dining car?" I asked.

The evening before I'd had my first dining-car experience. When I was growing up in Thomasville, we lived only a block from the Southern Railway mainline tracks. I loved seeing the steam locomotives when I was a child, and by the time I was 11 or 12 I knew the schedules of every passenger streamliner that came through town. I'd ride my bike up the hill to watch the trains and fantasize about being on one someday, going off to some exotic spot.

I was especially taken with the dining cars. One train came through headed north just about dusk every day and I often would go to watch it. The lights would be bright in the dining car and white-jacketed black waiters balancing big trays over their shoulders would be carefully placing dishes on white tablecloths before the fortunate passengers. How wonderful it must be, I thought, to dine in such luxury as the world passes by. And my first such experience the night before turned out to be as grand as I had imagined.

The conductor in Savannah laughed at my question about the dining car.

"Not on this line," he said.

"I have two meal vouchers," I told him.

"Won't do you a lick of good here, son."

I asked how long it would take to get to Ozark.

"We should have you there by dark."

That was more than 15 hours away, and I didn't have any food.

"Will we be able to get something to eat?" I asked.

"Oh, we'll make some stops. You'll be able to eat."

The car was dimly lit and shabby, the seats worn and dirty, and I was one of only a dozen or so passengers. Soon after we departed the station, the train slowed to a stop, then began backing up. We were picking up the other cars the conductor had mentioned—a string of box cars and toxic tankers. I was riding a freight train to Ozark. All across the state we stopped at sidings to drop off some cars and collect others, creating long delays.

An hour or so after dawn broke we stopped at what appeared to be nowhere to pick up more cars. The conductor announced that we could take a break and get something to eat. We just had to trek across an open field to a two-lane road that paralleled the tracks. An old unpainted country store awaited us. It was covered with faded signs advertising Tube Rose Snuff, Chesterfield Cigarettes, Tom's Toasted Peanuts, Royal Crown Cola and other treats. I had a Dr. Pepper and a stale honey bun in a cellophane wrapper for breakfast.

About mid-morning the conductor came around to tell us that hot box lunches would be available down the line but we'd have to pay for them now so he'd know how many he needed to order at the next stop.

"What's in them?" I asked.

"Usually fried chicken," he said, "best chicken you'll ever eat."

I anted up the three bucks. About an hour later the train jerked to a halt alongside a small frame house with a rusty tin roof. A woman and two boys hurried to the train carrying stacks of white cardboard boxes. The conductor placed the stacks on two front seats and handed the woman the cash he'd collected. She was smiling broadly. I got the feeling that the conductor ate for free.

I opened my box to find a thigh, a wing, a hunk of cold cornbread, and the biggest mound of slimy boiled okra I'd ever encountered. I liked fried okra well enough but boiled I couldn't bear. Just as an experiment I tried to lift a huge pod with the plastic fork that came inside the box but it slid off quickly. I was afraid that if I could get one to my mouth it would slip right through me without pause.

Did I mention that this car was not air-conditioned? That this was mid-July and the heat was unbearable? It was especially difficult for me, because I was in dress khakis, long-sleeve shirt and tie required. We rode with the windows open, which helped a little, but not enough.

Darkness was indeed looming when we finally reached Ozark and I was the sole remaining passenger. The original conductor had left hours earlier and another had replaced him. No passengers were waiting to board at the small, oddly shaped depot. Not a person was in sight. The place was shut tight. A mangy, skinny dog barked forlornly from the sagging porch of a small house on the other side of the track.

A sign directed incoming Army personnel to a phone on the wall with a direct connection to Fort Rucker. A driver would be sent for me, I was told. I sat on my duffel bag to wait in the pale light of a single bulb. This clearly was not Times Square. Forty minutes later an Army sedan pulled up. I hefted my duffel bag into the back seat and crawled into the passenger seat beside the duty driver, a laconic specialist fourth-class. He asked where I was coming from.

"Fort Slocum," I told him.

"Never heard of it," he said.

I asked how long he'd been at Rucker.

"Too long."

"What's it like?" I asked.

"I guess it's all right if you like airplanes and helicopters."

I got the feeling he might not care much for either. I'd never been around any, so I couldn't know whether I liked them or not. I had another question.

"What do you do for fun around here?"

"Drink mostly."

Fort Rucker, I soon discovered, was a sprawling place. Once we passed through the eastern entrance, not far from Ozark, it still was a long drive, miles and miles, to the main part of the post. When we began to see regimented structures I was disappointed. They were the same drab yellow wooden buildings that had contributed so greatly to making Fort Jackson so dismal.

But when my driver pulled to the curb to deposit me at Headquarters Company barracks I was pleasantly surprised. It was a two-story modern brick building with rows of broad windows, though utilitarian in design. It looked almost new. The duty officer, a second lieutenant, was expecting me. He told me I was being assigned to the Public Information Office (PIO), and gave me the number of the squad room on the second floor in which I would be residing with others assigned to PIO.

I was in another new place, not knowing a soul, feeling very much alone and wondering what lay ahead.

4

I REPORTED TO PIO in the big white frame headquarters the next morning, and was pleased to discover that the person who ran it was a civilian, a former newspaper man. I came to think very highly of him. His last reporting job had been with *The Birmingham News*. One story I was told about him was that he had written about the attack on popular black singer Nat King Cole in April, 1956, by a small group of Ku Klux Klan members while Cole was performing before a white audience at Birmingham's Municipal Auditorium. The Klansmen had shouted, "Nigger, go home!" My new boss reported this and closed the article this way: "Cole, born in Alabama, was home."

PIO had many responsibilities. It produced Fort Rucker's weekly newspaper, *The Army Flier*, along with a daily radio broadcast of post news and events for WIRB, a 500-watt AM station in nearby Enterprise, the only town in the world with a statue honoring the boll weevil, a ravenous insect that wiped out cotton crops early in the century, prompting local farmers to switch to profitable peanuts. Occasionally PIO provided 16-millimeter film of post events to TV stations in Dothan, 25 miles to the south, Montgomery, 80 miles to the north, and Columbus, Georgia, near the Alabama line 100 miles to the northeast. Columbus adjoins Fort Benning, home of the infantry, and units from the two forts often were engaged in joint operations.

My primary job would be writing for *The Flier*, and despite my lack of experience in journalism and my scant knowledge of the military, I was determined to make the best of it.

WHEN MY CO-WORKERS IN PIO discovered that I never had flown except in my dreams without mechanical assistance, they decided that needed to be remedied. How could I write knowingly about aviation if I never had gotten off the ground?

I was wary about this because I was convinced that flying was natural only for birds, insects and the occasional fish. I had little confidence in motor-propelled vehicles because the only one I'd owned, albeit briefly, a 1950 Ford coupe during my junior year in high school, broke down regularly leaving me stranded (and constantly broke). As frustrating and inconvenient as that was, I reasoned it was not nearly as dangerous as being in a vehicle that could break down in mid-air and leave you permanently stranded, possibly in many pieces.

One of the advantages that Fort Rucker offered was that everybody stationed there could go to Cairns Airfield and catch a free hop to any place a pilot was heading and willing to take them. All Army pilots, no matter their assignments, had to get in a certain number of flying hours, and many did this on weekends. One Saturday morning, two of my co-workers cajoled me into going to Cairns to see what developed. We hadn't been there long when three young lieutenants passed by. One of my new friends hurried after them.

He returned with a smile.

"They're going to Fort Benning," he told us. "They said we could go along."

Each would be flying an L-19 Bird Dog, a two-seat reconnaissance plane that had seen a lot of dangerous duty in the Korean War and would see much more in Vietnam. After the pilots had filed their flight plans, they came back to meet us.

"Which one's the cherry?" one of them asked grinning.

My friends pointed to me.

"Well, you can fly with me," he said, "I'll try to make it an experience to remember."

That turned out to be quite an understatement. I really didn't want to do this but I couldn't back down without appearing to be the utter coward that I suspected myself to be. I had to marshal all the willpower at my means to climb into that confined back seat and strap myself in, my knees almost blocking my forward vision. As we pulled into position for take-off, the pilot turned to me with a warning.

"If you throw up, you clean up."

I should have realized then what lay ahead.

We were the first to take off and were quickly in the air. Off to the left I could see much of Fort Rucker and the town of Enterprise growing smaller as we climbed. Both looked better from above.

Soon we had reached altitude and all three planes joined in a V formation, mine in the lead. The pilots were chatting casually by radio. Although the ride was a little bumpy, it was not nearly as frightening as I expected, at least as long as the engine kept running. Indeed it was satisfyingly beautiful gazing upon the earth from such a height. But that was quickly to change.

About 10 minutes into the flight, without warning, my plane suddenly went into a steep dive. Blood rushed to my head and I held on for dear life realizing that it likely was a futile act. The other planes followed. For the next 15 minutes the pilots played tag, swooping close, banking sharply, diving and climbing, laughing all the while. Bird Dogs were not designed for acrobatics but these guys seemed determined to push them to their limits. I closed my eyes and began to think of all the things I should have done before committing to my first flight, which I now feared might also be my last. I would have needed a much longer ordeal to complete that lengthy list.

To my immense relief, the pilots regained better judgment as we neared Fort Benning and fell back into formation before we began gliding to gentle landings. When the plane finally rolled to a stop, I had no doubt that I was pale enough from fright to resemble the ghost I feared I might become. I wanted to get out and kiss the tarmac, but thought that might be a little overly dramatic.

The pilot turned to me with a grin.

"Whatta ya think?" he asked

"I think I may take a bus back," I said.

By the time I left Fort Rucker for other assignments some eight months later, I would be an experienced flyer, although still a jittery one. I couldn't recall how many hours I'd spent in the air in a wide variety of planes and helicopters but it was a lot.

ONE THING I NEVER HAD thought to be of interest was politics. But that began to change after John F. Kennedy won the Democratic Party presidential nomination in Los Angeles on July 13, 1960, during my last week at Fort Slocum. He accepted the nomination on Friday, July 15, my 19th birthday. I, along with other classmates, watched his acceptance speech on TV and was impressed. My dad was a Democrat and so were most of the other adults I knew although none had any involvement in politics other than talking about it. Democrats had great power in the South in part because poor Southerners credited Franklin D. Roosevelt with bringing the country through the Great Depression from which so many had suffered so deeply. Democrats had won the presidential vote in North Carolina every election since FDR first won in 1932, nine years before I was born. That would continue until Richard Nixon beat Vice President Hubert Humphrey in 1968, nearly six years after I left the Army.

Nixon, too, was vice president when he ran against Kennedy in 1960, and I watched their first debate—the first presidential debate ever televised—in the TV room of our barracks at Fort Rucker. Not everybody there was pulling for Kennedy, but almost everybody agreed that Nixon, who recently had been hospitalized with an infection after banging his knee on a car door during a campaign stop in Greensboro, N.C., looked awful and performed weakly. I became a strong supporter of Kennedy but could do nothing to benefit him. Although I was old enough to risk my life in service to my country, I was considered not to have judgment enough to help choose my commander-in-chief because of my age. I wouldn't be able to vote until the 1964 election. I still resent that I missed the only chance to vote for JFK. It didn't cross my mind at the time how decisions Kennedy would make in the White House soon would be directly affecting my life.

Two of the drawbacks during my time at Fort Rucker were KP (kitchen police) and guard duty. It wasn't possible to get out of KP. The best you could hope for was that you would end up on the serving line instead of scrubbing massive pots and pans, pealing 50-pound sacks of potatoes, or cleaning the grease trap. But after a few unpleasant tours of guard duty, I realized it was possible to get out of that and I began plotting to do it.

Guards were drawn from all units, and those summoned to guard duty had to undergo inspection before they were hauled off in the back of a 3/4-ton truck to the guard house. The officer of the day usually conducted that inspection. Guards stood at attention, M-1s at their side. Each was inspected individually for condition and function of weapon, neatness of uniform, polish of boots and brass. Each also was questioned about chain of command, weapon and ammunition specifics, and other matters of military importance. Each day a supernumerary was picked, the person who looked and performed best. He got to stay in the barracks and fill his time as he pleased, although he remained on call. Everybody else went off to the guard house to spend much of the night marching around buildings and lonely fields in the dark with unloaded M-1s on their shoulders.

One guy was known throughout our company for regularly being picked as supernumerary. I cornered him one day to see if he would reveal his secret. It was simple, he said. He bought an extra uniform, had it form-fitted and permanently creased by a tailor in Enterprise. He also bought a second set of combat boots he kept polished to a mirror finish and wore only for inspections. He shined his brass every day, kept his M-1 in immaculate condition, clean and well oiled. He gave me a booklet with answers to the questions frequently asked at inspection.

I gave it a try, and it worked. I became supernumerary every time I was called to guard duty. Unfortunately, that had an unforeseen side effect. It got me appointed to the post honor guard. I had to practice regularly, and that required more time than I would have spent on guard duty, although that was during working hours, not long dark nights.

The primary function of the honor guard was to attend funerals. We wore dress uniforms and white gloves for that. At that time, any veteran could request a military funeral and it would be provided. We buried veterans of all services in Alabama, the Florida panhandle, Mississippi and parts of Louisiana, flying to almost all of those destinations in a plane designated for our use. We numbered 15, six pallbearers, seven riflemen, a command sergeant and a bugler. I was a rifleman. We each fired three blank rounds at the cemetery for the 21-rounds salute. The saddest and most memorable of these occasions came in Louisiana where we buried a homeless alcoholic World War II veteran in a pauper's grave. We were the only people present except for two guys from the funeral home who delivered the body and two guys who had dug the grave and were lurking under a tree on the edge of the field waiting to shovel dirt onto the cheap wooden box that served as a coffin. Nobody was there to receive the folded flag that had covered the coffin. That was a lonely grave to leave, and I've always wondered what that veteran's story was. But he wanted us there, and we all felt that he had allowed us to do something important.

ALTHOUGH THE HONOR GUARD disrupted my work at *The Army Flier*, that continued to be my main function and growing interest. The PIO director must have seen some potential in me, because he regularly offered encouragement and advice. One day he stopped by my desk with a book in hand.

"Here," he said, "you may want to read this."

The book was *Some of My Very Best* by Jim Bishop, a nationally syndicated columnist and author of two major bestsellers, *The Day Lincoln Was Shot* and *The Day Christ Died*. (He later would write many more.) I hadn't been a reader of books, but this one would have a big effect on me.

Bishop wrote about his family, his dogs, personal experiences, odd characters and fascinating people. Each column was a story, all the same length. Some were funny, some sad, some deeply moving, all entertaining. It hadn't crossed my mind that you could tell stories in a newspaper instead of writing formula reports. This was the seed that would set me thinking that working for a newspaper might be a meaningful and fun career.

MY WORK WITH *The Flier* gradually adjusted me to associating with officers, and I frequently was put in close presence with some of the post's top commanders, including the two-star commanding general, Ernest F. Easterbrook. These officers often were part of the events I covered, although I don't recall ever speaking with any of them. On some articles my byline appeared, but I couldn't have imagined that any of those commanders had taken notice of me.

One day, however, the PIO officer came to me and said that I was scheduled to undergo training to learn how to operate projectors of all types. I didn't know until I finished the training that I was about to become projectionist for the commanding general.

General Easterbrook was an impressive man, lean, with a thin face, a high forehead, a long neck and an impressive Adam's apple. He had a stern visage, a chest full of ribbons and the command bearing that a general is expected to present. He often spoke at community functions, and he liked to use images to tell the story of Army aviation, which he clearly loved.

I was more than a little nervous about this assignment. I had no doubt that anybody who screwed up and made the commanding general look bad was not apt to have a bright future in the Army, or even to get promoted beyond PFC, the rank I had achieved a few months earlier. But the job turned out not to be difficult. I just had to pay close attention.

When I was to assist the general, I first had to find out from the command sergeant major what projection equipment was required. Usually it was a slide projector, once when the topic was about future construction at the post, an overhead projector. I would gather the slides or other images, check out the necessary equipment, load it into one of the vehicles assigned to PIO, drive it to the site of the talk and have everything set up by the time the general arrived. He would get there early enough to mingle with community leaders beforehand, and during that time he would drop by to see me to make sure that I had my copy of his talk, marked exactly where each image was to appear, and to let me know if he'd made any changes. Luckily, I never screwed up. And a couple of times the general even made a point of coming by afterward to tell me, "Good job."

AFTER I HAD DONE this several times, the command sergeant major came to see me one day to tell me that I was to be at the general's office at 7 that night for a meeting. He didn't know what it was about, but it wouldn't involve any projection equipment. This was unusual and I was wary about it. I appeared as ordered, but the general wasn't present. Instead a major I'd never seen was waiting for me.

He introduced himself and said he was from the U.S. Military Academy at West Point. He invited me to sit for a chat. He told me that the Army had a program that allowed some active duty enlisted men to be inducted into the academy each year. He went on to explain how it worked before telling me I had been recommended as a potential candidate. My first thought was: Obviously, this guy has never seen my high school records.

As unexpected as this development was, I actually had undergone something similar late in basic training. I was one of five trainees pulled out of ranks one day and told to report to our executive officer, a martinet I despised. He greeted us with a smile, something I hadn't thought possible, and informed us we were being given a wondrous opportunity—OCS, Officer Candidate School. We could commit to 14 grueling weeks of intense training at Ft. Benning, and if we made it through, we would emerge as 2nd lieutenants.

I must have appeared slack-jawed in amazement, mainly because there apparently was one thing Sgt. Coon hadn't lied to me about. I actually was considered to have the potential to become an officer. But at this point I'd already learned everything I wanted to know about the Army and I liked nothing about it. To avoid more trouble, I responded by saying this was something I needed to think about.

I wasn't so diplomatic with the major from West Point.

"I'm not interested," I said.

He seemed taken aback.

"May I ask why?"

"I just know the Army is not for me, and I would be doing a disservice both to myself and the Army if I pretended otherwise."

"Well, I appreciate your forthrightness," he said.

After that, I never again was asked to assist the general at one of his talks. I don't recall thinking anything about it at the time. But after I began this memoir, I did some research about General Easterbrook. He was the son of a chaplain who became the Army's Chief of Chaplains. At 18 he joined the Virginia National Guard and from there won an appointment to West Point. He must have been very proud of that. He became the son-in-law of General "Vinegar" Joe Stillwell and served as his executive officer in the China-Burma-India Theatre in World War II. He trained and led Chinese troops in their effort to free Burma from the Japanese and later commanded the 475th Infantry Division that reopened the Stillwell-Burma Road. He went on to distinguished service after the war and I found references from people saying he was the best commanding officer they ever served under.

I'm sure West Point meant a lot to General Easterbrook, and I wonder if it was he who recommended that I be considered as a prospective candidate and if my outright rejection had caused him offense.

SATURDAY, MAY 20, 1961, was Armed Forces Day, and as usual Fort Rucker put on a big celebration. The highlight was an air show at Cairns Airfield attended by several thousand people that morning. My friend Bruce Eberhardt, a radio guy, and I were to do the primary coverage not only for the *Flier*, but for outlying newspapers, radio and TV stations.

As soon as I had finished my article about the event and Bruce had taped radio reports, we collected photos and film from photographers and departed in an army sedan to deliver these materials to newspapers, radio and TV stations in Montgomery and Columbus. We didn't know the exact location of the TV station in downtown Montgomery and were looking for it when we encountered a traffic jam as we neared the Greyhound Bus Station.

Crowds were on the sidewalks and police cars were parked nearby. We had no idea what was going on, but we noticed that some in the crowd were looking at us. One or two began pointing, others glaring. Traffic barely was moving and we were stuck. We had no clue why we were becoming the object of attention and began to get a little uneasy. Suddenly, somebody stepped off the sidewalk and hit the back fender of the car with his fist, yelling something we didn't understand. Another guy gave us the finger. This was hardly the reception we were expecting on Armed Forces Day. Not only did police not intervene, they glowered at us too.

Not until we found the TV station did we learn what was going on. Just a couple of hours earlier, a bus carrying Freedom Riders seeking to integrate transportation facilities had arrived. A mob was waiting in hiding, armed with baseball bats and metal clubs. The Freedom Riders, along with reporters and cameramen, were attacked and beaten. Nearly 20 minutes passed before police showed up.

Bruce and I were aware of the Freedom Riders. We had read news accounts and seen the photos of the Greyhound bus that had been attacked and set ablaze by Ku Klux Klansmen on a highway near Anniston six days earlier, but we did not know that more Freedom Riders were on their way to Montgomery on this day.

As it turned out, two ill-informed Army enlisted men on an errand were the only discernible federal presence at the Montgomery bus station in the wake of this historic event. And the surly crowd of onlookers surely suspected we were there because of it and didn't like it. If we had arrived a little earlier we might have been dragged out of our car and beaten too.

Bruce and I made it safely out of town. But we ran into more trouble in Columbus. After dropping off our materials at the newspaper and TV station, we stopped to eat in a downtown restaurant. Just after our meals were served, MPs came in and arrested us for being out of uniform. We were in work khakis, short sleeve shirts, no ties. But dress khakis and ties were required in Columbus. The MPs weren't interested in explanations. They hauled us to the stockade at Fort Benning, where we were held for several hours before somebody finally confirmed that we actually had been working and had committed no criminal acts. This became my only memorable Armed Forces Day.

Two weeks after my experience in Montgomery, I was summoned to the orderly room after supper. I thought I would be told that the honor guard was scheduled for another funeral. Instead, I was handed a package of orders. Within days, I would be on my way to the Special Warfare Center at Fort Bragg, North Carolina, only about a hundred miles from Thomasville. There I was to undergo three weeks of training in psychological warfare, after which I would be sent to a unit called U.S. Army Broadcasting and Visual Activity Pacific in the Ryukyu Islands.

I'd never heard of these islands. The next day I went to the library and learned this: the Ryukyus are a string of volcanic islands stretching from Japan to Taiwan in the East China Sea. The largest of those islands is Okinawa, where the last major battle of World War II was fought. That was where I was headed. I had no clue what I'd be doing there but I soon was to learn that my duties were to switch from seeking truth to, in some cases, creating deliberate deception.

5

NOTHING WAS VISIBLY SPECIAL about the Special Warfare Center at Fort Bragg. It was just as dismal as Fort Jackson. I didn't know what to expect, and that would continue for days after I arrived in early June, 1961.

Nobody seemed to know that I was coming, or what they were supposed to do with me. And I turned out to be not the only person in that situation. Others kept trickling in until we numbered, I think, seven or eight. We were put into an empty barracks building and told to wait until somebody figured out something. The problem appeared to be that a major reorganization of some sort was underway, as is often the case in the military. Although no explanations ever were forthcoming, there was much ongoing confusion, and we were just its incidental victims.

Psychological warfare, the subject we were supposed to be studying, is as old as human conflict. As long as people have fought wars, they have tried to figure out ways to fool or influence the enemy by whatever means.

The first Army unit to bear the name Psychological Warfare was the 14th Battalion, which was a mobile radio broadcasting company. It was created at Camp Ritchie, Maryland, at the end of 1943 and later took part in operations in the Alsace region of France along the Rhine and the mountainous Ardennes Forest of Belgium during the Battle of the Bulge, the biggest and bloodiest battle of World War II. But it wasn't the only Army unit practicing psychological warfare at that time. Another was the Ghost Soldiers, a top-secret group that actor Douglas Fairbanks Jr. had a hand in creating. Technically, it was the 23rd Headquarters Special Troops and its purpose was deception. It was made up of engineers, sound technicians, actors and artists, including future clothing designer Bill Blass. It set up fake encampments and used inflatable tanks, howitzers and recordings of battle sounds to fool Germans into thinking they were besieged by troops that didn't exist. The Ghost Soldiers served in more campaigns in the European Theater than any other unit and were credited with saving the lives of many Allied soldiers, sometimes at the cost of their own.

In the spring of 1945, General Dwight Eisenhower, supreme commander of Allied forces, publicly stated: "Without doubt, psychological warfare has proved its right to a place of dignity in our military arsenal." Yet, soon after the war the 14th Psywar Battalion was deactivated, as were the Ghost Soldiers, who would remain secret for half a century.

By 1949, only seven people in the Intelligence Special Projects Branch of the Far East Command were involved in psychological warfare, hoping to create a plan to revive it. Everything changed for this group on June, 25, 1950, when communist North Korea invaded the south. Within three days, their purpose was sealed and leaflets were being dropped over occupied areas of South Korea assuring residents that the United States and other nations would be coming to their aid.

The war prompted the Army to create the 1st Radio Broadcasting and Leaflet Battalion to serve in Korea. A psychological warfare center and school also was established at Fort Riley, Kansas. In April, 1952, that unit was moved to Fort Bragg where a new group was being created to perform some of the secret, behind-the-lines work of Office of Special Services (OSS) officers during World War II. These two units were joined and would become known as the Center for Special Warfare in 1956. By that time, the 1st RB&L Battalion had been deactivated and no psychological warfare unit had existed for two years. But a new psywar command structure was formed in Hawaii that year. It was called U.S. Army Broadcasting and Visual Activity, Pacific. From that a new 14th Psywar Battalion was established in Hawaii. It began moving to Okinawa in 1958, and the move was completed just two months before I received orders to join it.

My training as a psywarrior turned out to be somewhat limited. I was at Fort Bragg almost a week before I sat in a class. The classes seemed to be thrown together in a slap-dash manner and were conducted by two harried second lieutenants, who apparently had just completed a two-month training course for officers who would be joining the 14th, where we were headed, or a new psywar battalion, the 13th, that was being organized at Ft. Bragg at that time. I remember little about what was taught except for id, ego, and super ego, Sigmund Freud's theory of how the brain works. That stuck with me for some reason, although I still get the three confused, perhaps an indication that my brain might not have been a good one for Freud's consideration. After a week and a half of these haphazard classes, a captain we hadn't seen before appeared to tell us that our training had to be cut short. We could depart and consider it free leave time, he told us. I made a hasty getaway to Thomasville, hoping to get in a little id exploring.

I FLEW IN AN airlines passenger jet for the first time on the initial leg of my journey halfway around the world to Okinawa. My destination was San Francisco, where I was to be taken to Travis Air Force Base to depart across the Pacific by means unknown. Those means turned out to be Riddle Airlines, a freight hauler out of Miami that had a contract for flying military personnel to the Far East much in the manner that freight is hauled, if freight can be discomforted. This would turn out to be the longest, most miserable flight of my life, more than 20 hours in the air. I don't know how many uniformed passengers of various services were on it, all male, as I recall, but we were packed into a propeller-driven DC-7 much in the fashion that chickens are jammed into wooden crates to be hauled to the slaughter house.

We flew to Anchorage, Alaska, where we disembarked for a couple of hours while the plane was refueled. We then struck out into darkness and followed the Russian coastline southwestward toward Tokyo. I was seated just behind the wing on the right side and could see the two engines belching fire through literally the longest night I ever experienced, as half my fellow passengers snored and the rest smoked cigarettes, filling the cabin with unbearable smoke. With a couple of hours still to go before we reached Tokyo, I was jolted to see one of the engines feathered for reasons unknown to the passengers. The long-delayed dawn brought the welcome sight of Japan's green islands, easing some worries. But as we descended toward Tokyo Bay to land at Tachikawa Air Force Base, another engine on the opposite side of the plane was shut down. I wasn't the only one alarmed at this point. We took a hard landing, bounced once and slammed back down, causing a section of a heavily loaded overhead storage rack to collapse before the pilot regained control. In all of the flying I've done, I was never so relieved to get off any aircraft.

We waited hour after hour for the plane to be repaired and refueled so we could continue on the last 400 miles to Kadena Air Force Base in Okinawa. After my arrival in a state of near exhaustion, I learned that two other people on the flight, both low-level enlisted men, also were headed to B&VA, neither of whom had been with me at Ft. Bragg. A staff car was sent for us and we made the acquaintance of one of the unit's wildest characters, who happened to be the duty driver that day. We would come to call him the Soba King, because he frequently returned drunk to the barracks late at night with a big bowl of fat noodles in hand and woke up people dangling noodles to tickle their noses. We were eager to know what the unit was like, but he only wanted to talk about the bars in the nearby village. He proudly informed us, to great wincing on our parts, that he had a bumblebee tattooed on the most sensitive area of his most favored appendage, although he didn't put it in quite those terms. He also warned us about somebody named Sumiko at the Club Mule in Yafuso, who should be avoided.

The drive from Kadena to Machinato, where B&VA was situated, was not a long one. There were no truly long drives in Okinawa. The island is only 70 miles from one end to the other and just a few miles wide in some spots. Military bases filled much of the center of the island (some 44,000 troops of all services were stationed there), and the bulk of the native population lived in the southern half, where Naha, the Capital and only real city, was situated. At that time the island had only one major, multi-lane highway, Highway 1, that connected Kadena to Naha. The Machinato Service Area, a part of Fort Buckner, my new abode, was only a few miles north of Naha. Our driver turned onto Perimeter Road, which skirted the sea. We passed the B&VA compound, a collection of low, flat-topped stucco buildings and Quonset huts enclosed in a high cyclone fence on the sea-side of the road, and half a mile farther along we turned left into the driveway of Headquarters Co., 14th Battalion, which sat on a sharp incline overlooking the sea, offering spectacular sunsets, one of its few redeeming benefits.

Okinawa, a stunningly beautiful island, was called "the Rock" by many who served there. The hilly, forested northern part of the island is underlain by volcanic rock, the southern part by coral. Caves are common. It has a sub-tropic climate, similar to that of Florida, and is highly susceptible to typhoons year-round. Buildings have to be constructed to withstand powerful winds. Barracks had flat roofs and were built of concrete sunk deep into rock, each two-stories and painted a vague pastel color. Behind our barracks, a little higher on the ridge, were those of the 173rd Airborne. Just to the south were the 1st Special Forces.

I was assigned to the second floor, where long rows of double-stacked bunks with mosquito nets were jammed together with barely enough room to turn around between them. I had been happy to learn that I would not have to face KP or guard duty. Everybody had to chip in a certain amount each month to pay Okinawan workers to handle kitchen duties and "houseboys" to keep the latrines and barracks spiffy. We still would have to face daily formations, physical training (PT) and regular visits to the firing range. But I was immensely pleased to learn that I would not be issued another heavy, bulky M-1. Instead I would have an M-1 carbine, much smaller, lighter, and far easier for me to fire and hit a target.

The next day, I reported for duty at the B&VA compound, which included a headquarters building, a research and intelligence building, a separate research library, a large radio section with studios and broadcasting facilities, a unit for loudspeaker teams, a printed media building, which included a large printing section, offices for producing a monthly Japanese language magazine, *Shurei No Hikari*, distributed throughout the Ryukyu Islands, and a bi-monthly publication called *Veritas* for U.S. troops on Okinawa, which I would come to believe was grossly misnamed, and an art department.

I was shocked when I was told where I was being assigned—the art department.

"Are you sure?" I asked.

"That's what it says here," said the sergeant who was checking me in.

I was going to become an Army artist after all, at least part of the time, even if I didn't make it as an artist officer with beautiful women chasing after me as Sgt. Coon had led me to believe.

6

VIETNAM WAS A PROBLEM for President John F. Kennedy from the day he was sworn into office on January 20, 1961. The country had been divided in 1954 when the defeated French colonialists departed. The North was ruled by communists in the Capital of Hanoi. The South supposedly was under democratic control, with the Capital in Saigon, but it was supported almost completely at the expense of the U.S. government. The president of South Vietnam was Ngo Dinh Diem, a devout Catholic who had spent years at a seminary in New Jersey while the French occupied his country. He had achieved office with strong support from Kennedy, then a U.S. Senator, also Catholic, as well as from Cardinal Francis Spellman, who was close to the Kennedy family.

Unfortunately, things weren't working out well for Diem. More than a third of the country was under control of the Viet Cong, communist guerilla fighters supported by the North, who were regularly lopping off the heads of village officials and creeping ever closer to Saigon. Kennedy believed that Vietnam was, as he put it, in "critical condition" requiring "emergency treatment." The question was whether Diem, who was considered to be corrupt as well as inept, was capable of dealing with the situation. The only U.S. troops in Vietnam at the time were a few hundred advisers sent by Kennedy's predecessor, Dwight Eisenhower, a President I had glimpsed after standing with my M-1 for hours on a sun baked parade ground near the end of basic training waiting for him to pass by in an open jeep.

Only days after taking office, Kennedy approved a counterinsurgency plan to spend $42 million to expand South Vietnam's army by 20,000 men and the civil guard by 32,000. The bulk of that money was to be used to arm, house, feed, and pay those troops. But some was designated for other purposes.

"Next to the $660,000 set aside for 'Psychological Operations,'" Richard Reeves wrote in *President Kennedy: Profile of Power*, "Kennedy scribbled, 'Why so little?'"

That scribble probably was why I had landed in Okinawa. Many upper-level Army officers had little knowledge or concern for psychological warfare (there were no career psywar officers), but when top military commanders saw that scribble they no doubt realized that the new president considered it vital and they'd better begin boosting psychological operations in the planning that already was underway for sending U.S. troops to Vietnam, which seemed inevitable considering Kennedy's views.

The new 13th Psywar Battalion, which was being formed at Ft. Bragg while I was there, wouldn't become active until eight months after Kennedy's scribble, three months after I left Fort Bragg. But if psychological operations by U.S. troops were employed in Vietnam, it would not be by this new battalion but by the 14th I now was joining. The 14th was being expanded in preparation for intervention and I was just one tiny cog in that.

Vietnam clearly was a major concern for B&VA, as well as for every other military unit on Okinawa, as I soon would learn. At the time of my arrival in July, 1961, 10,000 Marines on the island were on alert to sail off the coast of Indochina in a show of force to discourage Hanoi from further intrusions into Laos and South Vietnam. The situation in Laos was even worse than in South Vietnam, but Kennedy already had decided that if he had to take a firm stand and commit troops it would be in Vietnam where U.S. interests were stronger. I soon would be dealing with these concerns myself.

MY ASSIGNMENT TO THE art department was just a matter of logistics. I still was to be an information specialist, writing copy for whatever projects the department was assigned. But when I asked the lieutenant in charge if I might also be allowed to do some art work, he said, "I don't see a problem with that."

Only two artists worked in the department when I arrived. They were Okinawan civilian employees, male, quite talented. Both were middle-aged, spoke English, and were friendly and helpful. A military artist also had been assigned to the department, but had not yet arrived. Eric Alberts, a lanky, reddish-blond-haired Spec. 4 from Texas, had been with me at Fort Bragg and we became quick friends. I was pleased that we would be working together. It would be a while before that happened, however. To Alberts' great misfortune he was coming by troop ship, an ordeal that would take nearly a month.

Before I started work, I had to train in printing and type setting. This involved learning to operate a 1250 Multilith offset press and attempting to master the Varityper, perhaps the most frustrating and confounding device ever created. Supposedly this contrivance would allow type to be set and justified in 300 styles and 55 languages with appropriate charts, fonts, knowledge and extreme patience. To my great dismay, I frequently would have to do battle with this fiendish monstrosity, and rarely did a day pass that I didn't want to throw it out the window.

One of the major functions of B&VA was preparing leaflets. Leaflets had played a big role in the Korean War, and would be even more important in Vietnam. More than 50 billion would be dropped in Vietnam during that war, an average of about 1,500 for every person in both north and south. Some actually would be effective, but most likely were used as toilet paper or fire starters. They certainly didn't lead to victory.

B&VA was already creating leaflets for Vietnam when I arrived, although no U.S. forces yet had been deployed except as advisers. All of these were designed and written in the art department. Their purpose was to win the hearts and minds of Vietnamese villagers and attempt to thwart the insurgency by luring Viet Cong to the other side with lucrative promises and safe conduct passes. I did the writing for many of these. I assumed that these leaflets were primarily training exercises and never was aware of any actually being used in Vietnam. Most, however, were general enough to be kept for future use. I was free to come up with my own ideas for leaflets and posters, but the majority came from other sources, usually Research and Intelligence, sometimes just from officers dropping by.

I remember a major coming in one day with a rough sketch he thought would make a good leaflet. It appeared to be some sort of bird tied to a pole by one leg. The message scribbled on it was this: "Where is your Air Force? Your Air Force is like a chicken staked to the ground."

When I noted, as politely as I knew how, that the Viet Cong had no air force and chickens don't really fly, the major became indignant.

"Well, goddamn it, it worked in Korea!" he snorted and huffed out, taking his half-baked chicken with him.

ALTHOUGH I HAD NO real concern about going off to war at this time, I was about to get a taste of what it might be like. Only a couple of weeks after arriving at B&VA, I was summoned to the orderly room and told to get my field gear ready. I was going to be a psywar liaison to Airborne and Special Forces in a major exercise with the Chinese Nationalist military in Taiwan, which still was ruled by Chiang Kai Shek, who had led his defeated army to the island after Mao Tse-tung and his communist forces won the Chinese Civil War in 1949. I would be gone for three weeks. I was instructed not to check out my carbine. I would be armed instead with a drawing board, sketch pads, paper, pencils, pens, ink, and a portable typewriter.

The next day I was in the back of a huge C-130 cargo plane loaded with a ¾-ton truck and trailer, a howitzer and another trailer consisting of two monstrous rubber tires filled with gas to refuel vehicles in the field. We were on our way to a military base just outside Pingtung City at the southern tip of Taiwan. I didn't know it then, but Taiwan has the largest, most highly concentrated collection of lofty mountains on Earth, 258 above 9,800 feet, the tallest, Yushan (Jade\'7d, at nearly 13,000 feet. After we landed, the first thing I noticed, following the shock of the incredible mid-summer heat and humidity, was a formidable mountain in the distance. It was called Beidawu, 10,144 feet high, and I would get to know portions of it intimately.

I soon was at a huge tent encampment in a broad field where I faced more confusion until I was pointed to a command tent where a Special Forces captain eyed me warily.

"What unit are you with?" he asked.

"B&VA," I told him.

"Oh, you're the psywar guy," he said, with what sounded to me to be disdain. "Where's your weapon?"

"I was instructed not to bring it, sir."

He rolled his eyes. "That won't do," he said. "We'll have to fix that."

I was not to stay at the tent encampment, I learned, much to my relief. Instead, I was assigned to a nearby Nationalist Chinese Army barracks with other support riff-raff.

Later that day, I was summoned back to the command tent, where the captain handed me a holstered .45 semi-automatic pistol.

"If you lose this, or fuck it up, it's going to be your ass," he said, "and you can take that as a promise."

I never had held a .45, much less fired one, and I wouldn't be able to fire this one because I was given no shells for it, not even the blank ones used in exercises. I'd never seen anybody but officers wearing .45s, so I dutifully strapped this one onto my utility belt and strutted around as if I were somebody, although the weight of it kept pulling my fatigue britches down, a distraction to my new self-importance. Nevertheless, this new acquaintance became my intimate companion for the next two weeks. I slept with it every night.

The following morning, I climbed aboard an HU-1 Iroquois helicopter, the first turbine-powered military helicopter. Troops would come to call it the Huey. It would become the iconic helicopter of the Vietnam War. I was familiar with it, although I never had flown in one. It had been in production for only a year and was just being introduced to service.

We flew straight into the mountains, which were steep and lushly forested. Roadways visible below soon gave way to hidden trails that could accommodate nothing bigger than a jeep. We hovered over a tiny village on the side of an impressive peak, where the masterful pilot set the Huey down in a clearing so small I thought it would be impossible. I was the only passenger disembarking.

A few U.S. troops and a Chinese Army translator were on hand, mingling with villagers, who, I had been told, were aborigines whose ancestors had been on the island for 6,000 years. There were several different distinctive groups of aborigines but all had fled to the mountains after the Chinese dominated the island, thus were called the Mountain People. I was to live among them.

A lieutenant who was present told me that I would have the use of one room of the two-room schoolhouse, constructed of wood, the only structure in the village with windows and a corrugated metal roof, likely a government project. The eight or 10 houses in the immediate vicinity were built of bamboo and thatch.

Before my arrival, an H-21 Shawnee helicopter, called the flying banana, had made a couple of trips to the village, lowering a sling filled with huge strapped blocks of C-rations in cardboard cases, along with a canvas tarp to cover them. The lieutenant informed me that I would be responsible for looking after this mountain of food that likely would be deemed inedible in other circumstances, some of it dating back to the Korean War. How I was to protect it was not explained. Without bullets I surely couldn't shoot anybody, and why anybody would want to steal the stuff was beyond my comprehension. He informed me that soldiers would be coming regularly on motorized platforms called Mules to haul the rations to others in the field.

The villagers appeared to be well-fed with wholesome food they produced themselves. They raised goats, pigs, chickens, ducks and geese. Small, and dark-skinned, they were friendly but shy and standoffish. I towered above them. I had no idea what language they spoke, but none spoke English. I would discover, though, that the oldest and friendliest man in the village actually knew a few words he'd learned from a missionary long ago and could play "The Old Rugged Cross" on a bamboo organ. No classes were presently being held in the schoolhouse, which also was used as a sort of community center. One night not long after my arrival one room would serve as the wedding night haven of a very young girl who just had been married with much pomp and celebration to a much older man, a night that consisted primarily of crying on her part. After I got set up in the room assigned to me, the other troops departed. I never had felt so alien and alone.

The village had no electricity, no telephones, no battery-powered radios, and no connection of any type to the outside world. I had not been given a field radio with which I could communicate. I was isolated. Just two years earlier, when I was happily making banana splits and extra-thick shakes in Thomasville, I couldn't have conceived that I would be in such a situation.

Rather than concern myself about it, I went to work. My job was to create leaflets that supposedly would be dropped on troops during the exercise. One was to be a newsletter, a single typed sheet with hand-lettered headlines. It would be called *News from Okinawa*. I had no way of knowing what news was happening in Okinawa, or anywhere else, so I would have to make it up. The whole idea was to mess with the minds of the troops. I was supposed to do four of these during the exercise, as well as some single-topic leaflets. I had been told that a helicopter would come regularly to pick up what I had created and take it to a place unknown to me where it would be printed, then showered on our troops from helicopters.

When I was at Fort Bragg, one of our instructors told us about a newsletter used in an exercise there that fabricated a car accident in Fayetteville. It reported that a woman and child had been killed and identification was being withheld because the husband was on a field exercise. Several troops, we were told, had come out of the field demanding to know the names of the victims, only to find themselves reprimanded for succumbing to propaganda. That was one idea I could steal. Many troops in Okinawa at sergeant level and above had their families with them. I wrote an elaborate description of an accident involving a bus and a car near Kadena, and along with dead mother and child, I included another child in critical condition, my own creative touch. What father wouldn't want to get back to that child?

The second article reported that the entire village of Yafuso had been declared off-limits after a deadly new venereal disease had been discovered there. Hundreds of troops were considered to be in danger. Early symptoms, I noted, were redness and itching, and the only hope for survival was early diagnosis and removal of the infected organ. I thought that might be cause for some troops to cry "medic!"

I felt that I had put in a good day's work after typing up the newsletter. By the time I'd downed a late supper of C-ration beans and franks and the stalest crackers in the Far East, washed down with cool spring water that flowed into the village cistern through bamboo pipes, darkness was descending. The villagers went to bed at nightfall, and I crawled into my sleeping bag on the school house floor entwined with my .45.

I expected to hear the clatter of a helicopter landing the following morning to pick up my brilliant fake journalism. I was eager to get it distributed and hear about troops swarming out of the field because of it. I already was thinking about what I would write for the next edition. But no other editions would be forthcoming. I waited all day and no helicopter came, although now and then I would see one flitting past. None would show up in days to come either. Apparently, the commanders of this exercise hadn't been informed of the Commander-in-Chief's fondness for psychological operations.

Late in the afternoon, two airborne troops appeared on a Mule to pick up a load of C-rations. They had no idea that I was a psywarrior. They thought I was just the C-rations guard.

"You got the easiest job out here," one of them told me.

I did indeed. As it turned out, I didn't really have a job. The only troops I encountered were the two guys on the Mule. They showed up several times daily. On one of their trips, they were laughing and boisterous, clearly drunk. They had bought some local hooch, they told me. I later learned it was called kaoliang, made from sorghum.

"This is some powerful shit," one of them said.

"Good, too," agreed the other with a big grin.

They offered me a nip, but I declined. They soon departed, the most boisterous one driving, the other perched precariously atop cases of C-Rations. That was the last time I saw them. I later was told that they had run the Mule and the C-rations off the mountainside and were hauled away in a medevac Huey—one way of attracting a helicopter, I guess, but I didn't find it appealing.

I did have unexpected overnight visitors once. All were officers, a lieutenant colonel, a smattering of majors and a few captains. This had been a day of immense change in the weather. It set off a lot of activity in the village. As dark, turbulent clouds moved in, the villagers began battening down. I figured they knew more than I did about what might be coming. The only thing I had to batten was the tarp over the ever diminishing pile of C-rations. I secured it as best I could and searched out some big rocks to put on top of it. At mid-afternoon, rain began, and I noticed that villagers were leaving in small groups. Most, I later learned, were taking refuge in nearby caves. I retreated to the school house as the rain grew heavier and the wind picked up.

By nightfall the rain was coming in torrents and the wind was worrying me. That was when I noticed something I hadn't seen before. Down the mountain to the west, headlights were moving slowly up the trail toward the village. The only lights I'd seen on the trail before were torches that the natives carried when they had reason to move around at night. Four jeeps soon ground to a halt in the clearing where the Huey had deposited me. They were filled with drenched commanders wearing ponchos, who had fled their collapsing tents in the hollows below, leaving lower grade troops to fare as best they could. They numbered perhaps a dozen. I never bothered to make a count.

I had a flashlight that I had used sparingly because I had only one set of batteries. I turned it on and opened the door. The wind almost flung the door back and me with it.

"Do you speak English?" one of the officers called as I wrestled with the door. He seemed surprised that somebody was there. I think he expected a response he wouldn't understand.

"Yes, sir," I shouted.

Three from the first jeep were headed toward me now. Others were climbing out of their jeeps or pulling out gear. I lighted their way with the flashlight.

The first through the door was a lieutenant colonel.

"Are you here alone?" he asked, as if he suspected I might be AWOL and hiding out.

"Yes, sir."

"Why are you here?"

"This is where they put me."

The others were crowding in now, making themselves at home. "How long have you been here?" the colonel asked.

"Since the exercise began," I said.

"What unit are you with?"

"B&VA, Fourteenth Psywar, sir."

"Oh, I see," he said.

After that, I was pretty much ignored. Officers aren't allowed to fraternize with enlisted peons, and some seemed to consider PFCs as sub-humans whose only purpose was to be ordered around and pushed out front if bullets were flying. This group was far better outfitted than was I. They had field radios and were able to get reports from hither and yon. They had bright gasoline lanterns, a propane stove, a coffee pot and other luxuries. They soon had the coffee pot percolating, and all were sitting around it in the floor, discussing the exercise and the storm. Nobody offered me coffee.

"Wouldn't you know we'd end up with a goddamned typhoon," one of them said.

That was news to me. If I'd known a typhoon was coming I could have written a hell of a scary story about it for the newsletter, even if nobody got to read it.

Since I wasn't invited into the conversation, I crawled into my sleeping bag with my .45 and soon nodded off. I don't know how long I had been asleep when I was startled awake by a loud crash, whipping wind, torrents of water. I saw flames. All was confusion. People were shouting. It took several moments for me to realize that I was trapped under a big tree limb that had ripped through the window and wall, striking a lantern and the propane heater under the coffee pot, sending both flying, spreading fire. My intruder guests were leaping about beating at the flames with sleeping bags and other gear. My sleeping bag was soaked, covered with leaves and shards of glass, but the limb had passed over me. I was struggling to get out from under it when one of the officers came and asked, "Are you alright?"

"I think so," I said, and he pulled me out.

By that time, the flames were out, and everybody was struggling to restore some order. The limb was pulled out of the window, and after a valiant effort, billowing ponchos were strung over the smashed window and wall blocking much of the rain and wind. But no comfort was to be found and nobody slept the rest of this night. A couple of hours later, the wind began dying down. By daybreak, for the most part, the storm had moved on and we stumbled out to check the damage.

The tin roof of the school house had held, except for one section over the second room, which was curled up. But the houses in the village had not been so fortunate. Their thatched roofs had blown away. Debris was everywhere. Trees and big limbs were down, and the trail passing through the village was blocked in both directions. My overnight guests were on their radios checking damage and issuing orders to create work details to deal with the cleanup. The military exercise came to a temporary halt. I joined with the officers helping the villagers collect debris and haul away limbs. After the trail had been cleared enough to allow the commanders to rejoin their troops down the mountain, I assisted the villagers gathering thatch to replace their roofs. I handed out c-rations to some, which they devoured voraciously, an indication, I suspected, of the desperation that calamity can bring. So far as I could determine nobody in the village had been hurt and I later learned that there had been no serious casualties among the sodden troops in the field. But 20 people in the southern part of the island died from flooding and mudslides caused by this category-two typhoon named June that had been worn down by Taiwan's mountains. It was the first typhoon of my acquaintance, but regrettably it wouldn't be the last.

Within a couple of days, most of the houses in the village had been restored and life was returning to normal. Nationalist Army engineers came to repair the schoolhouse roof and replace the smashed window. With little to do, I spent much of my time as I had before, wandering nearby trails sightseeing. I had found a spectacular waterfall, high and narrow, that I enjoyed because I could bathe there in privacy in the cold waters of its pool. I was there when large flights of Hueys began sweeping through the pass above me in early afternoon. In the distance I heard explosions and the rattle of automatic gunfire. I didn't know what was going on but I thought I'd better get back to my post, which was a couple of miles away, all uphill and precipitous.

Before I had made a mile, breathing heavily, a massive amount of gunfire erupted nearby. It seemed to be coming from the area of the village. I wasn't sure whether I should continue on and hid off the trail for a while until the gunfire subsided. After that I crept on warily, slipping from tree to tree hoping I wouldn't be noticed. When I got within sight of the village, I could see armed people in uniforms milling around there. I was hesitant and took a break behind a tree. When I attempted to dart to another tree for a better view, I realized I'd been spotted. Somebody was on an overlook motioning for me to come on, yelling out something I couldn't understand. I thought I could be in trouble. I was out of uniform, for one thing. I was bareheaded, but my trusty .45 was on my hip. I approached cautiously, only to be met by an angry airborne master sergeant in full battle gear.

"Where is your helmet?" he demanded. "Why aren't you with your unit? What are you doing with a .45?"

PFCs, he went on to proclaim, aren't issued .45s. He appeared to believe I had stolen it.

I attempted to explain my unique situation but he wasn't buying it. I finally got him to accompany me to the schoolhouse so I could show him my helmet and other gear and the remaining C-rations I was supposed to be guarding. I even showed him my unpublished Okinawan newsletter.

To his credit, he concluded that I was telling the truth. He informed me that the exercise had just ended. What I had been hearing and seeing was the grand finale. I didn't bother to ask which side had won. I only wanted to know when we would be returning to the base camp. Withdrawal would begin tomorrow, he told me.

The next afternoon, I climbed into a Huey with all my gear and soon was turning my trusty .45 over to the Special Forces captain, who seemed disappointed that I hadn't lost it. Two days later, after helping break camp and loading vehicles in unbearable heat, I was on my way back to Okinawa.

7

I NEVER HAD FELT close to history, perhaps because history didn't interest me until I began getting personally acquainted with some of it. You couldn't set foot on Okinawa without soon becoming aware of the devastating events that occurred there only 16 years before my arrival. Indeed I would meet numerous people who still had intimate memories of the horrors of it.

Not only was Okinawa the scene of the last major battle of World War II, it also was the target of the biggest of the Pacific campaigns. Taking the island and its airfields was deemed vital to the eventual invasion of the Japanese homeland only 340 miles away.

Native Okinawans long had been subjugated by the colonialist Japanese and that became even more drastic as the war progressed. As spring arrived in 1945, nearly 110,000 Japanese troops were on the island and thousands of Okinawans had been conscripted into their service, including 20,000 men in a home defense corps. By mid-March, the U.S. and Royal Navies had assembled an armada of more than 1,300 ships around the island. An Okinawan co-worker described it to me as if he were still seeing it, calling it the most awesome and fearsome sight he'd ever witnessed.

On March 18, the armada fell under assault by kamikaze (suicide) pilots. My friend watched many of these attacks, always wondering how many people were dying in each dramatic explosion. Nearly 2,000 planes and pilots would be sacrificed in these attacks in coming weeks. Thirty-six ships would be sunk and another 368 heavily damaged. Nearly 5,000 Navy men would die and almost that many more would be wounded, the greatest loss in any battle in U.S. Naval history.

Three days after the kamikaze attacks began, the armada began bombarding the island to "soften it," as the Navy euphemized, for invasion. Okinawans would come to call this the "typhoon of steel." Some sought refuge in caves, where over the coming three months many would die caught in battle, others from suicide or murder by the Japanese. About a third of the population would be killed, perhaps as many as 150,000 people, the second largest civilian loss of all the battles of World War II, topped only by Stalingrad. Another third would be injured, left hungry, untreated.

The invasion began on April 1, Easter Sunday, at 8:30 a.m. Army and Marine troops came ashore to little opposition along the middle beaches of the island's western side. Within two hours, they had secured the two airfields. Before the day was out more than 60,000 troops and vast amounts of heavy equipment including tanks and artillery would be ashore. But the land battle still was to come.

This was a fight the Japanese couldn't win and they knew it. Their goal was to destroy as many ships, planes and men as possible to hinder the expected invasion of the homeland. On land, their strategy was to defend the inland ridge lines that divided the island from north to south. Most troops were in the south, deeply dug in, protected by caves, tunnels, concrete pillboxes and blockhouses. Heavy artillery could be rolled out of caves on tracks and quickly withdrawn. The artillery barrages on American fighting men were unprecedented.

Much of the fiercest fighting took place along the Machinato Line, not far from where I now was stationed. That included Sugar Loaf Hill, Horseshoe Ridge and Half Moon Hill, but the focus was Sugar Loaf. The battle for that rounded mound, only about 50 feet high and 300 yards long, within sight of Naha, would consume 10 days in May and result in 7,547 Marine casualties. Wave after wave of Marines went up that hill only to be beaten back. Out of one company of 240 men, only two survived. Hand-to-hand combat was common.

When the battle for Okinawa ended on June 21, three months after it began, 7,613 of the 183,000 U.S. troops were dead, another 30,000 wounded. Fewer than 10,000 Japanese soldiers had been taken prisoner. The rest died in battle or killed themselves. Four thousand Japanese aircraft were destroyed (compared to 768 for U.S forces), along with 16 ships, including the mighty Yamato, one of the two largest battleships ever built (its sister ship Musashi was the other) and the last in the Japanese arsenal. Both sides lost their commanders, the two top-ranking officers killed in World War II. On the day after his remaining troops surrendered, General Mitsuru Ushijima committed seppuku, a samurai tradition of self-disembowelment by sword for shame, followed by decapitation. U.S. commander, Lt. General Simon B. Buckner Jr., son of a Confederate Army general who became governor of Kentucky and a candidate for Vice President, died three days before the battle ended when he was hit by a fragment from an artillery shell. The fort where I now resided was named for him.

Buckner, however, was not the most famous person to die in the Battle of Okinawa. That was the beloved war correspondent Ernie Pyle, who won the Pulitzer Prize in 1944 for his dispatches from the European Theater. He was killed on April 18 on the small island of Ie Shima, just off Okinawa's Mobutu Peninsula in the northwestern part of the island.

The 77th Infantry Division had invaded Ie Shima two days earlier and was cleaning out the remaining Japanese troops. Pyle and three soldiers were riding in a jeep driven by Lt. Col. Joseph Coolidge. They were on a road that had been cleared of mines and was thought to be safe. A Japanese machine gunner began firing from a nearby ridge. Coolidge slammed the jeep to a halt, and all five occupants dived into a nearby ditch. When the shooting stopped Pyle and Coolidge poked up their heads to check the situation.

"Are you alright?" Pyle asked Coolidge.

At that moment, the machine gunner opened up again. Pyle took a single bullet in his left temple just below his helmet. He died on the spot. The others were not hurt.

Pyle was buried on the island between two fallen troops. A stone marker was erected where he was killed: "At this spot the 77th Infantry lost a buddy, Ernie Pyle." Pyle's body later was disinterred and moved to Okinawa. When the National Memorial Cemetery of the Pacific opened in Honolulu in July, 1949, Pyle's was one of the five bodies buried there on dedication day. The others were two Marines, an Army lieutenant and an unknown soldier.

I knew about Ernie Pyle and his death when I arrived in Okinawa, but I wasn't aware that he had died on Ie Shima. Our unit regularly raised money to provide food, clothing and necessary services for needy residents there. I hadn't read any of Pyle's work at that time but that would change. I eventually would read all the books published under his name and about him. I would come to have a deep personal relationship with his memory, about which I will write later. My greatest regret about the year I spent in Okinawa would be that I didn't take the ferry to Ie Shima (now called Iejima) to pay tribute at the spot where he died.

THE EXCURSIONS THAT MY friends and I took around Okinawa made us more keenly aware of the effects of war, and considering the world events that were unfolding at the time, we all knew that the possibility of being thrust into combat was looming over us as well.

Only on a few occasions would that threat seem imminent. A more immediate threat came a couple of months after I arrived on Okinawa. A super typhoon named Nancy was headed toward us. It developed on September 7 off Kwajalein Atoll in the Marshall Islands far to the south and east of Okinawa and began moving westward on a path toward China. Within two days it had become a category 5 typhoon and its path was slowly turning northward. On September 12, it was just off Okinawa, where it stalled. On that day, a weather plane flew into its eye and recorded a sustained wind speed of 215 miles per hour, the highest ever for any typhoon or hurricane in the northern hemisphere to that point. Nancy would remain a category 5 typhoon for five and a half days, another record. In my humble opinion, it spent entirely too much of that time stalling off Okinawa before making a sharp turn to the right and heading northeastward to Japan. Compared to Nancy, Typhoon June, which I had endured only five weeks earlier in the mountains of Taiwan, would be considered little more than an irritant.

Compared to current technology, weather prediction was still primitive at the time, but we had plenty of warning to prepare for the storm. The ridge on which our waterfront barracks stood was high enough to protect us from flooding short of a tsunami. A barrier reef a few hundred yards offshore took the brunt of the ocean's force and spared us from significant breakers, leaving us mainly with greatly increased tidal ups and downs. While the barracks were safe from storm surge, the B&VA compound was only a few feet above sea level and subject to flooding. Vehicles and equipment that could be damaged had to be moved to safer locations. Files and machinery needed to be stashed above any potential flooding levels, although those could not really be known since this was an unprecedented storm. Preparations at the barracks mainly amounted to shutting down the mess hall and bringing in enough c-rations, flashlights, lanterns, candles and other paraphernalia to get us through the days it would take to get power restored. As the storm grew close, we were restricted to barracks.

I don't know what the wind speeds were that hit Okinawa but they had to have been in excess of 157 mph, the minimum for category 5. I can assure you that winds like that make a frightening and constant fury, as does the heavy rain driven by the wind as it slams against obstacles. Some of my barracks mates slept during this, but that was not possible for me. As I recall, the storm hovered over us for more than a day before finally setting out at a quickening pace toward Japan. My upper bunk on the second floor was at a vertical line of windows facing the sea. These windows usually remained open since we didn't have air conditioning. While the storm was making up its mind about which direction to take, the wind beat relentlessly on the windows. Nothing was visible but the rain. A few windows failed and wind and rain blew in, causing bunks to be moved out of the torrents. The windows in front of my bunk held, but the wind was so strong that the rain seeped in around them, running down the wall. We had two or three inches of water on the second floor and had to slosh our way to the latrine when necessity demanded. Water was even deeper on the first floor. The stairway from the second floor had become a waterfall. Mostly, we stayed in our bunks and hoped that the building had been anchored well enough to withstand the relentless beating it was taking. We only could lie there and hope for the best. This gave me a sense of what it must have been like for Okinawans hunkering in caves during a far more terrifying, human-created "typhoon of steel."

We got a brief break when at least a portion of the eye passed over us. I remember the wind beginning to lessen and then to calm. Suddenly a peek of sun appeared, and we tentatively stepped outside to see what was still standing. No structures appeared to be affected. Huge waves were breaking dramatically over the distant reef, and storm surge had covered the road beneath us and obviously had entered the compound down the road, although, as we later would learn, producing no serious damage.

That was not the case for much of the island. Many homes and businesses received significant damage. Low areas were flooded at levels not known to memory. Many crops in the southern part of the island were destroyed. But the storm killed no one on Okinawa.

Nancy was moving at 65 mph when it hit Japan near Osaka on September 16 and ripped the island nation from one end to the other. By the time it had crossed the northern island of Hokkaido, it had left 172 people dead, 19 unaccounted for, more than 3,000 injured. The government described the damage as "phenomenal." Nearly 12,000 houses were destroyed, 32,000 damaged, 280,000 flooded. More than a thousand fishing vessels and ships had been sunk, 566 bridges washed away, 2,000 roads destroyed. Nancy was so destructive that the Japanese gave it a special name, 2nd Muroto Typhoon, one of the six worst typhoons on record.

Blessed though I was to have survived a history-making typhoon, given a choice I think I would just as soon have been denied the honor by missing the whole show. After it passed, we had to turn our attention back to the prospects of a war into which we were being inevitably drawn.

From the time he was sworn into office eight months earlier, John F. Kennedy had to make decisions that led to military actions and international crises. The first was a planned invasion of Cuba by a brigade of CIA-trained exiles seeking to overthrow communist dictator Fidel Castro. Dwight Eisenhower had approved the plan in 1960. Kennedy, who had taken a strong stand against Castro during his campaign, ordered it to proceed shortly after his inauguration. The bungled invasion came to be known as The Bay of Pigs. It began with the bombing of three Cuban airfields on April 15, 1961. Two days later the brigade landed in the area that gave the folly its name. Within three days it was overcome by Cuban forces. More than 120 exiles died in action. Hundreds more were executed. All the rest, more than 1,200, were captured, tried for treason and sentenced to 30 years in prison.

The invasion became a major embarrassment for Kennedy and the United States. It not only strengthened Castro's position but tightened Cuba's relationship with Russia. More importantly, it emboldened Soviet Premier Nikita Khrushchev, who saw Kennedy's abandonment of the hapless invaders as a sign of weakness. Within a few months that would lead Khrushchev to create a major crisis, this one in Berlin.

Three years earlier, Khrushchev had demanded that the U.S., Britain and France withdraw from Berlin, which was surrounded by Soviet backed East Germany. The matter had been simmering since and was becoming a major issue for the communists because more than a thousand East Germans were fleeing into West Berlin every day to escape oppression. Khrushchev decided to confront Kennedy at a summit meeting in Vienna on June 4, when I was arriving at Ft. Bragg. If the Western powers didn't withdraw, he vowed, he would sign a treaty with East Germany closing all access to West Berlin.

Kennedy left the meeting feeling that he had been savaged by Khrushchev and believing that Khrushchev thought he wouldn't stand up to him.

"We have to see what we can do that will restore a feeling in Moscow that we will defend our national interest," he told James Reston, *The New York Times* Washington bureau chief who had arranged an interview soon after the meeting. "I'll have to increase the defense budget. And we have to confront them. The only place we can do that is in Vietnam. We have to send more people there."

From the Bay of Pigs crisis, three others would grow. And two of those would affect me.

In a televised speech on July 25, Kennedy revealed that he wanted to increase military spending by $3.25 billion, add 217,000 members to the armed forces, triple the draft, and get authorization making it easier to call up reserves and extend the tours of those already serving. The speech angered Khrushchev. Within three weeks, the East Germans began building a wall around West Berlin to block access. That would lead on October 26th to a tense face-to-face standoff between 33 Soviet tanks and 30 U.S. tanks at Check Point Charlie. Military forces in Europe and the Strategic Air Command were put on high alert. By this time, Kennedy and Khrushchev were communicating through an emissary. As the standoff continued, both decided that this was not worth a war. Kennedy sent a message that if the Soviet tanks pulled back, U.S. tanks would be gone in 30 minutes. After 20 hours, the Soviet tanks began to depart and the confrontation ended. The wall remained and many East Germans would lose their lives trying to get over, around, or through it. But U.S., French and British forces retained access to West Berlin.

My friends and I had been keeping close watch on the Berlin situation. We had two primary sources of news in Okinawa—*Stars & Stripes*, the military newspaper published in Tokyo, and the Armed Forces television and radio networks which broadcast on Okinawa. These were sources, we suspected, that weren't likely to provide information the government didn't want us to know but did convey the worldwide fear this crisis had sparked—that it might evolve into nuclear war. We were keenly aware that if that happened, Okinawa, our major military base in the Far East, from which B-52 bombers with nuclear bombs could fly, would be a certain early target. What we weren't learning about in the news were developments in Vietnam and the President's intentions there. These could have serious personal implications for us.

THE SITUATION IN VIETNAM was growing steadily worse, and pressure was building for the U.S. to make a stronger commitment. Experts sent to analyze the situation kept bringing back grim reports. On September 18, nearly 1,000 Viet Cong seized the provincial capital Phouc Vinh, 55 miles from Saigon, released 250 prisoners, seized all weapons and ammunition and beheaded the province chief and his deputy. That prompted President Ngo Dinh Diem to bring up the possibility of sending American troops. On October 5, the Joint Chiefs of Staff reported that nothing short of outside intervention could prevent the fall of Laos and South Vietnam. Four days later the Joint Chiefs reported that at least 22,800 men from the South-East Asia Treaty Organization (SEATO) would be needed to disrupt Viet Cong supply lines, 13,200 of those from the U.S. Two days after that, Kennedy met with the Vietnam Task Force he had formed following the Bay of Pigs disaster. No decision was reached on the SEATO intervention, but Kennedy did authorize sending a dozen old planes and a few hundred "Jungle Jims," U.S. troops disguised as civilians, to make reconnaissance flights and support ground attacks, accompanied by Vietnamese observers. These were the first troops Kennedy ordered to Vietnam.

A week before Christmas, in response to continuing pressure from Diem and others, Kennedy sent two helicopter companies from the Philippines, 400 men and 37 helicopters. That brought the number of American troops in Vietnam to more than 2,000, all classified as advisers. At first they were not allowed to use their weapons. On December 20, a new order came. They could use their weapons, but only in self-defense. Two days later, a Spec. 4 from Livingston, Tennessee, James Thomas Davis, was killed on a mission. Some 58,000 more would suffer his fate before the United States made a disgraceful retreat in defeat 13 years later. Although I couldn't have imagined that outcome at the time, I did know that I didn't want to become one of that war's statistics.

8

VIETNAM WAS HAVING A deteriorating effect on B&VA, but that wasn't the only problem the unit was facing. The other was pathetic leadership.

The commander of B&VA was Col. Rollins S. Emmerich, who appeared to be a bumbling fool with little knowledge of psychological warfare or any ability at its implementation. Blessedly, he was rarely seen or heard from, and I don't recall a single encounter with him. His primary interest appeared to be the bowling leagues that he promoted within the unit. What none of us knew at the time was that he might have had more burdensome concerns on his mind as well as his conscience, if he had one, which was questionable.

When the Korean War erupted in June, 1950, Emmerich, then a lieutenant colonel, was a top advisor to the South Korean Army. As communist North Korean troops surged southward, panicked South Korean officials ordered the slaughter of tens of thousands of northern sympathizers out of fear that they would join enemy troops. Some were women and children. Most of the bodies were dumped in mass graves.

At the end of June, 1950, Emmerich was with South Korean troops in the port city of Buson, where about 3,500 communist sympathizers were being held in a prison camp. When Emmerich heard that a military commander planned to execute these prisoners to keep them from joining the invaders, he informed him that the arrival of those troops wasn't as imminent as the commander feared and that "atrocities could not be condoned."

"Colonel Kim promised not to execute the prisoners until the situation became more critical," Emmerich later wrote. "Colonel Kim was told that if the enemy did arrive to the outskirts he would be permitted to open the gates of the prison and shoot the prisoners with machine guns."

Most of those prisoners were executed, and those executions had taken place just 11 years before the man who gave permission for them became my commanding officer.

None of this was publicly known until 2008 when a Korean newspaper uncovered a 78-page classified report that Emmerich wrote for Army historians. It was the first evidence that the U.S. military had sanctioned such killings in Korea. Obviously, the Army had chosen not to penalize or reprimand Emmerich for permitting mass murders of civilians, a war crime. He later was promoted to full bird colonel and allowed to retire with honor. He never had to suffer any public embarrassment for his actions because the disclosure didn't occur until 18 years after his death in 1986.

THE PERSON WHO ACTUALLY ran B&VA was an ambitious lieutenant colonel who was commander of the 14th Psywar Battalion. He was a petty tyrant and relished the role. He was a bit rotund with a round blank face, big-rimmed glasses and a Rudolph nose that frequently glowed. Although his pale spindly legs seemed inadequate to support the rest of his body, he preferred Bermuda shorts with his work uniform. The sight of him was not a pleasant one. My friends and I called him Blubberbutt. To my dismay, his office was just a short distance from the art department and I frequently had to encounter him in the hallways. If he ever had a friendly or jovial impulse, he never displayed it.

Blubberbutt was anal retentive, obscenely meticulous. Everything had to be in order, done just so, immaculate.

There were some things about which Blubberbutt was totally obsessive. One was rocks, another snails. Okinawa, of course, was a rock, still is a rock, and likely will remain one. That's why most troops called it "The Rock." It had a tendency to produce many smaller rocks, some of which seemed to pop out of the ground or wash up on the beaches. Blubberbutt wanted pavement, concrete and grass, no rocks, inside his compound.

Like many Pacific islands, Okinawa also was overrun by snails. The giant African land snail, to be specific, the largest and most invasive snail on Earth. They grew to be as much as eight inches long, their shells greenish-brown and ugly. They prowled at night. You couldn't walk from the barracks to the PX or the service club after dark without crunching them underfoot and having to clean the slimy mess off your shoes. How these snails got from Africa to Okinawa is still debated. Some say they were brought as a food source, although it's hard to imagine why anybody would want to eat one. They carried the larvae of the rat lung worm and anybody who didn't cook one long enough or with enough heat could get an infected brain and suffer a wretched death. However these despicable snails got to Okinawa, Blubberbutt was determined not to allow them inside his compound. But the snails seemed to have little concern for military dictates or the cyclone fences that enclosed the compound.

Each day, Blubberbutt saw to it that lower-ranked troops were assigned to details to clear the compound of rocks and snails. Rocks were tossed over the fence, where they appeared to be forming low walls so vast were their numbers. Snails had to be hunted down, smashed with entrenching tools and their slimy carcasses tossed over the fence for seabirds and crabs to feast on.

These weren't the only details to which we regularly were assigned, however. There also were details for picking up cigarette butts, spot painting trucks in the motor pool, and any other fixation that seized Blubberbutt's constricted brain. One day, Eric and I were assigned to spend the afternoon spot painting three-quarter-ton and deuce-and-half troop carriers. As we were working, Eric happened onto a very big snail seeking refuge from the sun. Almost instantly inspiration hit.

Eric picked up the snail and painted its shell with the olive-drab paint we were dabbing on rust spots. He left the snail in my care while he went to the art department and returned with a small brush and little bottle of white paint. When the paint on the snail was sufficiently dry, he decorated it with a star and "U.S. Army" underneath it. Thus was the first U.S. Army snail inducted.

So impressed were we with the results, we began hunting other snails. Before the afternoon was over we had a small cardboard box filled with 18 or 20 U.S. Army snails. We took the box to the art department and hid it. When the work day ended, I remained at my desk and Eric at his art table, pretending that we had a deadline project to finish and needed to work late. When we were sure the building was clear, we took our box of snails to Blubberbutt's office, granted them their freedom and closed the door. We hiked back to the barracks, laughing all the way. We didn't know what to expect the next morning.

When we arrived for work, we passed the Sergeant Major in the hallway. His desk was in a reception area just outside Blubberbutt's office. He was on his way to the printing department and had a look of panic on his face. We later learned that he had fetched two printers to capture and execute our brave, experimental psywar snails without granting them so much as a formal hearing. Later, these same two guys were seen going into the colonel's office with buckets of soapy water, brushes and towels to remove the myriad mucous trails and excrement the snails had left in their night of explorations.

I later asked one of the printers what was going on in Blubberbutt's office.

"Somebody let some damn painted-up snails loose and he just went batshit crazy," he said. "Sergeant Major said he came dancing out of his office swinging his briefcase and screaming, 'Snails! Snails! Snails!'"

"Why would somebody do something like that?" I asked.

"Beats me," he said, "but if I find out who it was, I'm going to kick his ass. I've wiped up all the snail snot I want to deal with for a while."

Eric and I thought that Blubberbutt might launch an investigation but he didn't, probably, we speculated, because he didn't want word of this to spread among other commanders on the island and make him a laughingstock.

THIS WASN'T THE ONLY stunt that Eric and I pulled during our time together in Okinawa. Another created a much bigger stir. One Sunday afternoon we were at the Machinato PX restaurant with our friend Bill Usher, a fellow North Carolinian whom we had nicknamed Tub. While we were there, dark boiling clouds began moving in, casting a pall on the day. We were seated at a table with a view of Naha Bay. I noticed that the backdrop of clouds had created reflections of the round, recessed ceiling lights on several of the big plate-glass windows.

"What does that look like to you guys?" I asked.

"I think we're seeing flying saucers," Eric said with a grin.

Flying saucers had been in the news throughout the country during the '50s. Some even had been spotted in Thomasville.

I had my twin-lens reflex with me, and I began taking photos of the windows. Some were close-ups of the reflections, others broader views that included the coast, the sea, and buildings just down the hill from the restaurant with what appeared to be a formation of flying saucers passing overhead.

"If these shots come out, we could have some fun," I said.

While Eric and Tub were returning to the barracks, I went to the service club to develop the film. I couldn't believe what I was seeing—flying saucers coming in low under the cloud cover in a tight diamond formation. There was no indication that any of these shots had been taken through a window.

I printed a stack of 8-by-10s and headed to the barracks. By the time lights out arrived, a good number of people believed that flying saucers had swooped over Machinato that day. Eric and I took some of the photos to work the next morning and people began passing them around and talking about them.

B&VA had lots of civilian employees from the States and Okinawa as well as other countries. We had a huge radio operation that broadcast into China and North Korea 24 hours a day with a wide range of programming, and we had actors, actresses, announcers, and interpreters from Korea, Taiwan, Hong Kong and other places. Many of these people made their way to the art department that day to see our photos and ask questions. Some of the Okinawan employees were more excitable than others. That may have been because some Okinawans were still fearful of going out in the rain because they thought it would cause them to absorb fallout from U.S. atomic tests in the Pacific several years earlier. We later learned that some of the Okinawan employees had asked to go home so they could protect their families from potential alien attack.

After we returned from lunch in the mess hall, our lieutenant stopped us outside his office to inform us that Okinawa's civilian-owned English language newspaper, *Morning Star*, had called. They had one of the photos, planned to publish it, and wanted to interview us. Before we could respond, the lieutenant's phone rang and he hurried to answer it.

"Yes," I heard him say. "Well, just one of them took the photos. You need to talk with him. He's right here."

He held the receiver out toward me.

"It's for you," he said. "You did take the pictures, right?"

"Who is it?" I asked.

"An Air Force UFO investigator from Kadena."

"Oh," I said.

The investigator seemed excited. How fast were they moving, he wanted to know.

"Well, they weren't exactly moving," I said.

"Were they hovering?"

"That's the appearance they gave."

"Do you think they could have been lights from ships or planes?"

"Not from ships or planes," I said and paused, realizing it was time to make the facts known. "More like the ceiling lights at the PX restaurant."

He didn't say anything for a few moments.

"You mean this is a hoax?" he finally asked.

"Oh, no," I said. "We were conducting an experiment in psychological warfare. We wanted to see if we could make people believe that an illusion was real. We just didn't realize it might get out of hand."

I apologized and he accepted with a distinct chord of disappointment. It's got to be hard being an UFO investigator and never being able to land one.

The lieutenant had been listening to my side of the conversation, and he burst into laughter when I hung up the receiver.

"I knew it was bullshit," he said, "but I never imagined that you could come up with bullshit enough to get out of it."

I thought we might be in trouble but the lieutenant was pleased with our little escapade. He fixed any potential problems by printing a widely distributed "Photos Never Lie" handbill with two of my dramatic shots. It noted that a majority of people who had seen the photos believed the images to be UFOs but also revealed the reality.

When I began researching for this memoir, I came across a website devoted to B&VA. It was created by Tim Yoho, who was a PFC at B&VA at the time I was there. He was in the radio section. I don't recall ever meeting him but one of his best friends was my friend Bill Usher. After leaving the Army Yoho got a Ph.D and was a professor of Biology at Lock Haven University in Pennsylvania for 30 years.

Some B&VA alumni have posted reminiscences at Yoho's website. One is Larry Hartley, an audio specialist, who also was there when I was, although I don't remember meeting him either. At the end of his reminiscence, Hartley wrote: "By the way, anybody from the 1961-62 time period remember the flying saucer scare that got some people worked up? The picture showed a number of saucer-like objects in the sky over the water. Later it was discovered they looked very similar to the lights in the Machinato PX reflecting off the window."

I was amazed that after more than half a century somebody would remember our little psychological warfare experiment.

MUCH OF WHAT WE had to deal with was not fun, however. That was largely due to the increasingly bad situation in Vietnam. The size of the unit was being boosted in preparation for that, but in bodies only. The facilities, equipment and jobs remained the same. That created crowding, especially in the barracks, as well as divisions of meaningful work. Tension and resentment began to grow. Training increased. Much if it was boring classroom stuff, but a lot was in the field, rehearsal for Vietnam.

I was assigned to learn how to drive the three-quarter-ton and two-and-a-half-ton trucks I had spent so much time spot painting. That training took place on rough trails along the rugged ridges in the central part of the island. I could handle the smaller truck OK, but the big one was a real challenge. I nearly turned one over during my first attempt at driving it. I still can hear my instructor, a sergeant, screaming, "You're going to kill us both!" before I brought it to a halt at a precipitous slant.

Nonetheless, I was licensed to drive the damn things and had to train regularly, dreading it every time. Some who knew me said they'd rather face the Viet Cong than ride in a truck I was driving, and I could understand why they felt that way. I frightened myself.

At one point, a large part of the unit was alerted to prepare to move out to an undisclosed destination. I was among those. None of us had any doubt that we were on our way to Vietnam. We spent two grave days loading up radio, printing and loudspeaker equipment, and in full combat gear, with my carbine close at hand, I drove a heavily-loaded deuce-and-a-half truck in a convoy to the docks at Naha Port, where a Navy ship awaited us. Once there, to our great relief, we learned that this was only an exercise. We actually weren't going anywhere. Not yet, anyway.

I soon was to learn quite a bit about the history of the situation in Vietnam. This was the result of another assignment. The two top commanders of Special Forces were coming to Okinawa on an inspection tour of our units. I was assigned to help prepare a report on the history of the situation in Vietnam

Okinawa's Soldier of the Month

and B&VA's potential role in preventing a communist victory there. The Intelligence section was in charge of the contents of the report and I was assigned there temporarily.

I worked for weeks on this project and eventually wrote most of the report that would be presented to the visiting generals. Initially, maps were the only illustrations, but I suggested that it might be enhanced with ink sketches of the top political and military leaders of both North and South Vietnam and offered to draw them. The sketches met with approval, and the commander of intelligence thought it might also be a good idea to do sketches of the generals who were coming to visit us so they could be used on a welcoming poster. I did the sketches and Eric and I created the poster in the art department.

Our visitors were Brig. Gen. W.B. Rosson, who served at the Pentagon as the Chief of Staff's assistant for Special Warfare, and Brig. Gen. W.P. Yarborough, commander of the Special Warfare Center at Ft. Bragg. Both had distinguished themselves in combat in Europe and North Africa during World War II. Yarborough had become commander of the Special Warfare Center in January, 1961, just months before I arrived there, and quickly saw its potential. In October he got President Kennedy to visit the center and convinced him to vastly expand Special Forces and sanction the wearing of green berets, which would become the famous symbol of those esteemed troops. Yarborough, who became known as the Father of the Green Berets, would retire as a three-star-general.

I remember well all the fanatical cleaning, rearranging and other preparations that Blubberbutt had everybody doing before the generals' arrival, but I have no memory of encountering them. However, a few weeks after the visit, I stopped by the mail room and was handed an Air Mail envelope. It was hand addressed to me and the name in the top left-hand corner was Brig. Gen. W. B. Rosson from his home address in Arlington, Virginia. I opened it and found a hand-written letter that began:

"Dear PFC Bledsoe,

"In the battle for men's minds there are many tasks to be accomplished. Accomplishment in turn relies heavily on the skill, motivation and dedication of those to whom the tasks are entrusted. Your fine effort is an outstanding example of all three."

Rosson, a West Pointer, would go on to become the longest serving top commander in Vietnam. He would retire as a four-star general.

Gen. Yarborough also sent me a similar letter, typed but hand-signed, adding that my sketch of him made an excellent souvenir of his trip to Okinawa. His letter was sent more formally through Army channels. It was forwarded to Blubberbutt, who had to send it on to me and sign off on it. I had been surprised by these letters because my name hadn't appeared on the report or the illustrations. I suspected it was the intelligence officer who had informed the generals of my work. I'm sure it wasn't Blubberbutt, who, I was certain, resented having to pass Gen. Yarborough's letter on to me. He had added no congratulations and never said a word about it when I passed him in the hallway.

THIS WASN'T THE ONLY recognition I received during this period. Twelve times yearly a competition was held in all Army units on the island to pick Soldier of the Month. The winners at each unit were sent to headquarters to compete for the position for the entire island. I don't recall how the candidates for this honor were chosen, but my name turned up on the list one month. I immediately sent my tailored, honor guard uniform off to the laundry and started spit polishing my inspection shoes and shining my brass. I sailed through the unit competition, but the headquarters affair was a little tougher. A single word would deliver me: roentgen.

The captain judging us as we stood at rigid attention, appeared to repress a smile when he began to question me after examining my meticulously clean carbine and looking me up and down. He already had flustered several others with his questions and I could tell that he was certain he was going to get me.

"What is a roentgen?" he asked sharply.

I wanted to leap for joy. I thought this moment never would come. My mentor at Ft. Rucker had told me that at some point I likely would face this question. It was a favored killer question, and I had carried the answer around for a year and a half without ever finding a use for it.

"Sir," I said sharply, "a roentgen is a measurement of radiation."

All merriment was instantly flushed from his eyes and replaced with a stunned look. He moved quickly to the next guy. After finishing his inspection, he returned in precise march-step, stopped in front of me, did a quick right face, instructed me to step forward and pronounced me to be Okinawa's Soldier of the Month.

"Nobody's ever answered that question before,' he told me afterward.

The PIO office of command headquarters sent a news release about this accomplishment to *The Thomasville Times*, and Wint Capel printed it in full. It didn't mention the question that granted me the honor. If it had that might have set off a stroke epidemic among my high school science teachers.

MY MOTHER SENT ME a copy of the clipping in a letter telling me that everybody was proud of how well I was doing in the Army, but in reality I wasn't doing well at all, although I would never let my parents know that. I still hated almost everything about it and I was angry that two years into my enlistment

I remained a PFC. Others I knew who had come into the Army at about the same time had long since become Spec. 4s. Some, including my friend Eric and my buddy-plan buddy Darrell, now in Germany (so much for the buddy plan), were about to reach NCO level. I was certain that Blubberbutt was keeping me from gaining rank and the extra income it would bring.

I did appreciate one thing about the Army. I was immensely grateful for the friendships it granted me. Some became especially close. Eric, Jim Lawler, Eugene Craig, Lester Blair, and I had formed a tight group that others began calling The Clique. We fancied ourselves to be an Okinawan version of the Hollywood group created by Frank Sinatra, Dean Martin, Sammy Davis Jr., Peter Lawford and Joey Bishop that came to be known as The Rat Pack, although they never called themselves that, favoring instead The Summit or The Clan. We thought The Clique was fine. At one point, as a joke, we bought identical beige blazers and had a formal group portrait made at a studio in Naha. It was an impressive, Hollywood-like publicity shot, but somehow over the years, much to my regret, I managed to misplace my copy. I do, however, still have my official Clique membership card, created and laminated by Eric.

Gene Craig had learned to speak fairly fluent Japanese from his Okinawan assistant while working in the library and was our off-base interpreter, allowing us to navigate well among the island's natives. With time we actually began melding into the local community.

Although he still was assigned to the barracks, Jim Lawler, who came from a more prosperous family than the rest of us, rented a house in a fairly nice neighborhood in Naha. That became our weekend retreat, the site of frequent raucous laughter and lengthy philosophical and political discussions, along with the usual bitching about the Army. The neighbors were receptive to us and impressed that Gene could speak Japanese so well. We wore civilian attire, shopped in local markets and ate in tiny restaurants where other military folks rarely ventured.

After Lawler had been in his house a couple of months, a neighbor across the street told him that he had a much smaller accommodation that he was willing to rent. It was beside his own house within a walled compound. Eric and I went to look at it. It was a traditional Japanese house with a single tatami-floored room, a tiny kitchen area at the rear with a small sink, a double-burner hotplate, a toaster oven and the littlest refrigerator I had yet encountered, but effective enough for keeping beer cold. The only other furnishing was a low wooden table on which we could eat while sitting cross-legged on the tatami. Running water was only in the metal kitchen sink. It came from a cistern on a stand beside the back door. Fresh water in Okinawa was captured from rain on red tile roofs and funneled into a cistern where it was filtered and fed by gravity to the faucet. There was no bath (neighborhood bath houses were communal and off limits to military residents), and the toilet was an indoor outhouse in a walled enclosure by the front door inside which a 50-pound sack of lime stood guard to tamp down odor. (Much of the city's sewage made its way untreated to the ocean through open "benjo ditches" and nothing could kill that stench.) When we found out the rent was only $14 a month, we accepted immediately. We went shopping for futons and pillows and moved in that day. I later bought a record player at the PX that would play 45rpm-singles as well as 33rpm-albums for entertainment. We had our own retreat from the turmoil in the barracks that gave us at least a slight sense of civility. Unfortunately, this little house would become the hatching ground for another venture that would lead to deep trouble.

9

CHARITY LED ME TO the distress I was about to encounter. I had a winter jacket that I had worn in high school and brought to Okinawa. Winter nights occasionally did get cool on the island, especially when the sea breezes were brisk, but I really had little use for the jacket. One day a huge box appeared in the barracks hallway near the mail room with a sign saying that clothing donations were needed for the poor on Ie Shima. Feeling big-hearted, I deposited my jacket.

Two days later, I was walking past the Sergeant Major's room. The door was partially open and I saw my distinctive, pale mustard-colored jacket on a hanger. Stealing, I had been taught, is wrong. Stealing from the poor is even worse. I went downstairs and searched through the clothing box. My jacket was missing. After formation the next morning, I went to the orderly room to report what I had discovered. I was told that the matter would be looked into.

When I returned for lunch in the mess hall, I was informed that the company commander wanted to see me. I reported as soon as I finished eating.

The captain said he personally had inspected the Sergeant Major's room and had seen no such jacket. Perhaps I had seen something else and mistaken it for that, he suggested. A PFC could get into serious trouble for making false allegations against a superior, he reminded me, noting that certainly was not to be expected from somebody who had been named Soldier of the Month for the entire island.

I didn't respond, but I suspect my tightly clenched jaw was betraying my anger. After I was dismissed, I went upstairs and questioned two houseboys who worked there. Both told me that the Sergeant Major had appeared unexpectedly at mid-morning and gone into his room. He left shortly afterward, they said, carrying a bundled laundry bag under one arm.

Had they seen the captain? I asked.

Yes, they said, he had come upstairs and gone into the room for a brief period about 30 minutes after the Sergeant Major left.

My anger over the jacket incident didn't dissipate. Instead, it started me thinking of a means to get out word about the plethora of growing problems within our unit and the low morale they were creating. An anonymous newspaper could do that, I thought. And from that idea I began to plot. My first co-conspirator, of course, was Eric, not only because he was my closest friend and confidant, but because I needed his expertise. The newsroom and production facility for this publication would be the tiny house in Naha that Eric and I rented.

At this point, I never had heard the term "underground newspaper." These would pop up by the score at U.S. Military bases in the late '60s and early '70s when the Vietnam War was at its height and opposition to it was burgeoning, even within the military. Some of the better known papers, such as *Vietnam GI* and *FTA* ("Fun, Travel, Adventure"), were almost professionally done, attained fairly wide readerships, and actually lasted for a year or two. I've found no underground paper in the military, however, that predates *The Harasser*, which appeared in spring, 1962, and could be the original underground Army newspaper. Presented as a weekly, it was far from technically professional, and its readership was greatly restricted because only 200 copies were produced and distributed in a single unit, B&VA. Readership was further confined because only one edition appeared. That restriction was imposed by the publishers out of a desire to remain out of prison.

The Harasser was only four pages, printed front and back, on legal-size sheets of pulp paper purchased in a Naha store. Eric drew the masthead, which included a triangular logo that said, "GET OUT ARMY," a play on an official logo "RE-UP ARMY." The paper was produced on a borrowed typewriter, and Eric hand printed every page using silk screen stencils. The pages were stapled, one of my jobs.

A major problem at B&VA was a grave division between top enlisted people and lower ranks. Because of the nature of a psychological warfare unit, many, if not most of the jobs required people who were smart, creative and often well educated. Most of the top sergeants had risen through completely different types of units and simply didn't have the intelligence and talents of the people they had to oversee. Not only did they not understand or know how to deal effectively with many of the people under their charge, they resented them, and in some cases hated them.

That explained the headline of the lead story on page one: "Terror Reigns as New Reign Begins."

It was about the company's new master sergeant who called a packed gathering of those who lived in the barracks to inform us that we were not meeting his standards. He threatened to ban houseboys, require everybody to rise 30 minutes earlier, face inspections every morning and regular rotations of latrine duty. Two days later, he issued an order that everybody be standing at attention beside his bunk after work for a GI party of intense cleaning. That order was revoked by the company commander after the mess sergeant complained it would disrupt the evening meal and cause problems for his Okinawan employees. The master sergeant's threats never panned out largely because it soon became apparent that he staggered back to the barracks drunk most nights and was so badly hung over the next morning that he rarely would have been able to carry out his early-hour inspections.

The mess sergeant didn't escape *The Harasser's* attention either. A short article reported a recent breakfast that consisted solely of sandwich bread and cold gobs of leftover potatoes. Usually, we at least got powdered eggs and hot oatmeal, but on this morning the power had failed, as happened often, and the emergency cooking equipment couldn't be used because the Okinawan employee who had the only key to the shed where the fuel was stored had not shown up for work.

The Harasser's only byline appeared on an odd article about rock gardening, aimed primarily at Blubberbutt. It was signed M. Twain.

One of the longer articles was devoted to dissatisfaction over the unit's policy that holidays, with the exceptions of Christmas and Independence Day, existed only for civilian employees and were not to be recognized or celebrated by anybody in uniform.

No article appeared about the Sergeant Major's theft of my jacket from the poor folks' box, which was not widely known, for the simple reason that I feared it would reveal the publisher's identity.

The most amusing piece, at least in my estimation, since I wrote it, was a satirical Broadway-opening style review of a two-day training session we had been required to endure at the Machinato Theater. This training included a full Saturday, usually a day free from work. The production was entitled "Organization, Mission, Functions and Capabilities of Psychological Warfare Units."

"The sets by the training section," I wrote near the end of the review, "were marvelous. Seldom in a production of this type does one experience such beauty....The diagrams were filled with such color that this writer was reminded of the beautiful charts in a sophomore accounting book."

Of the star performer, a captain, I wrote: "So removed did he appear to be that he even flubbed his lines numerous times. He did convince the audience of his apathy."

His best line came, I noted, after taking his bows and asking if there were questions (and this actually happened).

"One inquiring soul asked the actor this: 'Sir, how exactly is our present unit organized?' Quipped the captain: 'That's a good question. You know, I've been working in that department for two years and still haven't come up with the answer.'"

That actually got a laugh.

The front page also had a "Chuckle of the Week" and another section called "Rumors of the Week." One of the rumors was this: "The compound fence will be moved in the near future so the colonel will have rocks to throw over the fence again."

The final page bore this notation: "This paper is published weekly with no affiliation to the Army. It is an experiment in psywar. It has a lesser purpose of establishing a morale in the unit. Criticisms in this publication are not intended to be personal." That last bit, like psychological warfare, may not have been completely truthful.

Eric and I produced *The Harasser* over a weekend at our little house, finishing it late Sunday night. We slipped the copies into the barracks well after midnight and stealthily dropped copies on every foot locker. We left small stacks in the day room, at the mess hall door, and by the vending machines. Then we crawled into our mosquito-netted bunks with smug satisfaction and waited to see what morning would bring.

People were slow to recognize what some of higher ranks later would call the subversion that had been slipped into their midst. At first not many seemed to pay much attention to the copies on their lockers as they went about their morning rituals. But by the time the mess hall had opened, the mood had shifted. Many people were reading *The Harasser* as they ate. Others were talking, or laughing, about it, speculating about who had produced it.

By the time formation was called, a new spirit was apparent. A whoop went up, something that never had happened before. The company commander came before us smiling jovially.

"I want to thank the publishers of *The Harasser* for my copy this morning," he said. "I know we all are enjoying it. I'd like to talk with those who had something to do with it after dismissal."

Unsurprisingly, everybody trooped straight to the buses, leaving him standing alone.

It didn't take long after we arrived at work to learn that Blubberbutt had been informed and reports circulated that he was enraged. He began calling officers into meetings. No officers in the unit other than the company commander had seen the paper because copies had been distributed only in the barracks. Many were curious about it. We had a new lieutenant who had become our section leader. He was a cut above most of the other officers, smart, talented and friendly. He treated us with respect and we liked him.

I was leaving the compound snack bar with a soft drink about mid-morning when I encountered him. He asked if I could get him a copy of *The Harasser*. I didn't know if he suspected that I might have been involved with it, but I was wary. I said I couldn't help him. By noon word leaked out that Blubberbutt had ordered all copies seized.

I had left a copy in my locker. When I got to the barracks for lunch, I placed it in an envelope, addressed it to my dad and included a note telling him to keep it in a safe place and tell nobody about it. I dropped it in the mail box on my way to the mess hall. Not a single copy was seen in the mess hall this time, but there was much conversation about Blubberbutt's reaction. Some people had hidden their copies. One said he'd mailed his to his congressman, and two more, I later was told, claimed they had done the same.

BEFORE THE DAY WAS out Blubberbutt had made it clear that investigations were underway. Not just internal investigations, but a much wider and more serious criminal investigation. To Blubberbutt, this harmless little exercise in humor, lightheartedly turning psychological warfare upon itself, was an act of sedition and treason, crimes that could be punished by death.

The paper itself was sedition to him. His basis for treason was an item in the Rumors of the Week section: "Units from the 15th will be moving to Thailand, Taiwan, Vietnam and the Philippines before June." The 15th was Headquarters Company within the 14th Battalion. This rumor, Blubberbutt claimed, was aiding the enemy by informing them of troop movements, something of which we had no knowledge. It also was unlikely that any of our enemies had been able to snag a copy of *The Harasser*.

To put it mildly, these were sobering developments. Eric and I had said not a word to each other about any of this as we worked that day but we both knew what we had to do. As soon as we got back to the barracks, we changed into civilian attire and headed for our little house in Naha. We gathered up everything we had used, the silk screen device, stencils, ink, rollers, left-over paper, took it to an isolated spot, burned it and buried the ashes. No physical evidence would be able to tie us to the paper. Only five of us knew anything about it, and we were nervously bound to secrecy.

A couple of days later, I returned to the barracks at noon and went upstairs to get something from my locker. The guy on the lower bunk next to my stack of bunks was emptying his lockers. We had a lot of people who got temporary duty assignments to our detachments in Korea and Japan, and sometimes to other places.

"Where are you going?" I asked.

"Downstairs," he said. "They told me I've got to move."

"Did they say why?"

"No. They just said move. And do it now."

When I returned to the barracks that evening, a new guy had been assigned that bunk and was stashing his gear in the lockers. He was a Spec. 4. He seemed friendly and introduced himself to me and several others who bunked nearby. He said he'd transferred from another unit and was looking forward to working in psywar. My first thought, naturally, was why didn't they put him downstairs?

The next day I learned that he was to be a clerk for the Sergeant Major and would occupy a desk just outside Blubberbutt's office, up the hall from the art department. That seemed a little too convenient to me.

The following night, my friend Bill Taylor and I went to the NCO Club, a nightclub and casino that welcomed even PFCs. Bill and I were attracted to the club's enticing rows of slot machines that could hypnotically erase any worries and concerns—and mine were growing dramatically at this point—as long as your nickels, dimes and quarters held out. That night I hit two watermelons and a bar and the machine began spitting out a hundred nickels. I looked around excitedly for Bill to let him know, only to see the new guy just two machines away.

"Congratulations," he said.

My delight was suddenly undercut by what I took to be verification that his real job was shadowing me.

BECAUSE ERIC AND I worked closely together every day, we both assumed that he likely was under suspicion as well, although we'd seen no definitive indications of it. Eric was a low-profile guy who rarely publicly expressed criticisms or complaints, a strength I couldn't claim. Because people were almost always around us, we had little opportunity to talk about private matters at work. We now had to be careful about everything we said and did and felt as if we had stumbled into Spy World.

One day I returned to the barracks after work and discovered a well-worn book on my bunk. Its title was *The Execution of Private Slovik*. I'd never heard of it. I asked around the barracks trying to find out to whom it might belong, but nobody claimed it. Nobody knew who had left it. I started reading it out of curiosity.

Eddie Slovik was a Polish Catholic boy from Detroit who had a harsh upbringing, little education and mental problems. He had been classified 4F by the draft board, but as World War II was entering its final throes, he was snatched up by the Army and sent to the front as U.S. troops were beginning their push into Germany. He was emotionally unable to handle combat, and after a night of heavy fire, he offered to do any job behind the lines but refused to go back into battle. He was sent to the stockade, charged with desertion and sentenced to death.

General of the Armies Dwight Eisenhower denied his appeal. Slovik was tied to a post in a snow-covered courtyard, a hood placed over his head, and shot to death by 12 members of his unit. He was the only American to be executed for desertion since the Civil War. The execution was supposed to set an example for other troops, but the Army kept it secret. Slovik's wife was never told how or why he'd died or what had become of his body. Not until William Bradford Huie, a brilliant reporter and writer from Alabama, dug out the story did it become known. His book had been published in 1954.

I didn't know whether the person who had left the book on my bunk had done it to inform, warn, or scare me, but it accomplished all three. I had no doubt that the Army could and would do whatever it pleased to anybody within its hold. And it didn't necessarily matter whether the person had done anything wrong, especially if the purpose was to cover up incompetence or corruption by people of higher ranks.

FOR ME THE BOOK increased the tension that been growing, but it was about to get even worse. Not long after I finished it, I was summoned to the company commander's office and informed that the duty driver was standing by to take me to Army Headquarters where I had been only once before. That time I'd returned as Soldier of the Month. Somehow I doubted that I would be bringing back any honors this time.

"What's this about?" I asked.

"You'll find out when you get there," he said.

When I got there, I was escorted to a room where two Criminal Investigations Division agents were waiting.

"I guess you know what this is about," one said.

"No, I don't."

I was scared, but trying not to show it.

"We need to ask you some questions about *The Harasser*."

"Are you planning to place charges against me?" I asked.

"We just want to ask you some questions right now."

"Well, I don't intend to answer any," I said.

"You don't have a choice," the other one snapped at me. "You have to answer the questions."

"Then I want a lawyer," I replied.

They looked at each other and excused themselves, leaving me to stew for about 10 minutes before they returned.

"Are you willing to answer our questions now?" one asked.

"No, I'm not," I replied.

"OK, you can go, but you'll be hearing from us again."

I wasn't sure what to do at this point. The duty driver delivered me back to the barracks in time for lunch. I encountered Eric on his way to the mess hall and took him aside to tell him what had happened.

"I don't think they have anything, or they wouldn't have let you go," he said. "They just wanted you to confess."

He was concerned about being questioned, too, and we agreed that if he did get called in, he should take the same course.

THIS EXPERIENCE GREATLY HEIGHTENED the tension and stress that I was enduring. I knew that neither I nor my family could afford to hire a lawyer, and I wouldn't trust one assigned by the military. I began thinking of other ways to deal with this.

The following morning I put myself on the sick call list and reported to the clinic near the Machinato PX. After a lengthy wait, I finally got to see a doctor. When he inquired why I was there, I told him that I had a lot of personal problems, was under a great deal of stress and wanted to see a psychiatrist. He informed me that getting an appointment might take a few weeks. He said he would see what he could find out and told me to come back the following day.

When I returned the next day, the doctor informed me that I had an appointment with a psychiatrist two and a half weeks hence at the big hospital near Kadena which served all military groups. He also gave me a small bottle of pills that he said would help keep me calm and functional, but he advised that I not take them while drinking. They turned out to have little effect on the problems I was facing. The stress kept building.

One night Bill Taylor, who knew nothing about my involvement with *The Harasser* and the problems it had brought me, invited me to go to a bar in Naminoue. He liked this bar because it had half a dozen ancient Mills slot machines and he'd won $10 on one of them. We ordered a couple of beers and hadn't been there long when the door opened and who should stroll in but my shadow. He came straight to our table, acting surprised to see us.

"Hey," he said, "can I join you? Let me buy you guys a beer."

Bill had no suspicions about this guy and was friendly with everybody. We chatted for a while, and Bill went to get dimes to play the machine he believed to be hot. While Bill was cranking away, my shadow turned to me and said, "Man, I really enjoyed *The Harasser*. It nailed these assholes. We need to put out another edition, and I'd be willing to help."

"I would advise against that," I told him. "That's not something I'd want anything to do with."

My calming pills didn't prevent an outburst that got me into deeper trouble. That came when a promotion list was posted on the barracks' bulletin board. I saw it at lunch, and once again my name wasn't on it. I simmered for a while before my anger began to boil. I collected my letters from the Special Forces generals, a copy of the report I had prepared for them, my certificate for becoming Soldier of the Month, and an outstanding job evaluation from the departed lieutenant who had overseen our section. My initial thought had been to try to get a meeting with Blubberbutt to show him these symbols of ability and accomplishment and demonstrate to him that since I by far had the longest time in grade of any PFC in the unit—and probably in all of Okinawa—I deserved promotion to Spec. 4. But when I got back to the compound, still simmering, I realized this was a futile plan.

Years later, as a reporter writing about murders and other heinous crimes, I heard from perpetrators that they didn't mean to do it, they just "snapped." On this day I snapped. My rage came to a rapid boil. I headed straight to Blubberbutt's office. I swept past the shocked Sergeant Major without a word and threw open Blubberbutt's door. He looked stunned and frightened. His face went white as I stalked toward him and tossed my documents on his desk.

"I want to know why I wasn't promoted," I demanded.

"You can't do that!" I heard the Sergeant Major crying behind me.

Blubberbutt's color began coming back, his face getting redder by the moment. He jumped to his feet.

"If you'd show some loyalty to this unit, you might get promoted," he said, jabbing an index finger toward me, his voice rising with each word. I had no idea what he meant. I thought I had shown loyalty to the unit by preparing a report that got letters of commendation from the two generals in charge of Special Forces and by being the only person ever to bring the command Soldier of the Month award to B&VA.

"If you had any loyalty to this unit it wouldn't be as screwed up as it is," I shrieked back.

At that moment it dawned on me that this probably wasn't the best way to get promoted, and it never would happen now. It also struck me that I had exposed my role in *The Harasser*. The not-so-funny "Chuckle of the Week" had been this: "America is the country where any little boy can grow up to be President, but only those the colonel likes can make Sp-4."

Unable in my fury to think of anything else to say, I snatched up my documents and turned to leave. The Sergeant Major was standing in the doorway but he stepped aside as I swept past him.

By the time I got back to the art department, I was raging. The two startled Okinawan artists jumped up from their drawing tables and took refuge in a corner. Eric wasn't there for some reason. If he had been he might have prevented this situation. In anger, I tipped over an empty drawing table where I sometimes worked and headed straight for that demon machine, the Varityper. It was heavy and I was struggling with it, fully intending to throw it out the window, when two big guys from the printing department came running in, Blubberbutt, the Sergeant Major and my shadow close behind.

"Stop him! Get him," Blubberbutt was yelling. One guy grabbed me from behind and the other began trying to wrestle the Varityper from me. I had a near death grip on it. I was intent on destroying that thing.

"Let me go!" I was yelling. "You can't touch me. That's assault."

The Varityper was wrenched from my hands undamaged, and would be able to continue its evil ways for years to come, much to my regret.

The guy who had grabbed me had both of my arms pinned now.

"I demand to see a psychiatrist," I yelled.

"Take him back to my office," Blubberbutt ordered. "The MPs are on the way."

I could see the firing squad lining up now. I told myself that I would reject the hood and stare them down, a vision their consciences would have to bear for the rest of their lives.

As the burly printers led me away, I glanced over at the Varityper sitting smugly on its desk. I could swear it was leering at me.

The MPs didn't waste time arriving. They conferred with Blubberbutt out of my hearing. I figured I'd be sitting in the stockade for quite a while and was trying to prepare myself for it. I told the Sergeant Major to inform the MPs that I had an appointment with a psychiatrist and that I insisted on being taken to the hospital. They could confirm that, I said, by calling the Machinato Clinic and talking to the doctor. I needed treatment, I told them, and I wanted it known that I was demanding it.

This brought on more conferring. Calls were made. Discussions continued while I sat brooding, overseen by the Sergeant Major and my shadow, who never said a word. I wondered if he would show up in the cell next to mine in the stockade still hoping to entrap me.

After a long delay and more discussion, the MPs came to me and the older one, a sergeant, said, "Okay, we're going to take you to the hospital." That left me to wonder why Blubberbutt had agreed to it.

"Do we need a jacket?" the other MP asked.

For a moment I didn't realize what he was talking about, then it hit me. A straitjacket. That surely would make an impressive exit.

"Are you going to behave?" the MP in charge asked me.

I had calmed myself into a serious state of concern by this point.

"I'll behave," I said.

THIS WAS A FRIDAY afternoon, and it was late by the time we got to the hospital, a high-rise near Kadena. The Nut Ward, as it commonly was called, turned out to be a rather pleasant place, despite the locked door and guards, who were Naval and Marine enlisted men dressed in medical attire serving as attendants. The MPs turned me over to a nurse, also a Marine, and one I instantaneously knew better than to challenge. I'd have been more inclined to take on the MPs. She gave me forms to fill out and got me officially admitted.

I asked when I might be able to see a psychiatrist.

"Not until Monday at the earliest," she said.

I was surprised to learn that I had a room of my own, although I had to share the bath with the occupant of the adjoining room, who turned out to be a major. In the Nut Ward officers, enlisted people, civilians and any others who might qualify to be there were equal, but the grim and disagreeable major, who seemed to be undergoing detox, wouldn't accept that and protested vehemently when he saw that a PFC was in the room next to him.

Compared to a stockade cell, I felt as if I had just checked into a luxury hotel. Nearby was a recreation room with comfortable chairs, a TV, books, magazines, games, including checkers and chess.

The supper hour was near and I learned that all the nut cases who were mobile, non-violent and reasonably coherent ate together in the cafeteria on the first floor, my neighbor, the major, not included. Isolated tables were set aside for us. We went in a group in distinctive ward attire, accompanied by our attendants. Others in the cafeteria looked on with curiosity and a degree of caution as we made our way through the line to our dining area. A few long-term patients in our group made weird faces and menacing feints toward some of the more blatant onlookers, all in good fun. I joined in their laughter about it.

On our way to the cafeteria that evening, I chatted with one of the attendants, asking what his job was like, whether he had trouble with any of the people on the ward, whether there was anybody of whom I should be wary. He was a Navy guy, very friendly, and I could tell that we could get along well. He asked what had landed me there since I had arrived in the company of MPs.

"I had an unpleasant encounter with a colonel and told him what I thought," I said. "You have to be a potentially violent lunatic to do that."

He laughed. "You don't have to stay on the ward," he said. "You know that, don't you?"

"What do you mean?"

"You can have full run of the hospital. There's a theater, a library, soda shop, PX, all kind of places you can go. You just have to make a request and have one of us go with you."

"Really?" I said. "Well, I'll make use of that."

That knowledge actually made for an entertaining and relaxing weekend.

I saw a couple of movies, spent time in the library. Sometimes the attendants would leave me unaccompanied and go do their own things. Back on the ward, I watched TV, lost a chess match with another patient, and amused myself by locking the major out of the bathroom we shared, just to hear him banging on the door, cussing, and storming down the hall to report me to the Marine drill sergeant nurse, who would warn me not to do it again, a time or two, I thought, with a hint of a smile.

I had no idea what to expect when I learned that I had an appointment with a psychiatrist Monday morning. From cartoons and movie stereotypes I thought I might have to stretch out on a couch while my bewildered psyche was prodded and analyzed, but that turned out not to be the case. We sat in chairs. He wasn't what I expected either. He appeared to be still in his 20s, also Army, a first lieutenant, likely drafted as soon as he'd finished his medical training. He seemed friendly. I had expected a silent nodder, perhaps chewing on a pencil eraser.

After introducing himself, he glanced through a few documents on his desk, then turned his attention back to me.

"So tell me how you came to be here."

"Well, it's a long story," I said. "It goes back to a recruiter named Coon who told me enough lies to get me to join the Army."

"I mean here, today. Didn't a recent event have a more direct effect?"

Obviously, he had a report prepared by the MPs, or maybe even Blubberbutt.

"Well, yes."

"Tell me about that."

I had no intention of bringing up the possibility that I could be facing the death penalty on fabricated charges of sedition and treason for putting out a four-page newspaper that displeased Blubberbutt. I wasn't going to admit that to anybody. I knew that one way or another it would be used against me.

"I just blew up and had a run-in with my colonel," I said.

"Do you blow up often?"

"No, not really. But if I have to stay around this colonel much longer, I probably will."

"Do you think you have a problem with authority figures?"

"I would say so, yes, especially incompetent ones."

"Well, let's look into that a little. Tell me about your father."

"Look," I said, "this doesn't have anything to do with my father. He's a wonderful man. I love him deeply. He's never mistreated me in any way. I'd do anything for him."

"What's it about then?" he asked.

"It's about the Army. It's about nonsensical colonels, stupid sergeants, and corrupt company commanders. I've had all I can stand and I don't think I can handle any more of it. I want out."

He chuckled, surprising me.

"Well, I'm looking forward to getting out myself," he said. "But let me see if I've got this right. You think that I can write a report and get you out on a medical discharge for psychiatric disorders. Is that close?"

"That's what I'm hoping," I said.

He smiled and shook his head.

"Ever heard of *Catch 22*?" he asked.

"No, I don't think so."

"Well, it's the title of a novel that came out a few months back. My father sent me a copy for Christmas. It's set in Europe in World War II. A bombardier, Yossarian, wants to be declared insane so he can get out of flying missions. An Army psychiatrist, Doc Daneeka, tells him that anybody who wants to get out of combat missions is being perfectly rational and can't be crazy. Catch 22. He's got to keep flying. See what I'm saying?"

"I'm afraid I do," I said, my disappointment evident. "If I want out I can't be crazy. If I'm not crazy you can't let me out."

"You've got it. Sometimes we just have to adjust to our situations, even if they're bad. How much longer do you have?"

"Eight months until my tour here ends, 10 months on my enlistment. But I've been told that if I get back to San Francisco with less than three months left, they'll discharge me there. I may try for an early out if I can get into college. That could get me out in seven months."

"Tell you what I can do," he said. "I'll write a report recommending light duty and maybe a transfer to get you away from the colonel."

I thanked him, even though I was pretty certain that the only transfer awaiting me was to the stockade.

I went to lunch with the other nut jobs, my last meal with them. When I got back to the ward, I was told that I would be discharged as soon as the paperwork was completed. I suspected MPs would be waiting for me but they weren't. I walked right out of the hospital and took a bus back to Machinato.

EVERYBODY WAS AT WORK at the compound when I arrived at the barracks, but the work day soon would be over. I went to the PX to pick up a few things. When I got back my friends seemed surprised to see me. They thought I was in the stockade.

"No," I said. "I was in the nut ward but they decided I wasn't qualified enough to stay."

"You should have called some of us as witnesses," one of them said, producing much laughter.

After supper, Eric and I went to the NCO club. Nobody had said anything about questioning him, he said, and he thought this whole thing might be backfiring on Blubberbutt. He told me that one of the guys who had sent a copy of *The Harasser* to his congressman had heard back from him that he had asked the Pentagon to look into the situation at B&VA. Eric also said that he'd heard that even officers within the unit had begun questioning the leadership and wanted to deal with problems. Indeed, within a couple of months, 30 men in one of our radio units would be moved to a transmitter site at Deragawa near Kadena, where they would live in the luxury of two-man rooms with a former chef running the mess hall. This would relieve some of the crowding in the barracks, as well as the work place at the compound, and help ease tensions.

I returned to work at the art department the following day, and nobody treated me any differently. My shadow was still around, but I skirted him as much as possible. I didn't hear a word about my little episode on the previous Friday, although the Varityper appeared to me to be wary about my presence. I didn't see Blubberbutt for a couple of days, and then only from a distance. I was, however, expecting to see CID agents at any moment. I thought that surely would be the case when I was summoned to the orderly room before formation on Friday, just a week after my encounter with Blubberbutt.

But to my immense relief, no agents were present. The clerk handed me an envelope.

"You've got orders," he said.

I tore open the envelope as soon as I got into the hallway. To my great surprise and delight, I was being sent on six months of temporary duty to our detachment in Japan on the outskirts of Tokyo. I was to depart from Kadena on Monday and report to work on Tuesday. My Doc Daneeka had come through for me.

10

So THANKFUL WAS I to be getting away from Okinawa and Blubberbutt that I really didn't care much about what lay ahead. I figured it had to be better.

The tiny base where our Japan detachment was situated had been constructed right after the war, and I never knew its original purpose. Most of the buildings were of wood, even though Japan often was in the pathway of typhoons, and earthquakes were not uncommon (on several occasions I would be shaken awake by tremors). The base had a single barracks, a small library, and an NCO club with 10-cent beer on Tuesday nights.

The B&VA detachment had only five low-level enlisted men in one room of the barracks. They were clerks and supply people. One was Jeffrey Meyer, a Spec. 4 from Sheboygan, Wisconsin. On the evening of my arrival, he took me to the NCO club and told me what I could expect: no formations, no inspections, no guard duty or KP, no physical training, no weapons issued, and no hassle from superiors, a perfect situation in my view. Do your job and you'll be all right, Meyer said. Most of the people working at B&VA were civilians.

The most important thing I learned that night was that the NCO club had only pinball machines, no slot machines. I wouldn't see another slot machine for six months, which would greatly increase my spending money, and the next day I learned that I also would receive TDY pay that brought my monthly income to about the same level it would have been if I'd gotten promoted to Spec. 4, about $120 a month, but you could get 360 yen for a dollar.

I reported for duty the next morning and met our master sergeant, who was tall and lean with graying hair and a soft Georgia accent, a very nice guy. If anybody had sent him warnings about me, he never let it be known. He filled me in about the purpose of the unit, which was to produce and distribute two monthly magazines, each containing only 30 pages. One was called *Freedom*. It was published in Korean and distributed free throughout South Korea. The other was called *Koryu*. English translation: old flow, traditional, classical.

Since the U.S. was forbidden by treaty to propagandize the Japanese people, it was a publication for Japanese employees of U.S. armed forces and other governmental agencies, published in Japanese with some English text, and read from back to front as were all Japanese publications.

The commander of the detachment was a warrant officer, a grade between non-commissioned and commissioned officers. He also welcomed me to the unit and showed no indications of having been informed that I was a demented troublemaker suspected of sedition and treason.

I was assigned as the sole staff writer for *Freedom*, but some of my pieces also would appear in *Koryu*. The editor of *Freedom* was Bernard Dekle. Everybody called him Deke and so would I. He was a former newspaperman with thin receding white hair, trim, and slightly disheveled. I soon would discover that he also had a touch of absent-mindedness. He was only a few weeks away from turning 57.

At our first meeting, upon learning that I was from North Carolina, Deke informed me that although he was from Georgia, he had started out in the newspaper business in North Carolina during the Great Depression, first at *The Durham Sun*, later at *The Charlotte Observer*, and had loved every minute of it. When World War II came along, he joined the Office of War Information, serving first in Cairo, then in Rome, Salzburg and Vienna. He later was transferred to Tokyo to become an information adviser to General Douglas McArthur during the occupation. He had remained in Japan after it again became an independent country in 1952, serving at several posts with the new U.S. Information Agency before becoming a psychological warfare editor. Deke was married to a famous Japanese actress, Mariko Niki, who played the lead female role of Lotus Blossom in the Broadway production of *Teahouse of the August Moon*, a major hit set in Okinawa, which won the Pulitzer Prize for Drama in 1954.

Deke would play an important role in preparing me for my future. My first assignment was to write a piece about Secretary of State Dean Rusk. Deke admired Rusk, partly because he was from Georgia and had worked his way through Davidson College in North Carolina before becoming a Rhodes Scholar at Oxford. He fought in the China-Burma-India Theater in World War II, rising to the rank of colonel, before returning to Washington to work at the War Department. In 1945, he joined the Department of State in the newly formed office of United Nations Affairs. It was he who suggested dividing Korea at the 38th parallel with the Soviet Union prevailing over the North and the U.S. over the South. In 1950, Rusk was named Assistant Secretary of State for Far Eastern Affairs. He was working at his office late on Saturday evening, June 24, when an emergency cable arrived revealing that North Korean troops had invaded the South. In Korea that was June 25. The communist troops had crossed over the

38th parallel at dawn. Rusk quickly informed President Harry Truman and other key people. He would play a lead role in getting the United Nations to defend the South. That was one reason he was highly regarded there.

Most of what I would write in my six months in Japan came from newspapers, magazines and books. We had a research section with encyclopedias, many books about Japan and Korea, lots of clippings and mail subscriptions to major newspapers and magazines. Our daily news still came from *Stars & Stripes*, the Armed Forces TV & Radio networks, and a daily English-language newspaper in Tokyo, *The Japan Times*. We also had the post library and full access to the research facilities at *Stars & Stripes*, which was in a very nice and popular section of Tokyo.

I don't recall how long it took me to research and write my piece about Dean Rusk, but I remember well the day I turned it in and the anxiety I suffered as I waited for Deke to read it. He had a glass-enclosed office in the corner, but my desk was in the larger room with four Korean translators and a couple of other civilian employees, I watched with great trepidation as he read.

I wasn't sure what to expect when I saw him rise from his desk, manuscript in hand, and head for the door. He came toward me smiling.

"Damn," he said, "they've finally sent me a writer."

Nobody had said anything like that to me before. But that, of course, didn't mean that I had done everything as well as it could have been.

Deke pulled up a chair and began going over the article with me. He started by suggesting that perhaps a vivid description of a South Korean sunset on the evening before the invasion of South Korea might not be the strongest way to begin an article about Dean Rusk's forceful actions to save the country when he learned of the invasion. The lead, he suggested, was just a couple of paragraphs below, when Rusk received the cable on a slow Saturday evening at the State Department. I could see his point. He went on with a few other suggestions. It didn't take me long to re-do the piece and get a thumb's up.

ANOTHER PERSON WHO WOULD make a big impression on me while I was in Japan was Tomoo (pr. Toe-Moe) Ogita. He was editor of *Koryu*, and he came to introduce himself on my first day at work.

Almost 20 years younger than Deke, he was Nisei, a second generation Japanese-American. He had been born in Los Angeles and attended public schools there, while also studying Japanese at a private school. He later attended the University of Michigan at Ann Arbor, where he taught Japanese. There is a gap in his history from the time World War II began until it ended. It is known that his family was put into an internment camp in Amache, Colorado, and that a photograph made in 1943 showed Tomoo there with them, but it isn't known whether he was interned.

That was something he never spoke about with me, and so far as I know not with anybody else with whom he worked. The next stage of his life would be in Japan, and it was Deke who told me about it.

"He was one of the first Americans to enter Hiroshima after the bomb was dropped," Deke told me. "Ask him to let you see his photos."

Tomoo never told me how he came to be a language and psychological consultant for the U.S. Strategic Bombing Survey and I've never been able to find that information. The first atomic bomb employed in war exploded over Hiroshima at 8:15 on the morning of August 6, 1945. Three days later another such bomb was dropped on Nagasaki. On August 15, Japan announced its surrender. That surrender was signed on the deck of the battleship Missouri on September 2.

The following day, the lead elements of the Strategic Bombing Survey made their way into Hiroshima to begin assessing the damage, and Tomoo was with them, apparently serving primarily as interpreter. He was 21 at the time, the same age I would turn two and a half months after meeting him. Photos and film shot by the military in Hiroshima after Americans gained access to the devastated city would be kept secret for many years, but Tomoo had his own camera and he was a great photographer.

Tomoo brought me two albums that not only contained his stunning photos of the devastation and horror in Hiroshima but also many from the Colorado internment camp. They moved me deeply, as Tomoo knew they would. (Those photos, along with many others made by Tomoo are now in the Special Collections of the University of California, Irvine, Library.)

Not long afterward, Tomoo gave me a paperback copy of *Hiroshima* by John Hersey. That thin little book, just 116 pages long, affected me even more deeply than his photos, and in different ways. It not only made the suffering in Hiroshima real and personal, it entranced me in the details and descriptions that made that possible.

Hersey had been a war correspondent for *Time* and *Life* magazines, both in Europe and the Pacific. He came to Japan after the war to write about the country's reconstruction for the *New Yorker* and went to Hiroshima to see the devastation. There he met a German priest, Father Wilhelm Kleinsorge, who had survived the blast. Father Kleinsorge introduced him to other survivors, and Hersey decided to write about them.

The piece he wrote was a little more than 30,000 words long. It filled the entire edition of the August 31, 1946, *New Yorker*, and it became a sensation. Two months later it was published in book form, and it would sell millions of copies over the years. Initially it was forbidden in Japan, censored by occupation forces, and Tomoo wouldn't get to read it until later.

It was the perfect gift for me because it came just as I was beginning to think seriously that I might want to make a career of reporting and writing, and no better example of those skills could have been placed in my hands.

The book simply tells the stories of six survivors of Hiroshima. All are introduced in the first paragraph, which reveals where they were and what they were doing when the blast occurred. The experiences and suffering of these six people not only would portray the ultimate horror of war but would lay bare how vulnerable and akin people are, no matter their race, nationality, religion, politics, or any of the other circumstances that divide people. In the face of suffering, it confirmed, we are little different.

The simplicity of this book, the details of how people cope in unimaginable crisis would affect the way that I looked at all stories in the future. It would guide my writing although I never could hope to match it. But this is the one book I've kept going back to, reading it many times, and it never has ceased to affect me.

After his experience in Hiroshima, Tomoo was assigned to the Civil Information and Education Section of General Headquarters Supreme Commander of Allied Powers as a researcher of cultural assets. That had to have been an immense relief, and it led him to one of the great loves of his life—Japanese and other Oriental art. I had little doubt that the slaughter and destruction he saw in Hiroshima made the beauty and creativity of art all the more appealing.

Tomoo undertook the study of Far Eastern art, learned to speak Chinese and Korean, and became an authority and major collector of Asian art, particularly Japanese. He invited me to his house for dinner one night to see some of it and hear him explain its origins. Although I had no real knowledge of Oriental or any other art, I was deeply impressed.

Tomoo told me that night that his dream when he retired from government service was to travel the world lecturing about Oriental art. He might not have completely achieved that dream, but he came close. He returned to California in 1968, six years after I left Japan and saw him for the last time. He lectured at numerous universities, created Asia Art Associates to authenticate and appraise art, wrote articles, contributed to books and illustrated others with his beautiful photographs.

As happened with so many people I knew in the Army, I lost touch with him. Not until I began working on this memoir did I learn that he died in 1983 at 59. I don't know the cause of his death, but many people who entered Hiroshima soon after the bomb suffered radiation sickness and later died of cancer. I couldn't help but wonder if he, too, hadn't become another casualty of Hiroshima.

ONE THING ABOUT JAPAN was very comforting to me. Although it was a culture alien to the one in which I had grown up in Thomasville, I felt at home in the landscape. Tokyo and Raleigh, North Carolina's capital, are almost on the same parallel. The seasons and the flora are much the same. I quickly was fascinated by Tokyo. On my first weekend in Japan, Meyer took me into the city to acquaint me with it. That required the preliminaries of learning about the subway system and the heavily compacted trains with their many stations and the attractions near them. I also was introduced to the multi-storied USO, a place of refuge from the crowds and hectic streets. It was in the famous Ginza in the middle of the city, one of the world's greatest centers for high-end shopping and entertainment, Tokyo's Times Square and Park Avenue.

On this visit I got my first look at the Imperial Palace and its moat, along with the posh Imperial Hotel where the wealthy and powerful congregated. For lunch, we checked out one of Tokyo's massive beer halls with tables that marched on forever and stalls with enticing foods all around the walls. That night Meyer took me to a place in Shinjuku with narrow alleys, scores of bars and vendors offering yakitori (marinated meat on skewers cooked over charcoal), roasted chestnuts and whole baked sweet potatoes among other treats. The sweet potatoes were just as good as those my grandmother kept in the warmer of her wood-fired cook stove when I was growing up. The yakitori was tasty, but a couple of months later Meyer and I gave it up after an article in *The Japan Times* reported that dozens of yakitori vendors in the area had been arrested for selling the meat of feral cats.

We finished off this full day after midnight at the only place in Tokyo, other than a military base, that I was aware of where you could get a cheeseburger. (The fast-food burger joints just beginning to spread in the U.S. hadn't yet gained a toehold in Japan.) This was a bar run by a retired U. S. Army sergeant, and it was frequented mainly by U.S. military folks and other burger-hungry foreigners. On a later night Meyer and I would have an interesting experience there. We were having burgers and beer after midnight when an attractive Japanese woman in a tight red dress came in and took a seat at a table for two. She ordered a beer, kept looking around the room and glancing out the big window at the neon glow. Meyer started giving her the eye.

"I wonder if she's waiting on somebody," he said.

She kept sipping her beer but nobody came to join her.

"I'm going to ask her if we can buy her a beer," Meyer said, and was out of his seat without awaiting my approval. She smiled broadly. They spoke for a moment and she rose from her chair, picked up her beer and headed toward our table. I stood as she arrived and Meyer pulled up a chair for her and went to get more beer. Up close, it was clear that she was older than we, maybe even 40, but she had disguised it well with heavy makeup. She spoke English well, as did many of the females who worked as hostesses in the bar district. Meyer returned with the beer and pulled his chair closer to hers. I had to go to the john and excused myself.

I was washing my hands when a young Japanese man, casually dressed, came in.

"Do you know who your friend is talking to?" he asked.

"No," I said. "We just met her."

"She's very famous," he said.

"Really? What does she do?"

"She sings, but that's not why she's famous. She was first Japanese person to have sex change operation."

Her name, it turned out, was Nagai Akiko, and she was a cabaret performer in the area. Her surgery had taken place 11 years earlier, a year before an ex-GI from the Bronx, George William Jorgensen Jr., underwent surgery in Copenhagen and became famous as Christine Jorgensen.

I had the feeling that Meyer thought his evening had been made but I didn't want to create a scene by interrupting his conversation and letting him know what I just had learned. I waited until she had to go to the john herself. Meyer looked stunned at the news but agreed that even though we had beers to finish, a hasty departure might be better than attempting to talk his way out of the situation.

During the six months I would spend in Japan, Tokyo greatly widened my experiences. Meyer and I went to a sumo wrestling match and Vegas-style reviews with bare-bosom show girls at the famous Nichigeki Music Hall. At Tomoo's suggestion I even took in a production at Kabuki-za, the ornate theater on the Ginza where the ancient form of Japanese drama Kabuki was performed. It was spectacularly staged with elaborate and colorful costumes and makeup, the likes of which could be seen nowhere else. As with opera that I would attempt to grasp later, I had no clue what was going on, but it was fascinatingly entertaining anyway. I have a book about Kabuki from Tomoo's personal library signed by him.

As much as I enjoyed Tokyo, though, it wasn't the Japanese city that I came to care most about. That was a heartbreak away.

11

MY FIRST TRIP TO Kyoto came on my second weekend in Japan. My friend Jim Lawler had taken several days leave and caught a hop to Tachikawa to visit me. He spent daylight hours touring Tokyo for a couple of days, and I joined him after work for shows and other entertainments. He also wanted to see Kyoto, the ancient Japanese Imperial capital, and we caught an express train there on Saturday morning. Kyoto was 230 miles to the southwest and the trip took about four and a half hours. Along the way, we got magnificent views of Mount Fuji, still lightly snowcapped, and a small portion of Lake Biwa, Japan's largest body of fresh water and at four million years one of the oldest lakes on Earth.

We had lunch in a noodle shop near the train station and were heading out to see the sights when we were approached by a friendly group of young people. They were students at Doshisha University, founded in 1875 by a Japanese scholar who had studied in the United States and wanted to promote Christianity in his own country. These students identified themselves as members of the English Speaking Society and wanted to know if we would let them practice their English on us. They offered to give us a tour of some of Kyoto's attractions just to talk with us. Their enthusiasm was so ingratiating that we quickly agreed.

Kyoto is Japan's third oldest city and surely the most beautiful. None can match it for temples, shrines and gardens. Because of these ancient structures and the city's historical significance, Kyoto had been spared the bombings that had left so much of Japan in rubble. The city lies in a lush basin with mountains on three sides, some of which protrude into the city. Our new acquaintances took us halfway up one of those small mountains, Otowa, to see Kyoto's most visited spot, Kiyomizu-dera, the Buddhist temple of pure waters. The temple, founded in 778, is a compound of many structures, including two elaborate and colorful gates, a three-story pagoda and a bell tower. But most impressive is the main hall, Hondo, one of Japan's national treasures. It has a magnificent veranda called Kiyomizu Stage, which stood on nearly 200 cross-braced broad pillars cut from Japanese Zelkova trees. Nearly 40 feet high, the huge squared logs were topped by floorboards of thick cypress. Not a single nail was used to build this elaborate platform which provides beautiful views of the mountains and the city below.

Three small streams merge below the main hall, each coming from a spring producing the pure waters to which the temple is dedicated. A stone waterfall had been constructed there, providing each stream its own sluice for emptying the sacred waters into the common pool below. Visitors could stand under the sluices and drink these waters for good fortunes, catching them in carved wooden cups on long handles. One stream represented success, another longevity, the third happiness in love. Our new friends encouraged us to take a drink, but we could choose only one stream and they wouldn't tell us which each represented. By pure happenstance, Lawler chose success. I got longevity. So far so good. I hope it worked out for Lawler, too, but I long ago lost touch with him.

Our next stop was Kyoto Gyoen, the national garden, which includes the old Imperial Palace. The emperor had moved to a new palace when Tokyo became Japan's capital in 1869, leaving this palace as a historic site. We didn't get to see inside because tours had to be arranged, but we got a sense of its grandeur and relished the elegance of the garden before our afternoon ran out. Doshisha University was just across the street and our new friends wanted us to see the campus. Before we parted, they offered to take us to see more of Kyoto the following day. Our train was to leave at mid-afternoon, and they agreed to meet us at our hotel at 10.

This time they numbered five. The previous day two females had been with the group, now only one. She was very shy and had said little the day before. Her name was Akiko. A couple of times when I had caught her eye, she modestly glanced away. This time the group took us to see the Golden Pavilion, with its two top floors covered with gold leaf, as well as the Silver Pavilion, which was supposed to have been coated with silver, but the designer had setbacks and never got around to that. Both temples dated back hundreds of years (1397 Gold, 1490 Silver). I never had seen a zen sand garden but the intricate one at the Silver Pavilion, supposedly designed by the famous monk Muso Kokushi, was impressive. We next visited Ryoan-ji, the Temple of the Dragon at Peace, to see its walled stone and gravel zen garden, perhaps the most famous in Japan. It was viewed from a covered seated position, and many people came there for meditation. Akiko noticed my interest in these gardens and talked to me about them. She spoke English well, though a little haltingly at first, but her shyness dissipated when she talked about gardens.

Before Lawler and I had to catch our train, we took the group to a late lunch to thank them for the good time they had shown us. As we were parting afterwards, they told us that they hoped we would return to Kyoto. Lawler said that would be unlikely for him, but I promised to visit again. They asked if I'd be willing to talk with the English Speaking Society when I returned, and without thinking, I said sure. Akiko gave me her home address and telephone number to let them know when that would be.

I HAD NO IDEA how to deal with the Japanese telephone or mail systems. I learned, however, that the USO could help. Employees would address letters in Japanese and put them in the local mail system. They also would assist in making phone calls. After I returned to Tokyo, I sent Akiko a letter saying that I was planning to visit again in two weeks and I would call her to confirm my arrival time.

Akiko and others from the group that had taken Lawler and me on our tours were waiting at the train station. They took me directly to the campus where I was to meet with other English Speaking Society members. I had expected this would be a couple of dozen people and that we would sit around and chat about whatever interested them. I was astonished by reality.

That was an auditorium with a stage, a podium and chairs behind it for dignitaries such as college officials and English instructors. People already were filing in and they appeared to be coming by hundreds. I clearly had underestimated how many students might be in the English Speaking Society, and I couldn't imagine what they would want to hear from me. I remembered telling Akiko and her friends that I was a writer for two magazines, one Japanese, the other Korean, without mentioning that my total output so far was a single article that hadn't yet appeared. They must have fallen under the misimpression that I was somebody. Now the pathetic soul I actually was found himself facing full-bore panic. My first instinct was to break into a gallop back to the station and catch the first train out.

I had not spoken before any group since my public speaking class at Fort Slocum nearly two years earlier, and in the back of my mind, I could hear my Information School instructor telling me, "Next time you get up here, you better have something to say." I didn't have a clue what that might be, and I couldn't think about it because I was besieged by welcoming strangers.

How I got through the next hour, I'll never know. I had entered a state of fear so transcendent that it removed my conscious being from the spindly confounded fool who had to approach that podium. I was completely unaware of whatever he may have said or done, thus am blessedly spared any memory of it. The two of us were reluctantly rejoined only after he had staggered pale-faced away from the podium to fading spattered applause. All I hoped at that point was that he hadn't brought up Blubberbutt. Those who came up afterward to say they had enjoyed my talk only confirmed what I earlier had been told about Japanese people—that they are among the most polite on Earth.

The students had arranged for me to stay at a small, traditional Japanese inn in an out-of-the-way neighborhood. It had only six guest rooms. You removed your shoes when you entered and sat and slept on tatami. My room was very much like the little house Eric and I rented in Naha, and I was very comfortable. The inn had only one bath. Guests sat on a small wooden stool to bathe and rinse, then soaked in water hot enough to produce a sweat in a deep wooden tub. The water was changed daily, heated for hours by a small wood fire. A kimono was provided to wear to the bath and back. Mine turned out to be more than a bit short.

The inn never had an American guest before, and the family who owned it seemed happy to have me and eager to please. Akiko went with me to check in and serve as translator. I learned that I would have the honor of being first to bathe and was shown the bath area. Before Akiko left, I asked if she would like to have dinner and she said yes. A couple of hours later, she returned to pick me up and I told her to take me to a place that she liked. That was a crowded and noisy Chinese restaurant with smoked ducks hanging in the window. We sampled several dishes previously unknown to me. We ate, talked, laughed and sipped hot tea for nearly three hours. Akiko was fearful that I wouldn't be able to find my way back to the inn, which was in an area of narrow alleyways, and she led me there. This time I took careful notice of all the twists and turns. The area was not well-lighted and I didn't want her walking home alone, so I insisted on accompanying her. She lived with her family in a walled compound on the street leading up Otowa Mountain to Kiyomizu-dera. We said goodnight at the gate and agreed to meet the next morning for more touring before I had to catch my train back to Tokyo.

When we said goodbye at the train station that Sunday I knew that I would be coming back to Kyoto as often as possible. I would have made the trip every week if I could, but finances wouldn't allow that.

DURING THOSE VISITS, AKIKO and I toured other temples and shrines and visited many gardens. We explored museums, art galleries, an exhibit of Bonsai, the art of miniature trees, and another of Ikebana, the incredibly beautiful art of Japanese floral designs. Akiko also took me to a formal tea ceremony conducted in a place created for that purpose. It went on for hours and included much bowing and attentive service by women in stunning kimonos. Exotic foods and numerous teas were served, including a thick tea unlike any I had experienced before or since, served in a special pottery container.

We went to movies on almost every visit. American movies with Japanese subtitles were very popular in Japan. *West Side Story* was a major attraction then. We saw it and quite a few others. *Rome Adventure* with Troy Donahue and Suzanne Pleshette became our favorite. We both loved the song "Al Di La," which was sung in Italian by crooner Emile Pericoli in a nightclub scene. During the performance Pleshette asks Donahue, "What does Al Di La mean?" He tells her it's hard to explain. "It means far, far away, beyond the beyond, beyond this world. That's how much he loves her in the song." The song became a big hit, even in Japan. But the biggest hit in the country at the time was called "Ue o Muite Aruko" (I look up as I walk) sung by Kyu Sakamoto. It was so catchy that it stayed in your brain, replaying itself over and over whether you wanted to hear it again or not. In the song, Sakamoto is looking up to keep tears from falling, remembering those spring and summer days, "But tonight I am all alone." Although unexplained loneliness and sadness were its themes, we both loved it, perhaps because it foresaw the future of our spring and summer days. The following year the song was released in the U.S., retitled "Sukiyaki" because the record label thought that was a Japanese word that Americans might recognize. It became number one on the Billboard top 100 chart, the only Japanese language song ever to achieve that status, and every time I heard it, it made me all the more conscious of my own lonely nights, and far sadder than anytime I had listened to it in Japan.

On all but two of my trips to Kyoto I stayed at the same small inn where I was always received enthusiastically. But a night came when I thought I might have overstayed that welcome. Eric had come for a visit, and I wanted him to see Kyoto and meet Akiko. She and some of her college friends took us on much the same tour that Lawler and I had enjoyed when we first met them. Eric shared my room at the inn. Being a new guest he was invited to be first to bathe. He returned to the room red faced from the hot soak, but relaxed.

"That was great," he said.

A few minutes later, I heard a commotion in the hallway. I slid open the door and stepped out of the room to see what was happening. A Japanese guest in kimono with towel and wash cloth in hand was standing by the bath entrance looking perplexed. The woman who ran the place was pacing back and forth, upset and apparently repeatedly apologizing to the guest. Her daughter, who could speak some English, had come to see what the problem was and I asked her what was going on.

"Your friend," she said, her exasperation evident, "he let out tub water."

Nobody else got to soak that night, and Eric remained red with embarrassment for the rest of our stay.

I MADE ONLY ONE trip to Kyoto when I did not get to see Akiko. That was because I was on an assignment from which I could not break away. More than 26,000 Japanese Boy Scouts were to gather at a Self Defense Forces base near the city of Gotemba at the foot of Mt. Fuji for their annual jamboree. But this time they had decided to expand by inviting scouts from 20 different countries for the first Asian Boy Scout Jamboree. Some of the 560 scouts coming from other countries would include Japanese Americans from California as well as scouts from Korea. I was assigned to write about the jamboree for both magazines. But Tomoo asked if I would undertake another duty. He had played a role in organizing a group of scouts from Los Angeles to attend, and he wanted me to serve as their escort for a visit to Kyoto after the jamboree and to get them safely back to Tokyo by train. A staff member from the U.S. consulate in Osaka was arranging the Kyoto visit and would accompany us there, but after that I was on my own.

I arrived at the camp on Thursday, August 2, so that I could be present for the opening ceremonies the following morning. All the scouts would be sleeping in tents in the scrubby hills around the base and cooking their own food over open fires, but I had a private room in the bachelor officers' quarters and a card that allowed me to dine in their mess hall. My first mission was to find my charges. All the foreign scouts were in one area with camping sites marked by signs designating their homelands. The U.S. groups included scouts from several California cities and towns and were under the charge of two adult scout leaders who had come with them. Japanese scout leaders who were U.S. government employees also were assisting them. My six charges were 13 and 14 years old and far more American than Japanese in attitude and action. Other than saying hi, they took little notice of me. I learned that the American Scouts would be among those chosen to greet Crown Prince Akihito and his wife, Michiko, when they arrived for the opening ceremonies the following morning and I was invited to join them.

The royal couple arrived by helicopter. The crown prince, who was 29, was wearing a business suit. His wife, the first commoner to marry into the Imperial family, was in pink, also western style. Waiting to greet them were politicians, government and military officials, as well as Scout leaders. Before taking the stage, the royal couple came over to be introduced to the scouts who had been selected to welcome them. None of the scouts in my group seemed to be particularly impressed that they were meeting the man who 28 years later would become the 125th emperor of Japan, succeeding his father Hirohito, who had surrendered to General McArthur.

I made one big mistake during the jamboree. I joined my group and others in an ascent up Mt. Fuji, which at 12,388 feet is nearly twice the height of North Carolina's highest peak, Mount Mitchell. Although it's a volcano,

Fuji had not erupted since December, 1707, which offered me a little comfort. As beautiful as the mountain is from a distance, up close, like many things, it's not quite as attractive. Composed of volcanic rock and dust it boasts little vegetation at higher elevations. Still, it attracts thousands upon thousands of people who want to climb it, particularly in July and August when its snowcap is missing. A good climber can make it to the top in about eight hours.

It took an hour or two before the scouts began to complain, but it wasn't until the wind picked up that their grievances became more frequent and emphatic. Black dust began swirling around us and before we realized what was happening we were overwhelmed. It was clogging my nose and beginning to fill up my ears. My eyes were burning and I barely could see. We turned back, making the descent as quickly as possible, coughing, gagging and gasping for breath. By the time we got back to the encampment, we looked as if we had just emerged after being trapped for days in a collapsed coal mine. Our hands and faces were black, as were the legs of the scouts in shorts. My hair was coated, my shoes uncomfortably clotted. I was able to brush off much of it, but when I got back to my room and headed for the shower, I discovered that the dust had sifted through my clothing, and much of my body was coated. It even had worked its way inside my watch and clogged the gears.

It wasn't until after this experience that I heard an old Japanese saying about Mt. Fuji: You're a fool if you don't try to climb it once, a bigger fool if you attempt it twice.

I didn't know what to expect regarding my duties after the jamboree ended on August 8, but it didn't take me long to realize that I wasn't to be envied. I have suppressed almost all of those unpleasant memories, but a couple still hang on. My charges and I were to have lunch at the home of a prominent Kyoto official. His wife had prepared the meal. It wasn't atypical for a hot summer lunch in Japan—chilled soba noodles, pickled daikon, ginger, tofu, and some items I couldn't identify.

"What is this?" one of the scouts asked as he looked over the array of dishes, his voice heavy with disdain.

The wife began trying to explain each.

"I'm not eating that," another boy announced.

"I'm not either," said a third.

None of the boys spoke Japanese and none had a desire for Japanese food. They declined everything. The wife was clearly flustered and didn't know what to say or do, and neither did the rest of us. The guy from the consulate who had arranged the lunch was extremely embarrassed, as was I, and we both were deeply apologetic as we departed.

By this time, the boys were in full revolt. They demanded cheeseburgers and no compromise was possible. I didn't know a single place in Kyoto to get a burger, and neither did the guy from the consulate, who spoke fluent Japanese. But he got on a pay phone to the biggest hotel in the city and finally got the chef, who said that given a little time he probably could pull together a dozen cheeseburgers. Instead of touring temples and shrines, we ended up in the hotel dining room witnessing a cheeseburger orgy, paid for, I'm certain, by U.S. taxpayers because the guy from the consulate picked up the bill. He was one happy person when he dropped us off at the train station.

From that point, these wild Californians, fueled by cheeseburgers, were my responsibility. I had to keep them together and try to herd them safely onto the train. That wasn't easy and I had to raise my voice more than a few times but to little avail, if any. I thought things might improve once I got them to their seats and the train was rolling eastward, but that wasn't the case. They were loud and raucous and soon were chasing each other up and down the aisle. At one point they were tossing a rubber ball over other passengers' heads and giggling about it. Nothing I said or did had the least effect on them.

I was slumped in my aisle seat attempting to pretend that I had nothing to do with them when I realized that somebody was standing alongside me. I looked up to see an elderly Japanese man, formally dressed.

"Excuse, please," he said with a smile, waving his hand toward the boys. "They look Japanese, but they don't act Japanese."

"You've got it right," I said. "They're thoroughly American and there's no cure for it."

To my immense relief, an unfortunate soul from the U.S. Embassy with a sign identifying himself was waiting to take charge of my wild bunch when we finally got to Tokyo.

"I hope you brought a rope," I told him.

MY NEXT TRIP TO Kyoto would turn into a stunning embarrassment.

Akiko had an older brother who loved jazz and was a big fan of Thelonious Monk. He was impressed that I was from North Carolina, because that was where Monk was from. She wanted me to meet her brother, as well as her parents. When I called to tell her which weekend I was planning to come, she said that her parents wanted me to stay at their home.

By this time I knew that her family was well-to-do. Her father was involved in several businesses, one of which was an ice skating rink to which Akiko had taken me. It was there that I discovered that my ankles were prone to flop in unexpected directions when it came to ice skating, and not even the double-bladed skates designed for amateurs could prevent it. I considered it a major success that I was able to get off the ice without the assistance of ambulance attendants. Akiko, a graceful skater, seemed to find this amusing.

I never had been inside the compound where her family lived. I thought it would be nice, but it was even more elegant than I expected. The house was big, traditional and extraordinarily beautiful, furnished with Japanese antiques and incredible scrolls, tapestries and other art. As Akiko and her parents showed me through it, I wished that Tomoo could see it. The house was surrounded by a garden that could compete with any I had seen in Kyoto. A stream ran through it crossed by three decorative bridges. Big koi lingered in deep pools, looking like works of art themselves, wearing intricate designs of red, yellow, gold, orange, white, blue and black. When Akiko clapped her hands the fish came to her.

At the back of the garden was a guest house with two bedrooms. That was where Akiko's brother lived. He was about my age and I was to stay in the guest house with him. He became my friend the moment we were introduced because I had gone to the PX in Tokyo and bought him a Thelonious Monk album.

Akiko's parents had invited other guests for dinner that night, two couples of about their age. All were cordial. They seemed impressed at the bits of Japanese that I could speak. With Akiko's help, I'd been working hard to improve my Japanese, even to the point of learning to read and write some basic symbols. I thought I was making a good impression and might have achieved that if not for an unexpected spasm.

Early in the year, I had fallen into a newly dug drainage ditch in Okinawa on a dark night and injured my left knee. I underwent three months of physical therapy, and the doctors thought I would be okay. I was for the most part, but every now and then, if my leg was under strain and I made a wrong move, my knee would lock up, my leg would shoot out, and I would be in agonizing pain.

We were seated on tatami at the big dining table and I made the mistake of shifting position. My left knee locked up. My leg shot out striking the table. I yelped in pain and began writhing on the tatami, struggling desperately to get my knee to loosen and bend. Akiko jumped up with a look of panic and knelt beside me uncertain what to do. Everybody else remained seated, apparently stunned. I couldn't imagine what her parents were thinking.

Finally, my knee began to bend, my pain slowly abated.

"I'm okay," I told Akiko. "I'm fine."

She helped me up and I took a few steps around to get out the kinks before we returned to dinner. Although everybody resumed eating, the incident clearly had changed the tone of the evening, and I was fearful that it had deeply embarrassed Akiko. The dinner ended sooner than it might have otherwise. The guests found excuses to leave.

Akiko and I walked in the garden later. I apologized profusely and explained why my knee had gone berserk. She told me not to worry, that her parents had not been offended, that they would understand. We ended our walk at the guest house, where even before we entered we could hear Thelonious Monk making magic on the keys.

When we stepped into the guest house I knew immediately why her brother lived there. Home stereo systems were just becoming popular then, but he had the best available, sophisticated for the time and capable of high volume and throbbing bass. He didn't speak much English but he had a better way of communicating. As soon as Akiko left, he went to a cabinet, pulled out a bottle of Suntory whisky and raised it high in his right hand, a big smile on his face, a welcome cure for my earlier embarrassment. He fetched two glasses and ice cubes and was generous in his pouring. We settled in for some serious jazz.

Well into our second drink, my new friend's leg suddenly shot straight out. He grabbed his knee, yelped as if in pain, and began writhing on the tatami. It startled me and it was a few moments before I realized that he was mimicking my earlier agonies and doing a masterful job of it. When I began laughing, he jumped up and became his sister, rushing to my aid, dropping to both knees, a look of panic on her face, her hands in the air, fingers aflutter, uncertain what to do.

We both were laughing uproariously and decided for our next performance we'd have another drink.

The next morning, Akiko's first words to me were: "It sounded as if you had a good time."

On my next trip, Akiko took me to Kobe, a nearby city on the coast that had been devastated by American bombers in World War II. Her married older sister lived there, and Akiko wanted me to meet her. She lived in a high-rise apartment with a great view, modern appliances, western furnishings and rugs on the floors, a complete contrast to the home in which she'd grown up. I now was acquainted with Akiko's immediate family. They all seemed aware that the relationship that we had developed was growing deeper and they displayed no obvious dismay or concern about it.

EVERYTHING WAS GOING WELL, except for one major complication. My time in Japan was running out. I had been learning much from Deke and gaining some confidence from his encouragement and support. Almost every issue of *Freedom* had at least two articles by me, and I had several in *Koryu*, although none bore bylines. I had written about the space program, Alan Shepard, Gus Grissom and John Glenn, the first three Americans into space. A day would come when I would stand on the gantry where Glenn entered the Friendship 7 capsule to become the first American to orbit Earth, and I would spend time with all of the original astronauts except Gus Grissom, who died on January

27, 1967, along with two other astronauts, in an accidental fire while preparing for the Apollo 1 mission, but nobody could have convinced me of that possibility at the time. We had a series about countries that were allies of the U.S., and I wrote about Afghanistan, Jordan and Sudan. Another series featured modern American authors, and I had the pleasure of writing about Robert Frost, Ernest Hemingway, and Mark Twain.

Years later I would become aware of a book called *Profiles of Modern American Authors* by Bernard Dekle, published in 1969 by Charles E. Tuttle Company. In it were the pieces I had written about Frost, Hemingway and Twain word-for-word with no acknowledgment. I also knew that other pieces in the book had been written by TDY writers who had preceded me. On the back flyleaf I read this about Deke: "While serving as Director of the American Cultural Center in Kobe he was faced with repeated requests for a convenient, easily readable book on the important figures of modern American literature—and finding no such book in existence, he decided to write it himself." I was taken aback by this, and although I maintained contact with Deke years later, I never said a word to him about it. I figured I owed him.

Deke had his quirks, although presenting the work of others as his own was not one I had anticipated. Every day after lunch, he would close the blinds in his office and stretch out for a nap on the sofa. Afterwards, with the blinds reopened, he would be hard at work at his typewriter. It took a while for me to realize that what he was working on wasn't for *Freedom* magazine. He was writing a novel about a red light district in a Japanese resort town. He called it *Night Angel Street*. He eventually asked if I would read some of the chapters and give him my opinion. He seemed pleased that I enjoyed them. The novel was published by Tuttle in 1965, three years after I left Japan, but I didn't find out about it until years later. It got good reviews, according to the publisher, although there must have been one bad one, because Deke filed a libel suit against *The Japan Times* for an anonymous review it published. Filing lawsuits for bad reviews could tie up some authors in court for life.

Despite Deke's flaws, my time in Japan and his influence made me realize that writing was what I wanted to do, and another development helped seal that conviction. On a dreary weekend when I didn't have the money to go to Kyoto and was feeling low, I wandered into the small library at the base. Near the front door was a shelf for new releases. One caught my eye. The title was *A Long and Happy Life*. The author was Reynolds Price. It was his first novel. For some reason, perhaps the promising title, I picked it up and learned from the flyleaf that it was set in North Carolina. I turned to Chapter One. The first sentence covered most of the page, more than 200 words long. It swept me into the lives of Wesley Beavers and Rosacoke Mustian, a young couple facing the complications of love and life decisions. I checked out the book, took it back to the barracks, stretched out on my bunk and started reading. I knew these people, these places. I read the book straight through, missing supper on the one night a month that the mess hall had t-bone steaks. I found myself talking to the characters. I didn't want the story to end. After I finished it, I lay looking at the ceiling marveling at what I had experienced. Mere words on paper had delivered me home and entangled me in the lives of people who never existed but were as real as people I'd known. Never before had I thought about the transforming power of words that this book revealed to me. It made me dream of creating some of that magic myself. I would come to consider Reynolds Price a genius, a dear and gentle person, and many years later, to my great fortune, he would become a friend and even write kindly of my work.

ON A WEEKEND IN late September, I was back in Kyoto. Akiko and I had become all too aware of the fleeting days that we had together. We were eating at a tea house that we both liked. Japan was a land of smokers. Each table had an ashtray and a container filled with matchbooks. Akiko and I didn't smoke, but we still had to suffer the smoke of others. Matchbooks were one of the most popular forms of advertising in Japan at that time. It seemed that almost every business had its own matchbooks.

While we were eating, I decided that those matchbooks might be used for better purpose. I picked up one, opened it, took out a pen and wrote this in it: "Will you marry me?" I closed it and slid it across the table.

I watched intently as Akiko picked it up and read the message. I thought her face might reveal her reaction, but it didn't. She said nothing. Instead, she picked up the pen, wrote a response and slid the matchbook back to me. I was almost too afraid to open it. When I did, this is what I saw: "Yes, if possible."

She was smiling, and I couldn't have been happier, but those were two big words, "if possible." We both knew that the obstacles ahead would be many and difficult to overcome, but we began talking about how to deal with them.

I was thinking about getting my discharge and returning to Japan. That was a little more than three months away at the time. But I needed a job to make that possible. I talked to Deke and Tomoo about it. Both had met their wives in Japan, but they had good government jobs. They thought that my chances of getting such a job were almost nil. I went to talk to an editor at *The Japan Times*, and another at *Stars & Stripes*, about the possibility of becoming a reporter but got no encouragement.

I had to report back to Okinawa and Blubberbutt's control of my life on November 1, and I intended to spend my last two weekends in Kyoto. Akiko was waiting at the train station when I arrived early Saturday, October 20, and by evening I was sick with flu symptoms and miserable. As Akiko attended to me we talked only a little about our situation. Too many factors were out of our control, and I was coming to the harsh realization that I had little to offer—little formal education, no money, and no job prospects. The coming week would bring even more complications.

AFTER GOING ON SICK call Monday, I began feeling better. I had to go to *Stars & Stripes* on Tuesday morning to do some research. I arrived a little before 9:30 to find people in the newsroom crowded around a teletype that was spewing bulletins. It was a little before 7:30 on Monday evening in Washington and President Kennedy had just gone on national television to inform the country that offensive missile bases had been placed in Cuba.

"The purpose of these bases can be none other than to provide a nuclear strike capability against the Western Hemisphere," he said.

He had ordered a "strict quarantine on all offensive military equipment under shipment to Cuba." That meant a naval blockade to stop Soviet ships that already were on their way, and all military forces were ordered to prepare for confrontation.

"It shall be the policy of this Nation to regard any nuclear missile launched from Cuba against any nation in the Western Hemisphere as an attack by the Soviet Union on the United States," the President continued, "requiring a full retaliatory strike upon the Soviet Union."

The world suddenly was under threat of nuclear war that might be imminent, making all other problems seem minuscule. But mine were about to worsen. Not long afterward, another bulletin came. The Pentagon had ordered a DEFCON-3 alert. All military leaves were cancelled, all discharges halted, enlistments extended indefinitely. The next day the Strategic Air Command would go on DEFCON-2 alert, ready to strike the Soviet Union as soon as word was given.

Out of the blue, I was reduced to even greater despondency. I wasn't certain which would be the worse fate—instantaneous nuclear combustion or indefinite servitude under Blubberbutt.

Over the next few days tension would increase steadily. Troops from Fort Bragg, Camp Lejeune and other points began moving to Florida in anticipation of invading Cuba. War ships were encircling the island. Polaris submarines armed with nuclear missiles began taking up positions near Russia. ICBMs in silos were primed to fire. B-52s carrying nuclear bombs were constantly in the air. In a letter to Kennedy Nikita Khrushchev proclaimed that the U.S. had no right to establish a blockade in international waters.

On the day after Kennedy's speech, the Organization of American States voted unanimously to support the blockade and called for the removal of all missiles from Cuba. After the vote, Kennedy signed the order to begin the blockade the following morning at 10. Twenty-seven ships carrying Soviet arms and supplies to Cuba were heading toward it.

At 2 a.m. on Thursday, October 25, Kennedy received another letter from Khrushchev by teletype calling his actions "banditry...an act of aggression pushing mankind toward the abyss of missile nuclear war...."

That afternoon, the U.S. Ambassador to the United Nations, Adlai Stevenson, confronted the Soviet Ambassador in a televised performance and laid out the evidence of the missile sites for the world to see. That evening, a Soviet-chartered Panamanian vessel, the Marucla, was stopped and searched. It was carrying no arms.

Meanwhile, work was proceeding on the missile sites. Top military leaders wanted to launch air strikes against them, followed by invasion. Kennedy was reluctant to take those measures yet and a stalemate between Kennedy and Khrushchev settled in.

We had not been restricted to base during this crisis, and even if we had been, I had no intention of spending my last weekend in Japan in the barracks. What could our little unit do? Hurl magazines at nuclear missiles? I was going to Kyoto.

THE JAPANESE HAD MORE reason than any other country to be fearful of atomic war because they had experienced its horrors. A pall lay over the country and it would dominate my last two days with Akiko, complicating the uncertainty of my situation even more. We still had no solutions for our future, but we were determined to enjoy our time together despite the sadness we knew separation would bring. We revisited some favorite spots, remembering happier times. We sat for a long time at the Ryoan-ji zen garden in silent contemplation. We visited and laughed with her friends at the university. And that night we ate again at the Chinese restaurant where she had taken me for our first dinner together.

On Sunday we spent time with her parents and brother, had lunch with them and walked in the garden. Afterward Akiko and I hiked up the mountain to Kyomizu-dera and descended the wide, steep, stone stairway to Otowa Falls. We used the same wooden cup to drink the pure water from the sluice promising happiness in love.

All too soon we were at the train station. Some of her friends had come to be with her but they stepped back and allowed us to say what we needed to say before I got aboard.

It was Japanese tradition to display no public physical expressions of affection. No holding hands, no hug, no kiss. We just stared soulfully and sadly into one another's eyes and whispered the same three brief words. I turned quickly and got onto the train. I managed to find a window seat near where she was standing. She saw me and came toward the window just as the train began to move. She was holding out her right hand, trying to reach the window. I could see that she was crying. I placed my hand on the window and as the train picked up speed she began to run beside it, still reaching out, but falling back as the train moved faster. Straining to look back, I could see her friends rushing to her and closing around her.

Kyoto was as spectacularly beautiful in fall as it was in spring. The maples and other hardwoods already were showing off their brilliant yellows, oranges and reds, but as they passed by the window my vision of them was blurred.

DURING MY TIME IN Kyoto, I had paid no attention to what was happening in the Cuban situation. But I later learned that as I was leaving Tokyo on Saturday morning, October 27, which was Friday night in Washington, Kennedy had received a lengthy letter from Khrushchev indicating that he was reconsidering the situation and wanted to make a deal. The Soviets were willing to stop more arms shipments if the U.S. would agree not to invade. No mention was made of removing the missiles.

Tensions grew greater the following day when a U-2 pilot flying over Cuba was shot down by a missile and killed. Lower flying observation planes were attacked by anti-aircraft fire. The Defense Department was preparing to begin the invasion at dawn on Tuesday morning.

Before Kennedy and his staff could decide how to deal with Khrushchev's proposal, a second letter arrived by teletype while it was simultaneously being read over Radio Moscow. This one offered to remove the missiles in Cuba if the U.S. would eliminate missiles in Turkey aimed at the Soviet Union. That would cause political problems for Kennedy, and he decided to ignore the second letter and respond to the first, offering to end the blockade if Khrushchev removed the missiles.

When no response came from Khrushchev, Kennedy decided to move ahead with the invasion. At 9 Sunday morning, (11 p.m. in Tokyo) Khrushchev backed down and ordered that the missiles in Cuba be dismantled and returned to the Soviet Union. The crisis was over. By that time I already was in my bunk in the barracks, tired and depressed, and didn't learn about the good news until the following morning. That removed one complication in my life. Still it would be a while before the order cancelling leaves and discharges would be rescinded.

Over the next three days, I would finish my final article for *Freedom* and read another chapter of Deke's novel. On Tuesday, the unit held a small going-away party for me, but I was too glum to enjoy it. On my final night in Japan, Wednesday, Tomoo and his wife took me to a famous garden restaurant in Tokyo where course after exquisite course was prepared before us. It went on for hours and we drank a lot of sake. It's still one of the most memorable meals of my life.

The next morning, a staff driver dropped me and my overstuffed duffel bag off at the train station, and I rode into Tokyo for one last visit to the USO. I had promised Akiko that I would call before I left and she was waiting at home. An employee who had put through many of my calls to this same number recognized from the duffel bag the importance of this one. Akiko answered after the first ring. We talked for 15 minutes, promised to write each other regularly, and said our final goodbyes. I was morose as I headed to the subway for the first leg of my trip to Tachikawa Air Force Base. Tokyo's subway system was far newer, cleaner, more accommodating than New York's. Music played, and just as my train approached, "Al Di La" came over the speaker system. I couldn't believe it. I felt as if I were in a movie. I melded with the jammed rush into the train. As it pulled away I still could hear the song fading into the distance as I headed far, far away, beyond the beyond.

EXCEPT FOR SEEING MY friends, I dreaded returning to Okinawa, and some of my friends already had departed. Gene Craig had returned to Iowa and was preparing to enter graduate school. Others were close to departure. I wouldn't be returning to the art department. Instead, I was assigned to the Japanese language magazine distributed throughout the Ryukyus, *Shurei No Hikari* (Light of the Land of Courtesy). Unfortunately, I still was only a few doors away from Blubberbutt, but I did everything I could to avoid him and managed to fight back all urges to antagonize him.

My main concern at this time was getting out of the Army, and I wanted it to be soon. It was possible to get out up to three months early to go to college. I decided to try for that.

The problem was that I couldn't imagine that any college might accept me. I hadn't taken SAT tests, and my high school records did not portray the type of student that colleges normally sought. Until I got to Kyoto, I'd never even been on a college or university campus. Another problem was tuition. I had no savings, although I had accumulated leave for which I would get paid, and I could apply that to tuition.

My parents suggested High Point College. It had several advantages. It was small, aligned with the Methodist Church, and was closest to Thomasville, only about 12 miles from home. That would allow me to commute to classes. My parents suggested that I write to the current pastor of First Methodist Church, the Rev. Orion Hutchinson, and see if he could help me. I don't know how he did it, but he got me accepted.

On the day the acceptance arrived in the mail, I filed for an early out. I was hoping for quick approval and within two weeks I got it. I thought I might be leaving Okinawa immediately. Not so. I was informed that I had to get a document from the college stating the date my classes would begin. That took another 10 days by air-mail. I turned it in as soon as it arrived. A few days later I was informed that early outs were granted only a certain number of days before classes began. I ended up staying four days longer in Okinawa than I would have if I had not gotten an early out. Catch 22. Blubberbutt's revenge.

During this convoluted process, though, one good thing did happen. A captain came to see me one day and asked if I would be willing to work with him on a private project. He was a helicopter pilot, and while he was stationed in Alaska, he and two other pilots had been caught in a sudden blizzard, a disorienting whiteout that caused all three to crash, but all survived. He had written a first-person account and submitted it to *Reader's Digest*. An editor expressed interest but said that the piece needed work.

I went to the captain's quarters after work the following Friday and remained until the early hours Monday. I quizzed him at length about details and wrote and rewrote for two days. When I finished, I felt good about it, and he liked it, too. We had not agreed on price, but he shocked me by giving me a hundred bucks, the first money I earned directly from writing. The article was titled *Whiteout, Terror of the Artic*. I never knew if it appeared in the magazine. Even if it did, like all the pieces I'd written in Japan, it wouldn't have borne my name.

After Christmas, I bade farewell to my friends Eric Alberts, Jim Lawler, and Bill Taylor as they left Okinawa. Lonely and forlorn, I returned to the barracks and crossed off another day on the additional page I had to add to my short-timer's calendar because of my "early out."

For much of the time that I had been in Okinawa, I frequently watched Pan-Am 727s taking off from Naha and climbing into the sky over the East China Sea, wishing that I were on every one.

The day finally came when that happened. I was headed to San Francisco, with stops at Wake Island and Honolulu, but I was wishing I was on my way to Japan.

Jerry Bledsoe | DO-GOOD BOY

12

IT DIDN'T TAKE ME long to realize that college was not for me. I knew it within the first week. It bored me and I felt out of place. I was older than others in my classes, and my interests were far removed from theirs. As much as I hated to admit it, the Army had forced an element of maturity on me, albeit perhaps a small one. Experience had become far more educational than classroom instruction, and I preferred seeking knowledge on my own terms. Studying for the purpose of passing tests and gaining grades seemed a waste of time.

Most of my professors were dull, or so adamant about their subjects they couldn't see beyond them, not to mention, as in the case of my religion professor, unwilling to be challenged. I did have a spirited English professor, Sam Underwood. He was big on Shakespeare, not one of my better subjects. His eyes, magnified by horn-rim glasses, were quick and his hands flashed dramatically as he spoke. He loved to prod and prick to provoke discussions and relished rousing reasoned arguments. His were the only classes to which I looked forward. I have especially fond memories of the last one. For my final paper I wrote a parody of Shakespeare as a sportswriter.

"I don't normally do this," Underwood said as he started class that day, "but I got one paper that I enjoyed so much I'm going to read it aloud."

Mine. And the class laughed in all the right places.

THE ENTIRE TIME I was in classes, I was looking for a newspaper reporting job. Only days after I returned home, I went to talk with Wint Capel, the editor of *The Thomasville Times*. He had a small staff and no positions open. He told me he was willing to let me write free-lance features but could pay only 10 cents per column inch. I counted the number of words in a column inch and it came to about 50. If I wrote a 1,000-word article, which is longer than the average newspaper column, I'd make a grand total of two bucks.

I went to at least half a dozen other newspapers, all for naught. The pompous editor of *The High Point Enterprise*, Holt McPherson, informed me that I had zero chance of writing for a newspaper. *The Greensboro Daily News* didn't have time for me, but Floyd Hendley, the managing editor of the afternoon paper, *The Greensboro Record*, advised me that I needed to start on a smaller paper where I could quickly learn more and get a wider range of experience. He even called an editor in Lynchburg, Virginia, on my behalf. That editor granted me an interview but no job offer.

On one of my final days at High Point College, I stopped by a bulletin board where local businesses posted job notices. A new newspaper was about to be published in High Point, I discovered, and it was seeking a circulation manager. Although I never had been a circulation manager I had known more than a few. I became a paper boy when I was nine, delivering *The Thomasville Tribune* every Tuesday and Thursday on foot, carrying the papers in a strapped cloth bag so heavily loaded that I had to constantly switch it from one frail aching shoulder to the other. I continued carrying papers until I was nearly 16, from age 10 blessedly by bicycle. At 11, I began delivering the afternoon *Twin-City Sentinel* from Winston-Salem, 20 miles away. At 15, I signed on as a carrier for *The Greensboro Daily News*, a morning newspaper that eventually would play a major role in my life. I figured I at least knew something about getting papers to readers' doors, if not effectively collecting from some subscribers. I scribbled down the telephone number and called. Without questioning, I was granted an interview that day. I should have realized that was an indication of problems to come.

The new paper was *The High Point Daily News*, which had not yet published an edition. The plan was to bring it out twice weekly before expanding to daily but that wouldn't work out and it would become perhaps the world's only weekly daily.

This was not a publication started by a journalist, or a person with any knowledge of the newspaper business. High Point promoted itself as the nation's furniture center. It thrived on furniture factories and three times yearly, spring, summer and fall, it hosted national and regional furniture shows, attracting manufacturers and retailers from far and wide. (Now the factories are mostly gone but the furniture shows, spring and fall, are international and huge, occupying most of the downtown area.) The founder of this newspaper owned a company that sold supplies vital to furniture making. He had grown wealthy enough from it to buy and install the finest Goss offset printing press available at the time, better than any at other North Carolina newspapers. He added a new wing on his supply business to house it.

If I had known many other things about him I likely wouldn't have gone for an interview. His name was Abel Gross "Pete" Whitener, a 1928 graduate of the University of North Carolina, where he had been a cheerleader and a member of the prestigious honorary society Phi Beta Kappa. Unfortunately, he also was a political fanatic, a member of the John Birch Society and an ardent fan of a Raleigh TV commentator named Jesse Helms, who would become North Carolina's longest reigning and most controversial U.S. Senator.

When I went for my interview, Whitener's goal for the first issue was only a month away, and he seemed overwhelmed and desperate. He hired me on the spot and I started work as soon as my classes ended. It didn't take me long to learn why he was so desperate. For one thing, the press was still being installed and was a long way from functional. And not only did Whitener have no circulation manager, he also had no reporters. He did have an editor, a timid and hapless fellow who seemed to have no idea what to do and had unwisely given up his job teaching at a small college in Pennsylvania and moved his family to High Point, apparently out of commitment to Whitener's political views. His new boss verbally abused him in front of others, and within a week of my arrival he was gone without explanation.

A short time later, a new editor appeared. I recognized him immediately: Hammett Cecil Jr. He and his father had published *The Thomasville Tribune* out of the back of their office supply store when I had been a delivery boy. I didn't get a chance to have a conversation with Cecil because I was out trying to round up innocent boys to hustle subscriptions and deliver copies of a newspaper that was nothing more than an expensive fantasy at the time. Soon, Cecil, too, was gone.

That was when I got pulled aside by Whitener and informed that he had found an experienced circulation manager and had a new position for me. He was fed up with namby-pambies posing as editors. Instead he wanted a strong triumvirate and I was to be part of it. He also had hired a new graduate of Dartmouth College to complete the power trio, a person he hadn't yet met, but who wouldn't arrive for another week or so. I knew exactly what this meant. With no knowledge of local government, politics or business, and no sources of any type, I'd have to come up with copy to fill the first edition.

WHITENER WAS A SCRAWNY little guy with veins that bulged in his neck and head when he was angry, which was often. His management style had two primary components: harangue and rage. And everybody under his direction experienced it at one time or another, some with great frequency. One of the new press operators had all that he could take one day and decked Whitener with a single punch, not only costing him his job but leaving him facing criminal charges on the same day his wife gave birth to their first child. He did, however, bring satisfaction, if not a touch of glee, to other employees.

It was a near miracle that we actually produced Vol. 1, No.1, a sample edition, on July 10. It was aimed mainly at potential advertisers and filled with free ads. Only two pages bore copy. I had managed to turn out an article about the summer furniture market, another about a family that had gone six months without running water due to incompetence and indifference by the city, along with a host of shorter pieces. It wasn't until July 25 that the first issue actually aimed at readers appeared. Fortunately, by that time the Dartmouth innocent had arrived to help me find copy, but Whitener, who fancied himself a writer, filled a lot of the space.

He wrote much as he spoke—every word in all-capital letters. On the front page was a big photo of himself gleefully examining a copy of the sample edition as it rolled off the press. Beside the photo was a large block of type bearing the huge headline, "A NEW VIEWPOINT." The article boiled down the newspaper's purpose, which, as best I could understand it, was to counter the distortions of other area papers. Up until that point I hadn't realized that was supposed to be my job.

Much of the editorial page was filled with a far longer, double-column, seemingly endless block of type headlined "COMMUNIST DEFEAT." I thought it must have something to do with the war in Vietnam, but I was wrong. It was about the great victory of the North Carolina General Assembly a month earlier when it passed a law banning Communist Party members and anybody who had pleaded the Fifth Amendment about communist connections from speaking on state-run university campuses. This became nationally known as the Speaker Ban Law and its attempt to stifle free speech stirred quite a controversy, along with demonstrations.

Whitener saw commies wherever he looked, and anybody who dared disagree with him on any topic likely would be branded one as well. It finally dawned on me that I inadvertently had allowed myself to be considered a warrior in the battle against communism, when all I wanted was to write interesting feature stories and objective news.

I made it through one more edition without losing my temper and getting arrested. But I quit on the spot a few days afterward when Whitener, in one of his ever-swelling rages, ripped off a layout page a story I had written about a city council meeting. He screamed at me that I was too soft on the council members, all of whom were corrupt in his mind. I should be attacking them, not making them look reasonable. In its place he pasted an article he had clipped from one of the right-wing publications that arrived by the dozens in the mail. I did learn one helpful lesson from this experience. Fanatics have little sense of reality and never can be convinced of it. Attempting to deal reasonably with one is a waste of time.

It was early August when I left Whitener to his despotic delusions. I'd been out of the Army for seven months. I was 22, without a job, had no money, and still was living with my parents. I had no classes to attend in the future or any idea of what I might do next. I also was in debt to a finance company because I had to buy a car, a clumpy black, '54 Dodge four-door, so I could get back and forth to work and go in search of stories. My prospects were looking dim.

Just before I went into the Army, my dad had started a small wholesale company, selling candy, chewing gum, tobacco products, headache powders and various other goods to small stores, cafes and gas stations from an old bread truck. The business had grown and now occupied a cinder-block warehouse next to a grocery store in Thomasville. Although he couldn't afford it, my dad offered me a low-paying job putting together call-in orders and making deliveries in a pickup truck. I took it reluctantly, because I had no other options. A few weeks later, I also got a part-time night job paying 80 cents an hour at Biff Burger, a 15-cent hamburger joint on South Main Street in High Point, part of a chain headquartered in Florida that had sprung up after McDonald's began spreading across the country.

From the time I got home, I had been corresponding regularly with Akiko. While I was at High Point College, we wrote about our classes and how much we missed each other. I still had hope that I might get back to Japan, or that she might come to the United States. But after I started working for Whitener, my letters to her dropped off because of the pressures and exhaustion of the job. Now I was too embarrassed to let her know what was going on and how grim my situation had become. Even with two jobs, I still had trouble putting money away. What l was making wouldn't get me back to Japan, and I wasn't acquiring any skills to make my future any brighter. I went a couple of months without writing, and unsurprisingly, her letters trickled away.

On Friday, November 22, I was making deliveries and returned to the warehouse a little before two p.m. When I pulled up to the dock, my mother emerged. She was crying. I thought something might have happened to my dad.

I leapt from the truck. "What's wrong?" I asked.

"The President's been shot," she said. "We heard it on the radio."

"Shot?" I said. "Is he dead?"

"They don't know."

I jumped back into the truck, which had no radio, and drove home as fast as I could. I headed straight to the black-and-white 20-inch cabinet-model TV in the den and turned it on. Walter Cronkite's solemn face appeared on the screen. Three shots had rung out in Dallas, he was saying, the President, riding in an open limousine, had been hit and taken to Parkland Hospital. There were reports that he was dead but no confirmation.

I sank into the sofa, where I would remain for the next several hours, shocked by the unfathomable and sick with sorrow. Cronkite was coatless in the CBS newsroom, three telephones on his desk. He repeatedly removed and replaced his heavy, black-framed glasses. The scene kept switching to a banquet room at the Trade Mart in Dallas where the President had been scheduled to speak and where people now appeared to be wandering in a communal daze. At one point a speaker began a prayer.

When the camera switched back to Cronkite, he mentioned that a young man had been taken into custody, then turned dramatically to another unconfirmed report that the President was dead and a priest had delivered last sacraments. As he spoke two young men were hunched over a teletype behind him. One suddenly ripped paper from the machine and hurried to hand it to Cronkite, who replaced his glasses as he glanced at it.

"From Dallas, Texas," he said, "the flash, apparently official. President Kennedy died at one p.m. central standard time, two o'clock eastern time,"—he paused, his voice catching, and glanced at a wall clock—"some 38 minutes ago."

He removed his glasses, then put them back on, wiping a tear from his right eye as he resumed his broadcast. I found myself sobbing.

I remained in front of the TV, soaking in the details, until I had to go to my second job and don my Biff cap and apron. Business was very slow for a Friday night. Most people, I presumed, were in front of their TVs, where I wanted to be. But the Miss Thomasville pageant went ahead as scheduled that night. And the big Christmas parade was held in the rain on the following morning, after a brief memorial service at the Big Chair, which included a prayer and the playing of taps.

Until I had to report to work at 5 p.m., I also spent Saturday in front of the TV, while the President's body lay in a closed bronze coffin in the East Room of the White House. I did the same on Sunday, which brought more shock and incredulity.

The TV was on NBC when my mother summoned us to Sunday dinner. I still could see it from the dining room table. The focus then was on the detention center in the basement of the city hall in Dallas. Lee Harvey Oswald, who had been arrested an hour and 20 minutes after Kennedy was shot and later charged with his murder, was to be transferred to a maximum security cell at the Dallas County Jail. An armored truck used for transferring cash between banks was waiting to deliver him.

I heard somebody on the TV say, "Here he comes," and got up to watch.

A tight-lipped Oswald, his hands cuffed before him, was being escorted by two detectives holding his arms. The detectives were looking straight ahead when a stocky man in a dark suit and a fedora lunged out of the crowd of reporters and onlookers, a .38 revolver in hand, and fired a single shot point-blank into Oswald's lower left side. NBC had the only live TV camera at the scene, and it was allowing the entire country to witness this incredible event as it happened. I yelled "No!" when the shot was fired. My family jumped up then, and we stood staring at the chaos in wonder.

The shooting took place at 12:21 p.m. Eastern Standard time, and Oswald died at Parkland Hospital at 2:07. The main article on the front page of *The Greensboro Daily News* from the Associated Press the following morning began this way: "Lee Harvey Oswald found merciless death lurking in a crowd today, just as President John F. Kennedy did 48 hours earlier."

What a lead, I thought. And no byline.

Before this mayhem occurred, the President's flag-draped coffin had been taken from the White House to the Capitol by horse-drawn caisson and installed on a catafalque in the rotunda. Ten minutes after Oswald's death, the TV cameras switched there as the President's widow, Jacqueline, and five-year-old daughter, Caroline, knelt beside the catafalque. Caroline reached tentatively to touch the flag that covered the coffin, while her mother gently kissed it. After that, thousands upon thousands of people began passing by the catafalque, paying their respects. I wanted to be there, too, but I had Biff Burgers to Roto-broil and dip in secret sauce that night.

Originally, the plan was for the coffin to be on display to the public only until 9 p.m., but the crowds were so huge that a decision was made to keep them moving through all night. For some reason still unknown to me, I felt compelled to be there. Biff Burger didn't close until 11 and we still had to clean up after that. But about halfway through my shift, I made a decision. I was going to Washington.

I called my younger brother, Phil, who was 13, to see if he wanted to go (my other brother Larry was in the Navy at the time). Phil was excited about it. A high school student named Ken who was working with me said he'd like to go too. If it was OK with his parents, I told him, it was OK with me. About midnight the three of us struck out in my well-worn Dodge. I drove all night. We arrived before dawn and magically encountered a car pulling out of a parking space behind the Capitol. Few people were on the street there, but as we hurried around the Capitol, we encountered the line. At two that morning, we learned, it had stretched for three miles. It had diminished greatly but it still was very long and we walked its length to join it. It was a bitterly cold morning and in our haste we had not dressed warmly, but we were willing to suffer the shivers.

Sunrise came shortly before seven, and just after 7:30 we saw police officers coming down the line, and people beginning to peel away. Some would continue streaming through the rotunda for another hour, but the police had determined a cut-off point in the five-abreast line, and those of us on the wrong side of it were out of luck. Our disappointment must have been heavy on our faces because a friendly cop stopped to ask where we were from. I told him we'd driven all night and had really been hoping to pass by the coffin.

"Let me tell you what to do," he said. "Leave right now and go to the northwest gate at the White House. It's on Pennsylvania Avenue. Station yourselves in front of that gate and hold your position. There shouldn't be too many people there now. Most of these people are going to stay here and hope they can see the coffin being removed. If you're at that gate and in a good position, you'll see more than you ever hoped to see."

We did just that.

The caisson bearing the coffin left the Capitol at 11 in a military procession followed by limousines carrying the family and others. Bells tolled as the procession entered the northeast gate of the White House and pulled to the portico. While choirs sang on the lawn and bagpipes played, a new procession was formed for the eight-block march to St. Matthew's Cathedral where the funeral would be conducted. The crowd around us was deep and huge now, and except for the occasional snuffle or cough, was reverently silent.

The march began at 11:35, led by military bands and honor guards followed by the caisson pulled by six white horses, with a seventh in the lead. In military tradition, soldiers in parade-dress uniforms sat erect in saddles on the lead horse and the three horses on the left. Behind the caisson was the caparisoned horse named Black Jack for General John J. Pershing, a horse without a rider, black boots reversed in his stirrups, a silver sword sheaved on his side. Black Jack apparently had been spooked by the situation. He was nervous, his eyes rolled, and the PFC who was his handler was having difficulty controlling him. I was fearful that he might break free and bolt into the crowds. The only sounds now were the muffled drums ahead of the caisson and the clatter of the horses' steel-shod hooves on the pavement.

The president's widow followed Black Jack, her face veiled. She was walking in step with the President's brothers, Bobby on her right, Teddy on the left, both in formal wear. I had been seeing these faces on the TV screen for days, and now they were just feet away from us and seemed surreal.

Behind them were other family members, including the President's brothers-in-law, Sargent Shriver and Jamie Auchincloss. Fifteen feet back, surrounded by Secret Service members, was the somber-faced new President, Lyndon Johnson, also in formal wear, his head bare of his familiar Stetson, his wife, Lady Bird, at his side. They were followed by a slow-moving limousine carrying the Kennedy children. This was John-John's third birthday.

Behind came a rag-tag group that was making no attempt to march in step: the foreign dignitaries. They were 14 abreast and in 16 irregular lines.

Ninety world leaders were among them. The only two major leaders not present were Mao Tse-tung and Kennedy's nemesis from the day he became President, Soviet Premiere Nikita Khrushchev, although Khrushchev had sent his deputy, Anastas Mikoyan. The one who stood out most to me was General Charles de Gaulle, President of the French Republic, who towered above all the rest, not only in height but in dignity. He was in full uniform on the first row. The most colorfully and lavishly uniformed leader, only a few feet away from De Gaulle, although far shorter, was Haile Selassie, Emperor of Ethiopia. Kings and Queens also marched among them, although I recognized none. Then appeared the Supreme Court justices, congressional leaders, White House staff members.

After the procession had passed, trailed by police officers on motorcycles, some in the crowd began surging after it. We remained in place, still in awe of what we just had witnessed. I don't remember the three of us saying anything, but I know we were deeply and permanently aware that we had taken part in a major historical event.

THAT, HOWEVER, WAS NOT the end of my compulsion. I felt drawn to Dallas, too. My Army buddy Eric Alberts was living near Dallas with his parents in a small farm house outside the town of Euless. His father, also an artist and sculptor, had taught at the University of Nebraska and worked on murals with his friend Grant Wood who gained fame for his painting "American Gothic." Eric had gotten a job as a technical illustrator drawing missile parts at Texas Instruments, a high-tech corporation in Dallas. He wasn't happy with it. We had been corresponding since he returned home, and he, too, was thinking of returning to Japan, even though he'd only visited for a few days. We wanted to see each other, and I was determined to see Dallas and experience the scenes of the President's assassination.

Just before Christmas, I quit my two jobs, got out what little money I'd put into the bank and two days after Christmas, I caught a ride to Ft. Polk, Louisiana, with a high school buddy, Chuck Tysinger, who was stationed there and had been home on leave. From there I took a bus to Dallas. Eric met me at the bus station and took me in search of a place to stay, which turned out to be a rooming house not far from downtown, where I would have quick access to city buses. My plan was to renew my quest for a newspaper job, but first I had to fulfill my compulsion.

I devoted days to that. I walked a good part of the route the President took to his death just so I could experience the sights that were among his last. I spent hours at Dealey Plaza, where the shooting took place, sometimes just sitting in contemplation on the winter–faded grass of the slight hillside that became known as the grassy knoll. I got a brief glimpse inside the Texas School Book Depository, from which Oswald had fired the fatal shots, before I was asked to leave. I visited the emergency area at Parkland Hospital where the President and his assassin died, the dock at the city hall jail where Oswald had been loaded into an ambulance. I sat through a grade-B movie at the seedy Texas Theatre where Oswald had been captured after murdering Dallas police officer J.D. Tippit.

I didn't know why I was doing all of this, and as I write this more than half a century later, I still don't know. Perhaps I was just being driven by a nascent reporter's frustrated instincts.

I discovered that Eric, too, was in debt. He'd bought a green Triumph TR3 convertible and we spent weekends touring spots of interest. One weekend we drove to Monterey, Mexico. We later discussed catching a freighter to Japan but the complications and uncertainties of that were profound and discouraging. While I was in Dallas, I wrote to Akiko, who had met Eric, telling her about my visit and our thoughts about returning to Japan. I received no response.

I spent weekdays searching for a newspaper job. I went to *The Dallas Morning News* and *The Fort Worth Star-Telegram*, where I was directed to personnel offices and allowed to fill out applications that I knew were hopeless. I also rode buses and hitchhiked to newspaper offices in nearly every outlying town without ever getting an interview. After six weeks, I was running out of money and immensely frustrated. I started looking for other jobs and landed one as salad boy at Bob's Big Boy. When I reported for work I was handed a red-checkered apron and a Big Boy chef's hat. I suddenly was struck with the realization that if I donned those gaudy accoutrements I'd be submitting to ultimate humiliation. I walked out, went to a pay phone, called my dad collect and asked if he'd wire enough money for me to get a bus ticket home.

On my first day back, I dropped by the Biff Burger. Art Miller, the manager, told me he'd just been promoted to oversee all five Biff Burgers in Greensboro, High Point and Burlington and his job was open. Would I be interested? The pay would be much more than I ever had made and I needed the money. I said yes. Two months later, I met a dark-eyed beauty named Linda Irene Boyd, who had grown up in High Point. Four months after that, we eloped to South Carolina in my newly purchased but problem plagued Austin-Healey Sprite. (We've been together ever since.) After a weekend in Myrtle Beach, I decided that I was going to make one final effort at getting a newspaper job—and to my great astonishment it panned out.

13

"Paternalism" was a word often bandied about with regard to Kannapolis, I learned after arriving there in September, 1964. Usually, it was reporters, academics, union leaders or other outside critics who applied the term. You rarely heard it from anybody who lived in or near Kannapolis, although it was hard to know who actually lived in Kannapolis because nobody knew where Kannapolis began or ended. It often was described, even by historians, as the largest unincorporated city in the country. But local historian Norris Dearborn questioned that. It all depended on how a town or city was defined. Ft. Bragg, for example, was far bigger with a much larger population. It wasn't incorporated, and it was only 120 miles away. Was a fort not similar to a mill town?

Some might claim that fear was responsible for keeping residents from complaining about paternalism. But others would maintain that a lot of people in Kannapolis had no complaints because they preferred it. Kannapolis had no mayor, no city manager, no city council, and no governmental bureaucrats relentlessly enforcing petty rules. Yet residents had police and fire protection, water and sewer service, garbage collection, street maintenance and other benefits for which they paid no taxes. Many millworkers and their families had comfortable, attractive company-owned homes with regular maintenance and yard upkeep at low rental cost.

The person who was ultimately responsible for providing and funding all of that, the benevolent paternal figure who presided over Kannapolis, was Charles A. Cannon, also known as "Mr. Charlie," "Uncle Charlie," and "The Skipper." It was Mr. Charlie's father, James W. Cannon, a former general store manager and cotton broker, who set out in 1906 to build a town on 600 acres of farmland near a small community called Glass in Cabarrus County. He planned to call it Cannapolis, for Cannon Town, but a year into construction, for reasons now unknown, the C got changed to K. He intended it to be a model town, built around a mill devoted to making towels. The town thrived after the mill opened in 1908 and went on to become known as the largest producer of towels in the country, causing it to be referred to as Towel Town.

J.W. Cannon had opened his first textile plant in nearby Concord, the seat of Cabarrus County government, in 1887, producing a coarse fabric that came to be called Cannon Cloth, used for many purposes. He soon turned his attention to becoming the first manufacturer of towels in the South. By the time he started building Kannapolis on the northern edge of Cabarrus County, he, along with partners, already had opened nine mills in Cabarrus and nearby counties.

Charles, the youngest of J.W.'s 10 children, had grown up in Concord, attended Fishburne Military School in Waynesboro, Virginia, and spent a year at Davidson College before marrying at age 19 in 1911. His father made him manager of a plant in the small town of Rockwell, south of Salisbury, and five years later, he was named vice president of Cannon Manufacturing Company and transferred to Kannapolis.

When his father died in 1921, Charles was left in control of 12 plants with some 15,000 employees and sales of $40 million annually, and he set about fulfilling his father's dreams. He brought all of the plants under control of a single company, took it public on the New York Stock Exchange and began expanding by building new plants to manufacture sheets and other products. As the company grew so did Kannapolis, and the son molded it into the model mill town that his father envisioned. Many southern towns with textile plants had mill villages, but none could compare to Kannapolis, where the company owned 900 acres in the center of town and controlled most aspects of community life.

BY THE TIME I arrived to start my new job at *The Daily Independent*, the population was estimated to be about 35,000, and the town seemed to be pleasant and orderly. The downtown business area—every commercial building owned by the company—had been remade into a Williamsburg-style village with a wide, tree-lined boulevard down the center.

One complication of the company's ownership of most of the town was that rental apartments weren't easy to find. After a frustrating hunt, Linda and I had to settle for three shabby rooms and a bath in the back of a rambling old farmhouse on the edge of Concord, seven miles away. That turned out to be a miserable experience, but our luck would change a couple of months later.

One of my co-workers, Z. Bright Tucker, the quietest and oldest person in the newsroom, whose job was to lay out the bulk of the paper and write headlines, told me that the apartment adjoining his in a duplex in Jackson Park, Kannapolis's first planned suburb unconnected to the mill, had become vacant. We went that day to see it and met Bright's wife, Lottie Mae. Both were in their sixties, and Lottie Mae was even quieter and more shy than her husband. Each apartment had four rooms and a bath with a small, screened back porch. The available one was bright, spacious, well-kept and we took it on the spot. The rent was $55 a month, and it was the nicest of the four places we'd lived so far.

I KNEW NOTHING ABOUT *The Daily Independent* when I reported for work. It would be a while before I learned much, and many years before I found out one meaningful fact. The paper began as a weekly called *The Toweler* in 1927. It was founded by James L. Moore, who was 19 at the time. After high school, he had worked in the mill, where his father also worked, but since the seventh grade, when he started his own little newspaper called *Tin Cup Noos*, his heart had been in journalism.

The paper struggled in the beginning, an indication that Cannon Mills was providing no support for it. But it began to grow in 1931 when Moore, who was nicknamed Jazzy, hired his friend Lawrence Gilliam to sell ads. In 1934, Moore hired Tom Wingate to be a reporter. A year later, the Kannapolis Publishing Company was incorporated. The name of the paper was changed to *The Independent* and Wingate became its editor. By this time there was no question that Cannon money was involved. Mr. Charlie's son-in-law, Robert G. Hayes, a Cannon Mills executive, was the company's vice president and secretary. This would raise questions about just how independent *The Independent* actually was.

The paper had become *The Daily Independent* in 1938, although it had no Saturday edition. When I arrived it had a circulation of more than 12,000. It was the largest paper in Cabarrus County and had won more North Carolina Press Association awards than any paper in the state with a circulation of less than 20,000. It also had another distinction. Sunday magazines were popular in many big city newspapers at the time, but *The Daily Independent* had the only locally produced Sunday magazine in the Carolinas, and that would be greatly beneficial to me.

I became the youngest person in the newsroom. Most of the others had been there for many years. The managing editor, Bill Workman, a chunky, florid-faced man who was easily agitated and often loud and abrasive, another son of a Cannon Mills worker, had become a cub reporter the same year the paper became a daily. He sat in the center of the room, his desk between those of two beat reporters, Franklin Scarborough and Charles Mathis.

I got only quick perfunctory introductions to co-workers when I reported for my first day at work. Mornings were frantic, with no time for formal introductions or chit-chat. Everybody knew my name because a short article had appeared in the Sunday edition announcing that I would be joining the staff and that I would be focusing on religion.

MY FIRST EFFORTS FOR the paper, however, had nothing to do with religion. After I had completed formalities in the personnel office and arrived at my desk, Bill Workman immediately gave me directions to the tiny building on A Street two blocks away that housed the police department on the street floor, a small courtroom on the second, and the jail in the basement. He wanted me to fetch reports of all arrests, criminal actions and traffic accidents that had occurred since Saturday night and turn them into news stories before 11. Although law enforcement officers in Kannapolis wore police uniforms with Kannapolis PD patches, they actually were sworn county sheriff's deputies. Cannon Mills bought their services by reimbursing the county for their salaries and paid all the expenses of operating the department. The company also determined who would be hired, promoted and fired, not the sheriff. During the time I was attempting to assemble all of the information Workman had sent me to fetch, I also was taking and writing obits and answering phone calls.

Only after lunch did I get to know my co-workers. One was especially happy to see me. That was Jim McAllister, the magazine editor. He was thirty-five, from Mt. Pleasant, a small town just south of Concord. He had joined the Navy shortly after World War II, then attended journalism school at the University of North Carolina at Chapel Hill on the GI Bill. He was the only person who ever won a major journalism award at the paper, a National Headliners Award for feature writing. Every week he had to fill the 12 pages of the Sunday magazine and he was pleased to see a new face eager to turn out copy. The magazine, a tabloid, had two major articles each week, the cover story and the center spread. There would not be many weeks in the coming 16 months when I didn't fill one of those spots, sometimes both.

My first story in the magazine appeared on the cover on the second Sunday of my employment. It was about a local magician called Leonardo the Great who had found the Lord and was giving up magic to become a traveling evangelist, setting up tent revivals outside small towns. One of the benefits of writing feature stories, McAllister told me, was that after they appeared the *Independent* had no objections to letting you sell them to other, larger newspapers. *The Charlotte Observer, Raleigh News & Observer*, and *Greensboro Daily News* were prospects. I typed up copies of my Leonardo piece and mailed them out. To my amazement, the *Observer* called and asked if I could provide a photo. I sent it, and my byline soon appeared in the state's most widely distributed newspaper that I now was reading every day. I got a check for twenty bucks, a big boost to a seventy-five-dollar salary. In coming months I also would have features prominently displayed in the Raleigh and Greensboro papers.

My mornings were devoted to turning out news articles, but afternoons usually were spent finding and writing feature stories, sometimes called people stories. Those usually were the most widely read items in the newspaper, and readers associated those stories with the name of the writer more than they did with news articles. I was amazed at how many fascinating and often entertaining people I was able to find. I was even more amazed at how willing and eager they were to talk. I don't recall a single person ever turning me down. But the story that would change the path of my career was about a mule.

WE HAD A MISERABLE January in 1965, with heavy snow and freezing rain. I had an awful time getting around in my Austin-Healy Sprite, which balked indignantly at cold weather and didn't cling well to ice. After one big miserable storm I walked to the police station on a Tuesday morning to pick up my usual reports. I was surprised to see a mule wearing a chain bridle tethered in the alley beside the police station.

"What's that mule doing out there?" I asked the woman behind the counter who usually had my reports waiting for me.

"I don't know," she said. "Some old man tried to take him up the steps to the courtroom. Said he was evi-dence."

I decided I'd better go up and see what was going on.

A black man named Robert Cauthen was on trial. He was 84, dressed in his Sunday best, including topcoat and a weathered hat that he held in one hand. He was standing before Recorders Court Judge Robert L. Warren with the assistance of a cane but without counsel.

A week earlier, somebody called Kannapolis Police to report that a mule had been left out in the ice and snow storm that had hit the area hard. The officer who answered the call found the mule tied to a tree in Cauthen's back yard. The mule was twelve years old. Her name was Rhodie, although Cauthen referred to her as Ol' Rhodie. She was draped in heavy snow and big icicles hung from nose to tail. The officer charged Cauthen with animal cruelty and, over Cauthen's objections, took Rhodie into protective custody. The officer snapped Polaroid shots of Rhodie that made her look like an ice sculpture before having her removed to a livestock dealer's farm. He had shown those to the judge before I got to the courtroom.

When I found a seat near the front, Cauthen was explaining that he had intended to build a shed for Ol' Rhodie before the cold weather set in but his rheumatism got the better of him and kept him from it. When he heard the ice storm was coming, he said, he pinned a rug on Rhodie as a coat to protect her.

"She ain't suffered," he said.

"Did you ask her if she had suffered?" asked Warren.

"I can tell by her looks," Cauthen replied.

At that moment, Rhodie brayed loudly in the alley, prompting laughter in the courtroom, even from the judge.

"You're not able to keep a mule if you're not able to keep it up," Warren sternly told Cauthen. "Here's what I'm going to do. I'm going to issue an order to keep the mule in custody until you build a shelter for it...."

"But, Judge, I need that mule to do my haulin'," Cauthen protested. "I ain't got no money, Judge."

Warren, whom I liked and considered to be an open-minded and fair man, fell silent and sat for a few moments in contemplation.

"Do you think you could build that mule a shed with ten dollars?" he asked.

"I might could," Cauthen said.

Warren reached under his robe for his wallet, pulled out a ten-dollar bill and passed it across the bench to Cauthen.

"If you can get a shed built in the next week, I'll have them bring Rhodie back to you and I'll dismiss the charge," he said.

I knew I had a heck of a story. I followed Cauthen out of the courtroom and got him to pose for a photo with Rhodie, who clearly was affectionate toward him.

"I'm gonna get you back, ol' girl," he kept telling her. "Don't you worry."

I rushed to the newsroom, dropped off my film at the photo department, and wrote the story as fast as I could. It turned up in the center of the front page in that afternoon's edition, with a big photo of Rhodie licking Cauthen's hand. "'Old Rhodie' Had Her Day In Court" was the headline.

The following morning I was back at my desk dealing with mundane news reports when the phone rang.

"This is Chuck Hauser," the caller said. "I'm the Carolinas editor for *The Charlotte Observer*. I want to use your mule story if it's OK with you."

"It's fine with me," I said.

"Is it possible that you could get that photo on a bus to me by this afternoon?"

I certainly could, I told him. The *Observer* played the story big the next day, and people in the newsroom and elsewhere were talking about it. After lunch, Charles Mathis, who was not an excitable type, came rushing into the newsroom as excited as any of us ever would see him.

"Your mule was just on *Douglas Edwards with the News*," he told me. He'd seen it at lunch.

Unbeknownst to me, Hauser had put the story on the Associated Press national wire (the Independent used United Press International and little, if anything, about Kannapolis ever appeared there) and not only was it now in newspapers across the country, it even made its way onto CBS.

Robert Cauthen was not aware of the attention he and Rhodie were getting and seemed not to be impressed when I told him about it two days later. That was Friday. I stopped by to see if he was making progress on his shed. I wanted to do a follow-up story for Sunday. I found Cauthen in the backyard in the same overcoat and hat he'd worn to court. He was standing amidst construction debris, staring at a completed shed.

It was crudely but stoutly built, mostly with scrap lumber grayed by time that had been scavenged around the neighborhood. Not only would it shelter Rhodie from the weather, it was roomy enough for her to move around in and provide a straw bed on which she could sleep. Cauthen said that neighbors had helped him finish it and he'd spent the judge's ten dollars on a roll of tarpaper roofing, nails, hinges for the door and other materials.

I went back to the office and called Judge Warren to tell him about this and get his reaction.

"I'll see that he gets his mule back tomorrow," the judge told me.

Cauthen was happy about that news but remained disgruntled about the whole situation.

"I ain't had a spot against my life in all these 84 years," he told me. "And I've took care of that mule. Why, she's as fine a mule as you'll find anywhere. I've just been scandalized."

That same day, I got another call from Chuck Hauser. He wanted to know if I'd be interested in becoming a regional correspondent for the *Observer*. I'd be a freelancer paid by the piece, but I'd be sending news items on a consistent basis as well as the occasional feature. I told him I'd have to talk with my editor. Wingate said it was OK with him. Hauser and I would work together for several months, always by telephone, before he left for another job, but that wouldn't be the last time I'd work with him, and Rhodie's story would be responsible for that.

ONE THING I NEVER had to do at the *Independent* was write about the Cannon Company or family. Only two people were allowed to do that—Tom Wingate and Bill Workman. That didn't bother me because those articles usually were dry and tedious, and the price of getting something wrong no doubt would the costly.

Early on, I had noticed a ritual incident in the newsroom at 11:30 every morning. Workman made a call, hunched over his desk talking in low tones, holding one hand in front of the mouthpiece so nobody could hear what he was saying. I wondered what was going on and mentioned this to McAllister .

"You don't know what he's doing?" he asked incredulously.

"No, I don't."

"He's calling the mill and telling them what's going to be in the paper that day. If it's something that might be sensitive, he even reads it to them."

I had no idea how much control of the paper the Cannons had and neither did other reporters. Because Jazzy Moore was president and treasurer as well as publisher, it appeared that he might have controlling interest. At least, that was what the paper wanted readers to believe to maintain its credibility. Not for years would the truth be known.

Moore retired in August, 1973, less than eight years after I left the paper. Four months later he died with his dog Missy in a smoldering fire that started during the night in his small, two-story brick house. He was 65. Three and a half years later, his heirs put his share of the paper's stock up for sale. He owned only 45.2%. The rest belonged to Robert G. Hayes and his wife, Miriam, Charles Cannon's daughter. Their new partner in the *Independent* was another native North Carolinian, Roy H. Park, who was building a media empire and would become one of the country's richest men.

NOBODY HAD TOLD ME that I could or couldn't write about certain things, and neither had anybody changed anything I had written without letting me know and explaining the reason for it. But I soon would encounter such a situation, and it would be the only occurrence. Now and then I had to cover a trial in Superior Court in Concord. One day, after turning in my article, Wingate summoned me to his desk as deadline approached. One of the people I had quoted was the attorney for the defendant.

"We can't use his name in the paper," Wingate told me. "If you have to quote him, just refer to him as the lawyer for the defendant. I'll explain it to you later."

He never did explain it to me, I suspect because it was an embarrassment to him. I held Wingate in high regard. I thought he was a wonderful editor and a fine writer. He was a man of high intelligence and character, thoughtful, gentle, decent, always considerate. His suggestions always improved my stories. But this bothered me deeply.

McAllister told me the ban had come about years earlier because the lawyer, Bedford Black, had the audacity to run for the legislature against one of Cannon's candidates. The story was more complex than that, but I wouldn't learn that until much later.

Black was forty-six when I met him. Although he had a sort of mournful look about him, he was genial and witty and I always enjoyed talking with him. He had come to Kannapolis when his father, a Wesleyan Methodist minister, was assigned to a local church. He became an outstanding student in high school and got a degree from Wake Forest while it still was a college and still in the town of Wake Forest. During World War II he became a technical sergeant in the Air Corps, putting in more than 1,600 flying hours, much of it over the

Hump in the Himalayas resupplying Chinese troops fighting the Japanese. (Charles Cannon's son, who was named for him, would be killed while flying a fighter plane over the Hump.)

After the war Black became one of the promising young people favored by Mr. Charlie, who loaned him money to study law. He later opened an office in Kannapolis and became deeply involved in Democratic politics. Unfortunately, he supported candidates for governor and the U.S. Senate that Uncle Charlie, also a Democrat, didn't like and he quickly fell out of favor. He was described as too unpredictable, too independent, which, considering the circumstances, he rightly seemed to take as a compliment.

In 1958, two candidates were running unchallenged for the State House of Representatives in the district including Cabarrus County. One was a superintendent at Cannon Mills, the other a lawyer who often represented the company and also was Mr. Charlie's first cousin. At the last minute Black entered the race and came out of it tied with Mr. Charlie's cousin. A recount was required, but out-of-town reporters discovered that the ballot boxes had been moved to a Cannon Mills warehouse, raising suspicions that garnered statewide news coverage. The boxes were taken to Raleigh for the recount, and Black emerged the victor by 21 votes.

During his two years in the legislature, Black did all he could to frustrate Mr. Charlie. He supported a minimum wage law that Cannon despised. He tried to change the tax evaluation procedures in the county, which allowed Cannon to pay much lower taxes than industries in other nearby counties. After his term ended, he got the state attorney general to rule that the county had to make public the financial arrangements of the Kannapolis Police Department, which had been kept secret at the mill's request. Black also began a movement to attempt to get Kannapolis incorporated and out from under Cannon's control, further irritating Mr. Charlie.

All of this led to Black's name being banned from the *Independent* in April, 1959. This not only got statewide attention, it went national. *Time* even wrote about it. The press was blaming Mr. Charlie for the ban, but he vehemently denied having anything to do with it. Nobody bothered to ask if his son-in-law, who actually controlled the paper, had issued the order. Jazzy Moore took responsibility for it, offering the pathetic excuse that Black was "publicity crazy" and trying to use the newspaper for his own purposes.

I had no idea that Black was such a rebel when I met him. If I had, I would have held him in even higher esteem. He was very helpful to me because I knew nothing about court procedures and the legal system and he was willing to take time to explain things to me. I always could call on him for help, but that wasn't the only reason I liked him. He also told me he enjoyed my stories. I don't know if the mill, or even Jazzy Moore, was aware of it, but Black often would hang out in the back shop at the *Independent* late on Saturday nights, chatting and laughing with the pressmen and Linotype operators, waiting to take home a fresh copy of the newspaper that couldn't bear his name.

Charles Cannon already had stepped down as president of Cannon Mills when I arrived in Kannapolis, but he remained chairman of the board and continued working in his office. On April 2, 1971, he suffered a heart attack at his office and died in the hospital he founded in Concord. His nemesis, Bedford Black, followed him less than three months later, on June 29th at age 53. He, too, was the victim of a heart attack and died in the same hospital as Mr. Charlie.

I had been gone from the paper for five and a half years at the time and was unaware of either death. When I learned about them years later, I couldn't help wondering if Black's obit made it into the *Independent*. I went to the library to check microfilm. Black died at 3 in the morning and I was happy to discover that his death made the front page of that day's edition. The article appeared under a two-column headline: "Death Claims Bedford W. Black." The 12-year Blackout was over. The article even was accompanied by a photo of Black wearing dark glasses and looking appropriately rebellious.

I'm pretty sure that Tom Wingate made that decision and that Black might have taken some pride in it.

In April, 1965, Jim McAllister showed up at my desk carrying a news release from the Public Information Office at Ft. Bragg. Special Forces would be holding a field exercise in the Uwharrie National Forest not far from Kannapolis that month. McAllister knew I had been in the psywar division of Special Forces and suggested that I write about the war games for the magazine.

He thought it would be timely because the war in Vietnam was really heating up at this point. On March 2, U.S. bombers began pounding North Vietnam in Operation Rolling Thunder. Three days later, Lyndon Johnson committed the first American combat troops to South Vietnam. Thirty-five-hundred Marines landed at China Beach to protect Da Nang Air Base. Twenty-one-thousand U.S. troops already were in Vietnam, all serving as advisers. At the end of March, Viet Cong troops stormed the U.S. Embassy in Saigon, wounding several Americans. Two days later, Johnson authorized sending two Marine battalions and 20,000 logistics people to the fight. On May 3, the first Army combat troops would arrive, the 173rd Airborne Brigade, my former neighbors in Okinawa, with whom I had participated in a field exercise in Taiwan in preparation for this eventuality. The American death toll would be growing soon.

There was no question that the people I would be writing about were preparing for their own roles in Vietnam. I met a first lieutenant from PIO in the town of New London, climbed into a jeep with him, and headed into the wilds of the well-worn Uwharrie Mountains, 500 million years old. The lieutenant took me straight to an ordeal from which I thought I had permanently escaped—lunch at an Army field kitchen. We were joined by several young officers who had been rounded up to talk with me, and the conversation quickly turned to Vietnam. All of these officers seemed eager to get to war. Combat brings excitement, medals and quicker promotions as well as gruesome death.

After lunch, the lieutenant took me to the 13th Psywar Battalion encampment and said he was sure that I could talk with the commanding officer. We pulled up to the command tent and I waited while he went inside. A couple of minutes passed before the tent flap opened and he stepped out with a lieutenant colonel. I couldn't believe what I was seeing.

Blubberbutt!

The one person on Earth I hoped I'd never have to lay eyes on again was only a few feet away, both of us in obvious states of disbelief. Neither of us offered a greeting, and my instinct to salute had long since evaporated.

Blubberbutt, with his addiction to authority, made the first move. He whispered something to the lieutenant and they stepped back into the tent. A few minutes later the lieutenant returned, red-faced and flustered. The colonel wouldn't be able to talk with me, he said, without explaining why.

I found this to be quite amusing. A bombastic, power-loving lieutenant colonel, .45 holstered on humpy hip, playing war games, turns heel and runs for cover at the sight of a troublemaking former PFC armed only with pen, pad and camera, my first real lesson about the amazing power of the press.

I NOW LOOK BACK on my time in Kannapolis as greatly beneficial and enjoyable, but August brought Linda and me the most meaningful and joyous event of our lives. She had become pregnant soon after we moved into our new apartment, and by August she was approaching delivery. We had just bought an aquarium and set it up in the living room with all the proper gadgets and pretties. We had filled it with water, put plants in it, and warmed it to the appropriate temperature. We were ready to introduce tropical fish into our lives. We had made an appointment on Sunday morning, August 1, to meet a couple I had written about who raised tropical fish so that we could pick out our selections.

But just as we were getting ready to leave, Linda started having labor pains. I, of course, wanted to race immediately to the hospital in Concord, perhaps with a police car running interference, siren blaring and emergency lights flashing, but she said no. She was insistent that we get our fish first. She'd put too much into this project to postpone it now. For some reason I had visions of her water breaking in a roomful of gaping fish and wondering what effect that might have on a baby, not to mention the fish or me.

Getting her in and out of the Sprite was not easy, considering the load she was carrying, but we got our fish, which were darting nervously in little plastic bags, returned to the apartment and let the bags float in the aquarium until the temperatures adjusted so that we could release them to begin checking out their new home. All of this was taking far more time than I expected and greatly increasing my anxiety. Finally, with the fish free, seemingly swimming happily, and Linda's pains growing more intense, she agreed to let me take her to the hospital.

"Are you OK?" I kept asking.

I'd read too many stories of babies being born in cars on their way to the hospital, and that was something I wasn't sure I could handle, especially in a Sprite.

"I'm all right," she kept saying. "Slow down. You don't have to drive this fast."

I was relieved when I saw Cabarrus Memorial Hospital looming on the north side of Concord. I pulled up to the main entrance to let Linda out and went in search of a parking place. I trotted back to the entrance and we headed to the admitting office.

The first question we got was: "Do you have insurance?"

We had medical insurance provided by the *Independent*, although I had to pay for Linda's coverage. But when we went to a maternity clinic we discovered that it didn't cover those benefits. The three doctors in the group were letting us pay their bills over time.

When I told the woman that we didn't have maternity benefits she informed us that we would have to make a fifty-dollar cash deposit and sign an agreement to pay the balance within a specified period. I told her I didn't have fifty bucks. Would eighteen do?

"Well, we can't admit her until we have the full deposit," she said.

I was furious, and near panic, but I didn't want to cause an uproar and upset Linda even more. I couldn't run to a loan office because none was open on Sunday. I didn't know where to turn. The only person I could think of who might be able to help was Tom Wingate. Noon was approaching and I knew where he would be—at First Presbyterian Church in downtown Kannapolis, where he was a Sunday school teacher and deacon. I left Linda in the waiting room, wondering if we'd still have to pay if she had the baby there, and drove back to Kannapolis breaking every speed limit. Services were just letting out when I arrived. I hurried up the sidewalk past departing parishioners, searching for Wingate. I spotted him standing just outside the entrance, chatting with another church member. He seemed startled when he saw me, as if he thought I might be coming to tell him that some big news story was breaking that required his attention. When I told him what was going on, he reached immediately for his wallet and looked into it as if he wasn't certain that he had fifty dollars. He withdrew two twenties and a ten and handed them to me.

"Call and let me know what's happening," he said. "We'll be praying for you."

I rushed back to the hospital where we impatiently completed the admission process and Linda was wheeled away to be prepped for the labor room. In those days, fathers did not get to participate in the birthing process, at least not in Cabarrus County, and I'm not sure I could have withstood it if they did. At Cabarrus Memorial, fathers also weren't allowed into the labor area. I was directed to a tiny waiting room outside the maternity ward furnished with a small plastic-covered couch, a few uncomfortable chairs, a couple of scruffy tables spread with tattered outdated magazines, and a penny Ford ball gum machine supporting Lions Clubs with its profits. I was the sole occupant. I didn't sit much. Mostly I paced the hallway, chewing ball gum to benefit the Lions until the flavor disappeared, but it had little effect on my anxiety.

Four hours inched by before one of the maternity doctors came out to tell me that things looked OK, the baby's heartbeat was fine, delivery could prove difficult because of the baby's size and Linda's small stature, but that was yet to be seen. He was certain that birth was not imminent and suggested that I take a break, go home, get something to eat and try to relax for a while.

I drove back to the apartment to fix a sandwich and pick up a book I was supposed to review for the Sunday magazine. When I walked into the living room, I saw that in our rush we had left the aquarium top open, and five of our fish, apparently not happy with their new accommodations, had leapt to their deaths on the floor. I took that as a bad sign, of course, but tried to put it out of mind after flushing away their tiny bodies whose brilliant colors had lost their sheen in death. I finished my sandwich and let Bright and Lottie Mae know what was happening before hurrying back to the hospital. I couldn't concentrate on reading and went back to pacing, my worry building with every step.

Midnight was nearing when another doctor came to tell me that birth still wasn't imminent and I should go home and try to get some sleep. He assured me that somebody would call if there were developments. I took his advice, had a beer and went to bed, but dozed only fitfully, tossing and turning. I got up at five, fixed a cup of instant coffee and headed back to the hospital. Still nothing was happening. A little after seven, I called Wingate to tell him I wouldn't be coming to work. He told me to take all the time I needed and tried to be reassuring.

At mid-morning I was joined in the waiting room for the first time by another expectant father. He was twice my age, a chatty, easy-going fellow who quickly recognized my fearful concerns.

"First time?" he asked.

I nodded and told him how long I'd been there.

"Nothing to worry about," he said. "Sometimes babies are just reluctant to leave that warm, safe place. They like to set their own pace. Everything will be fine. You can count on it. This is my fifth time."

At about 12:30, a grave-looking doctor appeared at one of the waiting room's two entrances. Both of us jumped up. The doctor asked my new acquaintance to step outside. I could hear the doctor speaking softly but couldn't understand what he was saying. Suddenly, I heard the expectant father erupt in a sob. A nurse who was standing by led him away. Only later did I learn that the baby was still-born. His wife's room in the maternity ward was across the hall from Linda's and Linda could hear her crying for hours.

I never had been so frightened and worried as I was after this. The nurses came frequently to check on me as the afternoon wore on and on. I was slumped in one of the chairs, my head in my left hand, eyes closed, elbow on the armrest, when I heard a male voice say, "Mr. Bledsoe…"

As I leapt up, my left arm flew out, my elbow forcefully striking the gum ball machine beside the chair. It rocked back, slammed against the wall and tumbled forward, the glass bowl shattering on the tile floor. Gum balls, red, yellow, green, black and white, raced in every direction. Nurses and others came running at the sound of the crash. I stood stunned and frozen in place looking at the mayhem I had created. I was afraid that if I moved I might roll off down the hall on gum balls.

"Well," said the doctor, "we've seen some excitement in this room before, but none that could quite match this."

He was smiling, and that was the most meaningful smile I'd ever seen. It told me everything was OK.

"It's a boy," he said, kicking aside gum balls to shake my hand. "And he's a big boy, nine pounds, five ounces, twenty-two inches long. No discernible physical problems. They'll bring him out and let you see him in just a little bit."

"How about Linda?" I asked.

"She's going to be fine."

Janitors with heavy brooms and big dust pans were cleaning up the broken glass and chasing after gum balls when a nurse brought out my son, wrapped in a blanket, and held him up for me to see for the first time. He had more hair, very dark, than I expected, and his face seemed multi-colored, almost bruised, perhaps the result of a rough entrance, I thought. His eyes were closed and he seemed at peace with the world. He had arrived at 4:05 p.m., more than 27 hours after Linda had entered the labor room, 30 hours after her contractions began.

"Isn't he beautiful?" the nurse said.

"That's exactly what I was thinking," I said.

It would be three more hours before Linda held him for the first time. She had been so heavily sedated that she wasn't even aware that she had given birth and was slow in coming out of it. This time his eyes, which appeared to be blue, like mine, were open and his color had improved. Later his eyes would turn brown to match his mother's. We named him Erik Albert for his godfather, my Army friend Eric Alberts, who was now studying at the Art Students League in New York and soon would catch a bus to Kannapolis to see his godson. We changed the c to a k in his first name to give it a more kingly feel, as in King Erik IX, patron saint of Sweden, though we had no connection whatever to kings, saints, or Sweden.

Linda and Erik remained at the hospital until Thursday when I took them home. With a new baby and an aquarium full of suicidal fish from warm climes to attend, our lives changed radically. But even more change was soon to come.

ON A SEPTEMBER MORNING, I came in to find Wingate with a grave look on his face. He took me aside for a private conversation. Jim McAllister had shown up at his house the previous night and resigned, effective immediately, he told me. Wingate had tried to talk him out of it, even asked if he could pray for him—and did—but McAllister was dealing with a problem of such magnitude that he felt he had no other option. Wingate needed my help in getting out the magazine that week, and I spent many extra hours seeing that it happened.

The next week, I learned that McAllister would not be replaced and the magazine, which had been a distinguishing feature for the paper for years, would be dropped. This was a major disappointment to me because most of the reader reaction I'd gotten, in addition to sales to other papers, had been from stories I wrote for the magazine.

There was much speculation in the newsroom about what had prompted McAllister's sudden departure, but nobody really knew, not even Wingate. About six weeks later I got a call from McAllister. He didn't want anybody to know that he was calling. He had a new job, he said, but asked me to keep that secret, too. He was now on the copy desk at *The Greensboro Daily News*, editing news reports and writing headlines. An old acquaintance from journalism school who recently had become managing editor of the *Daily News* had given him the job. That was Chuck Hauser, for whom I had worked at *The Charlotte Observer*. Until that moment I didn't know where Hauser had gone. McAllister said that he and Hauser had been talking about me, and Hauser told him that if a reporting position opened, he intended to offer me a job. He just wanted to alert me.

I tried to pump some personal information out of McAllister but he was reluctant. He was living in a cabin in the woods near High Rock Lake in Da-

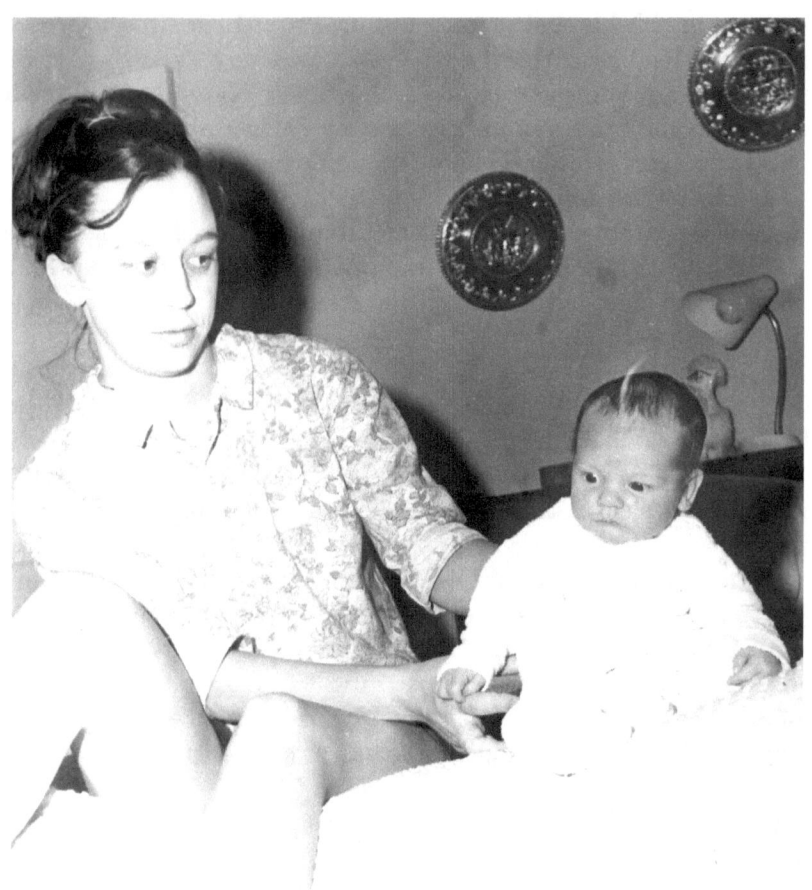

Linda and Erik shortly after his birth

vidson County, I learned, and didn't have a phone there. That was about all I got out of him. Not until much later did I find out what actually happened.

McAllister had a serious weakness—a roving eye for females, and a keen instinct for those who were vulnerable. It was a problem that would plague him all the way to his death bed, dying from cancer at 55, where sadly it would become all too transparent and embarrassing. This failure of character led to multiple relationships over the years and ended with him living in different locations with three women at the same time, none aware of the others. The complexities of this were too difficult to imagine, much less manage. In this case, however, only one woman was involved, and an irate new husband had come looking for McAllister with a 12-gauge shotgun. The woman and her young child were now living with McAllister in the cabin in the woods. He had begun using an assumed name, Jim Brown, except at the *Daily News*, where his copy editing job kept a byline from revealing his identity and where he might be found.

My call from Hauser came early in December. He had an opening for a reporter in the High Point bureau. Would I be interested? I said yes. Not long afterward, I drove to Greensboro for an interview with Hauser and the new city editor, Irwin Smallwood. The job offer came soon afterward. I dreaded having to tell Wingate about it and give my notice.

"I expected this was coming," he said. "I think you're doing the right thing, even though I hate to see you go. I believe you have more potential as a reporter and writer than you ever could fulfill here, and I expect great things from you."

I was overwhelmed. I'd never received such a vote of confidence, and I felt that whatever potential I possessed, Wingate had contributed much to creating.

My final piece in *The Daily Independent* appeared on Sunday, December 19. It was a Christmas story set in Thomasville, based on the Christmas when I was ten and got my first bicycle, making my newspaper deliveries so much easier and more enjoyable. It took up much of the feature page with a long jump inside. The headline was "The Christmas The Angels Came." The sub-head: "For Several Young Boys, It Was A Yule That Will Never Be Forgotten."

I was eager to know Wingate's reaction to the story after I turned it in, and I kept surreptitiously glancing across the newsroom as he read it. When he finished, he laid it down, removed his glasses for a few moments, put them back on, picked up the typed pages and walked over to my desk.

"Nice piece," he said.

That was all I needed to hear, but a couple of hours later, I got an even more encouraging response.

Typesetting technology was in transition during this period. Two women who worked in a small office just off the newsroom had to type every article into a device that transferred it to a perforated paper ribbon that was fed into a Linotype machine to produce the metal type.

Bright Tucker came over to my desk with a little grin.

"Well, you've done it now," he said. "Both of those women back there are crying their eyes out over your story. They can't even get their work done."

Thirty years later, I rewrote that story as a novella titled *The Angel Doll*. It became a bestseller, even was published in Japan, among other countries, was excerpted in *Good Housekeeping*, and later made into a movie.

One of my signings for the book was in Kannapolis, I looked out over the crowd and saw Wingate coming in the door. I hadn't seen him since I'd left the *Independent*. I went straight to him and hugged him.

"I think I may have told you that you might have some potential," he said with a grin.

"In big part, because of you," I said.

Soon after that I was at another signing in nearby Salisbury when I looked up and saw my tenth grade English teacher at Thomasville High, Millie Modlin, in the line. I hugged her, too, and introduced her to the crowd.

Later, several women gathered around her to chat. I heard one say, "So you're the one who taught him to write."

Mrs. Modlin, as I always had known her, hesitated for a long moment.

"Well," she said, "he did sit in my class for a year."

SEVENTEEN YEARS PASSED BEFORE I returned to Kannapolis again, this time to research for this memoir. I was in for a shock. I hardly recognized the place. Only a few churches and the old Gem Theater downtown seemed unchanged. The transformation was so radical that it almost was unbelievable

The buildings that housed *The Daily Independent* were gone. So was the newspaper. It had merged in 1996 with *The Concord Tribune* to become *The Independent Tribune*. As I write this, it is published only three times weekly and is owned by Berkshire Hathaway controlled by Warren Buffett, one of the richest persons in America, far richer than Mr. Charlie could have dreamed of being. Everybody I'd worked with at the *Independent* was dead, except for Charles Mathis, with whom I've had no contact for nearly half a century.

Gone, too, was the monstrous Cannon Mills plant, the beautiful headquarters building, the big YMCA, and the huge neon cannon sign, all imploded and the debris hauled away. Town Lake in front of the plant had been drained and filled with dirt. In 1982, Cannon Mills was sold to billionaire David H. Murdock, the owner of Dole Foods, who apparently didn't want the civic responsibilities Mr. Charlie had coveted. Two years later, Bedford Black's dream was realized when Kannapolis was incorporated and no longer under the control of Cannon Mills. In 1986, Murdock sold the mill to another textile manufacturer, Fieldcrest, but kept the real estate surrounding it. Pillowtex bought the combined companies in 1997. By this time America's textile companies were in precipitous decline due to lower-cost competition from China and other countries.

The end for Cannon Mills, which once had employed nearly 25,000 people, came on January 30, 2003, when Pillowtex went bankrupt and nearly 8,000 people were let go, almost 5,000 in Kannapolis and nearby areas, the biggest one-day layoff in state history. I couldn't imagine what had become of all those people, some of whom I might once have known, many of whom had devoted their lives to the mill.

Murdock bought back the abandoned and dilapidating mill at the end of 2004, announced his intention to partner with corporations and universities to build a research center devoted to human health, and went about imploding all the mill's structures. When I returned to start my research, three impressive research buildings employing a few hundred people stood where the mill once had been, but much of the 300 acres was just growing weeds.

Many of the Williamsburg-style buildings that Charles and Ruth Cannon had constructed downtown were still there, although more than a few were vacant. The small building that once had contained the police department, jail and courtroom had become a music museum owned by record producer Mike Curb, although it later would move to larger quarters.

One thing that struck me was that visitors to Kannapolis would find no indication of the model mill town it once had been. A small state historical marker on Cannon Boulevard miles from downtown, is the only hint. It states this: "James W. Cannon 1852-1921. Textile pioneer; founder of Cannon Mills, 1887, and Kannapolis, 1906, leading manufacturer of towels. Grave 2 mi. S." I found no visible recognition of Charles A. Cannon, who guided the company to its great success, actually built modern Kannapolis and ruled it for half a century.

I did, however, discover a new beautifully designed garden downtown, right beside the old police department-jail-courtroom. In the center of it is a nine-foot, 900 pound bronze statue on a huge circular base of polished granite. It's called Dale Earnhardt Plaza.

When I came to work in Kannapolis, Dale was a thirteen-year-old kid helping his daddy, Ralph, work on race cars in a garage behind their modest frame home on Sedan Avenue. Dale went on to become a legendary NASCAR champion called "the Intimidator" and died in 2001 in a crash on the last lap of the Daytona 500. The statue does seem a bit intimidating as Earnhardt stands, arms folded in a keep-your-distance fashion, even though he's slightly smiling.

I don't think that Dale Earnhardt created any jobs in Kannapolis, but he did become its most famous son. City leaders say that his statue attracts a lot of visitors, especially when the big races are held at Charlotte Motor Speedway, just 20 miles away. It seems unlikely that many race fans, or any other visitors, would be attracted to a statue of Mr. Charlie. In our current culture, fame apparently matters more than building cities, producing goods and providing jobs and income for thousands of people.

14

The Greensboro Daily News was undergoing drastic change when I was hired to be a reporter in its High Point bureau in December, 1965. Greensboro was the third largest city in North Carolina, and the *Daily News* had wide distribution across the state and a reputation for excellence, although that reputation had been based on earlier periods. Recent years had offered flimsy evidence of it, with the exception of the sports and editorial pages.

The *Daily News* had been started as a Republican-populist morning paper in 1909 and had a succession of owners in its early years. One was Edwin Bedford Jeffress, who not only would guide the paper to success but also became mayor and one of Greensboro's most prominent citizens. He formed the Greensboro News Company and in 1930 bought the afternoon paper, *The Daily Record*, which had been founded in 1890 and had a much smaller circulation. In 1934, Jeffress suffered a debilitating stroke which made it impossible for him to work. His son Carl, one of five children, ran the company after his father became incapacitated. In 1947 the company opened a radio station, WFMY-FM, and two years later a TV station, WFMY, which went on the air September 22, 1949. (I well remember the excitement that WFMY's early broadcasts stirred in Thomasville. Few people had TVs, and Holton's Furniture store on Main Street put a small set in its big front window where crowds gathered nightly to gaze upon the faint, flickering images, although the sound couldn't be heard.)

After E.B. Jeffress's death in 1961, his children began thinking of selling the company. Both newspapers were losing money, and only the profits from the TV station were keeping them afloat. The News Company's three-story brick building at the corner of Davie Street and Friendly Avenue was deteriorating, the press and other gear outdated, the management aging and slack. New leadership, new staff, new equipment and eventually a new building would be required to put the papers back on track.

FRANK BATTEN WAS THE person who would deal with those problems. Batten was only 27 when he became publisher of *The Virginian-Pilot and Ledger-Dispatch* in Norfolk, Virginia, newspapers owned by his uncle, Samuel L. Slover, called "the Colonel." Batten had been only a year old when his father, a bank auditor who married into a wealthy family, died. His mother, Dorothy, was the sister of Slover's wife, Fay, and Slover moved mother and child into his mansion and reared Frank as if he were his own son. A graduate of Culver Military Academy in Indiana, Batten entered the U.S. Merchant Marine Academy near the end of World War II and served on a troop transport in the Atlantic before enrolling at the University of Virginia in Charlottesville. While at the university, he worked summers as a reporter at the *Ledger-Dispatch*. He earned a master's degree in business administration at Harvard in 1952 and returned to Norfolk to work at various jobs at the newspapers before replacing his uncle as publisher in 1954. He inherited the newspapers following Slover's death in 1959.

Batten wasn't satisfied with owning just Norfolk's newspapers. He wanted to expand, and in 1964, he began building what would become a communications empire that would include creating the Weather Channel and make him a regular on *Forbes* magazine's annual list of the 400 richest Americans. Buying the Greensboro News Company and a cable TV system in Roanoke Rapids, N.C., were his first steps.

The deal in Greensboro was completed on January 19, 1965. Batten paid $17,164,975 for the company, and had to borrow $10 million to do it, a loan he'd be able to pay back in just three years with the swift turnaround of the newspapers. One of the problems at the Greensboro papers, as Batten saw it, was "wall-to-wall unions," which included the Newspaper Guild in the newsrooms. One of his first moves was to begin planning to stymie the unions, training company managers and others in Norfolk to fulfill all the jobs necessary in case of a strike, but none developed.

Editorial changes were quick in coming. The editor of the *Daily News*, H.W. "Slim" Kendall, who was in his late 60s, stepped down to the new position of contributing editor, kept his office and continued writing his Sunday column. He was replaced by Bill Snider, who had served as Kendall's associate editor for 14 years. Snider had grown up in Salisbury, received a journalism degree from the University of North Carolina in 1941, and served in the India-China-Burma Theater during World War II. Snider picked Chuck Hauser, a Korean War veteran, as the new managing editor. He had another person in mind for city editor.

Greensboro was Irwin Smallwood's hometown and he had come to the *Daily News* in 1947 straight out of the University of North Carolina, where he had been sports editor of *The Daily Tar Heel*. Smallwood had won many writing awards, including first place awards in the national golf writers' competition three years in a row. He was associate sports editor when Batten bought the *Daily News* and didn't know what to expect from the new management.

Smallwood went to the editorial department every day to check out the exchange papers from around the state. Soon after learning that Hauser was coming, Smallwood was leafing through the exchange papers when Bill Snider came over to chat.

"You ever give any thought to leaving sports?" Smallwood remembered Snider asking him.

His answer would affect the rest of my life.

"As a matter of fact," he said, "I have."

Smallwood knew Hauser. They had worked together at *The Daily Tar Heel* when Smallwood was a senior and Hauser a freshman. Hauser arrived in late May, shortly after Snider spoke with Smallwood. A week or so later, Smallwood was called in by Snider and Hauser and informed that he would be the new city editor. Within a few weeks, they began making major changes in the newsroom, upsetting many of the settled old-timers, and the newspaper took on a new life.

When I met Hauser and Smallwood for my interview both impressed me. A few days later they offered me the job in the High Point bureau and I accepted. I would be making $90 a week, with five bucks extra for working in a bureau, thanks to the Guild contract. I had a strong desire to impress and please my new editors, and I had a plan for that. I showed up at the bureau a week early to work without pay so I could acquaint myself with my duties and meet some of the people I would need to know. When I began my official duties the following week I got a surprise. The bureau chief, Doug Kerr, was leaving to take a furniture industry job. A week later, Smallwood called to tell me I would be the new bureau chief. I had only sixteen months of daily newspaper experience and never had supervised anybody in my life, or had any desire to do so. Fortunately, I was starting out small. The only person I would be overseeing in the beginning was Doug Kerr's wife, Jane, who also had a newspaper background, and was being hired to work part-time, just two days a week.

The High Point bureau also was responsible for covering Thomasville, my hometown, as well as Davidson County where it was situated. That job was open and it would be a while before it was filled by another female reporter, who was nearly twice my age and had become convinced that Thomasville was under control of "the mob." She turned out to be no more easily supervised than the mob might be. That would be a problem for the future. For now, I essentially would be covering two major areas of *Daily News* circulation mostly on my own, and I was going to be one busy fellow.

My new position gave me a responsibility that I immediately recognized as a wondrous opportunity. The bureau chief was required to write a column called "High Point Notebook" for the Sunday edition. It traditionally had been used for short items announcing upcoming meetings and events, along with leftover bits of information, governmental and otherwise, that were not important enough to justify a news story. I intended to take "High Point Notebook" down a radically different path. I'd turn it into a personal column, and I wasn't planning to ask permission. I'd just do it and see what happened. I was well aware that unlike other papers of its size the *Daily News* had no regular local-front feature columnist, and I thought that was a shortcoming that needed to be corrected.

I HAD BEEN STRUCK by the lack of humor in most newspapers and thought something should be done about that as well. In my first few weeks on the job, a huge snow storm hit. Such snows in the South nearly shut down everything, but reporters, like cops and fire fighters, still had to report to work. It took me three hours to make the eight miles to the office from the house Linda and I had bought in the Randolph County hills. I could find no news breaking and was left with nothing more to write about than my travails with tire chains and getting to work. I was surprised when this attempt at humor appeared on the front page with an illustration by editorial cartoonist Bob Zschiesche, whom I hadn't yet met but who later would become one of my closest friends.

Only a few weeks later, I found myself caught in the madness of a George Washington Birthday sale at a local department store (I couldn't have imagined how many things could be priced at 22 cents or 22 dollars). I was telling Smallwood about my experience during our daily telephone conversation about what he could expect from High Point that day.

"Don't tell me about it," he said. "Write it."

That piece, too, ended up on the front page, this time with a caricature of me overloaded with sale items and a headline that read, "It's No Lie, He Didn't Buy Any Cherry Trees."

I got a few letters from readers about that one, which encouraged me to attempt more humorous pieces. I soon realized that I would have no shortage of material because High Point offered innumerable opportunities for ridicule and poking fun.

One was an art exhibit which raised a ruckus. Complaints were made about a painting that was decried as offensive and pornographic. Hearing this, and expecting something titillating, I, of course, wanted to see the painting. It already had been removed from the show when I got there, but at my insistence, the sponsors let me into a back room to get a glimpse of it. I was shocked.

It wasn't at all what I hoped. It was a look straight down into an apparatus that is found in every bathroom. The one you sit on. And there wasn't anything in it but water, albeit with a slight yellowish tint.

I wrote a "High Point Notebook" describing the painting and agreeing fully with those who had demanded that it be removed. There was no end to the harm that might be wrought if such clearly pornographic material was allowed to be publicly displayed, I proclaimed, especially to the young. Why, in no time parents of teen-aged boys in High Point surely would be finding plumbing manuals hidden under their sons' mattresses.

AN EVEN MORE RIDICULOUS situation would provide me material throughout my time in the High Point bureau. This was the boob law, and I mean that in more ways than one. The city had annexed an area on Greensboro Road that included a drive-in theater. The theater had not been doing so well until the owner discovered a sure-fire draw—really bad, cheaply made, grade B movies that literally created traffic jams. That was because all of these films featured attractive, well-endowed young women who were willing and eager to expose their endowments. The name of the theater was The Pointer, but as I pointed out, it would have been more aptly named Two Pointers Drive-In.

The Pointer's huge screen was visible from the road and every night cars lined the highway on both sides. They clearly were occupied by people who wanted to catch periodic glimpses of mountainous close-ups of undraped female breasts at no charge. Sound was not a necessity for these movies. The city maintained that this situation created a hazard for other drivers, but when city fathers attempted to solve the problem by erecting no-parking signs and handing out tickets the situation only grew worse. The former parkers, many of them teen-aged boys, began driving slowly back and forth in front of the theater, backing up traffic. The theater owner, Vincent Furio, offered to build a taller fence but the city claimed that would be a violation of zoning ordinances.

Instead the city council enacted a law making it illegal to display images of nude or semi-nude persons on screens and billboards visible from a public road. Furio was quickly arrested and convicted in Municipal Court. He appealed and kept right on showing the movies that infuriated the council. All of this happened before I came on the job, and it was a few months before I would start having my fun with it. That came after a Superior Court judge overturned Furio's conviction and his ruling was upheld by the North Carolina Supreme Court, which said the law was too vague to be enforced. The city council was quick to initiate action.

"I think that thing's obnoxious," Mayor Carson Stout said of the drive-in, "and it can be stopped one way or another."

If a mayor could get rid of whatever he chose to deem obnoxious, I feared that I, too, might soon be banned from High Point.

But the mayor would find that stopping the Pointer wouldn't be as easy as he anticipated, and I would be the foremost obnoxious contributor to his frustrations.

At the council's instruction, City Attorney Knox Walker quickly drew up a more specific new ordinance:

"It shall be unlawful for any person, firm or corporation to project, cause to be projected or permit to be projected upon any public motion picture screen within the city limits, any picture of a female person over the age of 12 years whose breast or breasts are nude."

I wrote a piece questioning whether this would make it illegal for schools, colleges or civic groups to show travelogues or documentaries in which bare-breasted natives appear, for hospitals to show instructional films for breast examinations and breast feeding. Wouldn't it also ban movies that included paintings or statues that depicted bare female breasts?

This did not sit well with the city attorney. He told council members and reporters that the law obviously wasn't intended to apply to any of the issues I had raised. Nonetheless, he rewrote the ordinance, supposedly to make it clearer. It now would only be illegal to show bare female breasts, aged 12 years and above, "upon any motion picture screen of a licensed theater." All other screens were freed.

I responded with a "High Point Notebook" pointing out recent films that would be illegal in High Point if this law won approval. They included: *Cleopatra* and *The Sandpiper*, both starring Elizabeth Taylor and Richard Burton; *La Dolce Vita* with Marcello Mastroianni and Anita Ekberg; *The Pawnbroker* with Rod Steiger; *A Fine Madness* with Sean Connery, Jean Seberg and Joanne Woodward; *The Blue Max* with George Peppard and Ursula Andress.

The Naked Maja, the story of painter Francisco Goya's romance with the Duchess of Alba, starring North Carolina's own Ava Gardner with Anthony Franciosa, apparently could not be shown because it opens on Goya's painting of the unclothed duchess with breasts pointing in opposing directions. Neither would it be possible to show *Dr. Zhivago*, with Omar Sharif, Julie Christie, Alec Guinness and Rod Steiger, because it had numerous scenes with statues of nude women. Also any movies that included shots of Grand Central Station, The National Archives building, the New York Customs House, The Louvre in Paris, the Medici Chapel in Florence, and many other structures could be barred because their facades included statues of women with the offending protrusions bared.

None of this was of any concern to the city council. One member claimed the law was justified because the Pointer, which he called "the worst cesspool we have," was "responsible for increased immorality, broken and unhappy marriages and moral decay." The new law passed unanimously.

A few weeks later detectives bought tickets at the Pointer to see *The Secret of Nina Duprez*. Their visit was expected because the film had been edited to eliminate bare breast scenes, but one little flash of less than a second got overlooked. As soon as it flicked across the screen, the detectives went to the projection booth, arrested the manager and projectionist, seized the film and shut down the theater. The police said they had acted on a citizen complaint.

A week later, a reader called to tell me he'd just seen a movie called *Lady L* in a downtown theater and he was sure it was a violation of the law. The movie, directed by Peter Ustinov, was about an elderly woman recalling her past loves. It starred Sophia Loren, Paul Newman and David Niven and was rife with paintings and statues exposing bare female breasts. I suggested that the reader call the police department and make a citizen complaint. He did.

I waited a day or two to see what the police might do. Nothing happened. I went to the police department and learned that detectives had called the theater manager to warn him that they would be in the audience, and although they had seen the images of bare breasts they had been advised by the city attorney that this was not a violation of the law.

I went to Knox Walker to ask why. The difference, he told me, was that the flash of a bare breast at the Pointer was a picture of a person, while the bare breasts at the downtown theater were paintings, which made them immaterial.

I, of course, could not resist a response to this. It included the following:

"The police are apparently using movement as a guideline in making arrests for violation of the law. In other words, unless the nude is a living, breathing picture, it's not a violation.

"Yet, there's no such thing as a 'moving picture.' People just seem to move in a movie. It's an optical illusion. A lot of pictures are being flashed on the screen in a hurry.

"This leads the confused citizen to ask a lot of questions.

"If movement is the guideline, would it then be okay to present a slide show of nudes on a theater screen? Or to stop the projector when a nude scene comes up and show it one frame at a time?

"If it's legal to show a picture of a picture of a nude, then would it be okay to show a movie in which a movie showing nudes is shown?

"After all, a movie is only a lot of pictures, and a movie of a movie would only be a lot of pictures of a lot of pictures of nudes."

I loved the headline that appeared over this column: "If Nude Stays Still The Law Will Too."

Nonetheless, the city attorney and the police department ignored my thoughtful analysis. I suspected I knew why. The law had been designed for only one purpose—to put the Pointer out of business—and technicalities would be found to exempt the supposedly respectable downtown theaters which could benefit from the Pointer being shut down.

The Pointer case didn't come to trial for nearly two months. The presiding judge was Byron Hayworth, a strong Quaker. The attorney for the two defendants argued that the law was unconstitutional, violated his clients' free speech rights and discriminated against them. He asked that the charges be dismissed. Hayworth put off a decision and waited 25 days before denying the request. Trial was set for two weeks later. Charges were dropped against the projectionist, but the manager was found guilty and given a 30-day suspended sentence. An appeal followed. The law remained in limbo and mountainous breasts still could be spotted after dark on Greensboro Road for the remainder of my time in High Point.

For my New Year's Day "High Point Notebook," 1967, I wrote a list of predictions for the coming year. This is one I included:

"I predict that the city council—which in 1966 banned lions from back yards and nude breasts from motion picture screens—will reverse itself on these two important matters and in 1967 make it illegal to show pictures of lions in theaters, or to keep bare-breasted women in the back yard."

Not long after I was reassigned to the newsroom in Greensboro at the beginning of March, 1967, Linda and I went to the Center Theater in High Point to see the movie *Hawaii*, based on the novel by James Michener. It was about missionaries bringing Christianity to the natives of those islands. And what did I witness on the screen? Running through the jungle lushness were native females with bare breasts galore, even jiggling. Being a good citizen, and recognizing a moving violation of law when I saw one, I left the theater and went straight to the police station to report the crime. The cops didn't seem to be too happy about it, but they took the report.

The following day, detectives went to the theater and watched the movie. This time the breasts clearly were not in paintings or on statues. They were in full movement.

The theater manager and projectionist were arrested. TV news crews had been tipped off (I wonder who?), and reporters and cameras were waiting outside for the perp walk of such egregious criminals. This time the news wasn't just local. It went national—and international. High Point, a city which considered itself a center of cosmopolitan enlightenment, home of the biggest, most fashionable furniture market in the world, had banned a movie about missionaries taking Christianity to Hawaii, which by city council standards was clearly pornographic and adding to High Point's cesspools. The city became the object of jokes and derision, which did not please the furniture industry. The law would quietly disappear. Never again would anybody in High Point be carted off to jail for showing bare breasts on movie screens no matter how much they may have contributed to broken homes or moral decay.

THE BOOB LAW WASN'T the only topic that caused me to stir reactions from readers while I was in High Point. As odd as it may seem, New York City was another. In early fall, Linda and I bought our first new car, a candy-apple red Ford Mustang. When we rode around in that beauty, we had the feeling that we were the objects of envy, obviously being admired for our fine tastes. In October, we decided to drive to New York to visit our friend Eric, the godfather of our Erik, who was 14 months old at the time and had just begun to toddle. We could show off our car and our son at the same time. Unfortunately, this trip turned out to be a little more trying and difficult than we anticipated.

Eric was now living and painting in the loft of an old building in lower Manhattan. It was one big room without furniture other than an Army cot that he slept on and a battered Army locker that he had salvaged off the street (he apparently had a bit more nostalgia for the Army than I did). Consequently, we were having to carry along sleeping bags, foam rubber pads to soften the floor, a big ice chest, food, camping gear and cookware, a collapsible crib, an assortment of toys, huge piles of diapers and other baby items. There was hardly room to move in the car. We left in the wee hours of Saturday morning, hoping to arrive in New York in time to attend the opening of Eric's first show at a small gallery that night. This was not to be, because of some serious miscalculations on my part.

I hated toll roads and had decided that I could save money by not taking any. When I encountered the first one at Petersburg, Virginia, I turned onto U.S. 1-301, which took us through endless small towns and scores of stoplights. I eventually ended up lost in Richmond, and how I managed to get out, I can't be certain. I considered it a miracle when I finally reached Washington and was comforted by the sight of the Washington Monument and the Capitol. After circling the Capitol a few times, I spotted a sign that said Maryland and took off that way, thinking I would be headed in the right direction. I had forgotten that Maryland lies south of Washington as well as north of it, and drove for nearly an hour before I realized I was going the wrong way. To compound our problems this wayward path took us into an area of Maryland where slot machines were viral, and that cost us another hour, while Linda fumed in the car with Erik and I lost enough nickels to have paid all the tolls to New York and back.

After getting so deeply lost in a very bad section of Wilmington, Delaware, that a fellow southerner at a gas station who told us we were in a highly unsafe area took pity and led us to the appropriate north-bound highway, I found myself squandering nearly three hours to make 50 miles through New Jersey towns. That was when I decided to give in to toll roads. When I finally made my way to the New Jersey Turnpike, I began to wonder why anybody would want to pay to get into traffic mayhem that would make the Southern 500 stock car race at Darlington seem like a Sunday afternoon ride.

Twenty hours and innumerable diaper changes after we had departed from Randolph County, we emerged from the Holland Tunnel into the chaos of Manhattan. This was my first visit to the city since I had left Fort Slocum more than six years earlier, and Linda's first. It also was my first attempt at driving in it.

The address to which we were heading was in an area where I never had been. We had trouble even finding a place to stop and study maps. After much futile and frustrating searching, we found the dismal, run-down street in the produce district, just a block from the Hudson River. The building was four stories tall, ancient, dirty and decaying. The ground floor housed the returns from street sales of *The New York Post*. A drunk was passed out on the sidewalk in front of the adjoining building, which was headquarters for the Cheese of the Month Club, which had a more than moldy appearance.

"I'm not sure this is a safe area," Linda said.

A big, hand-lettered sign bearing my name had been taped to a door with peeling paint that led to stairways. On it was a note from Eric with a number to call. With Linda and Erik locked safely, I hoped, in the car, I found a pay phone not far away and dialed the number. A gruff voice answered, "Yeah." It sounded as if the person had been rousted from sleep and wasn't happy about it.

"Is Eric Alberts there?" I asked.

"No. He had to go to Columbia University. He left a number for you."

I called that number and got another unfamiliar voice, but Eric, whom for years I had called E, while he called me B, was with this person.

"B," he said, when he came to the phone. "Where are you?"

I told him that we finally had found his building. It turned out that Eric, who had amazing skills with his hands (he carved intricate scenes in peach pits, for example) was helping a friend build a model for a big architectural project and suggested that we drive up to the university. He was only 116 blocks away. Exhausted from 20 hours on the road and more frustration than I could handle, I was in no condition to traverse Manhattan from south to north on a Saturday night, but I foolishly undertook the challenge and miraculously made it without passing out or getting hit by any wild taxis.

Eric and his friend had finished their work for the night by the time we arrived. And with Erik in my arms protesting loudly to all of this disruption to his routines, we admired the model and chatted with the budding architect, before rearranging the car, squeezing Eric into the back seat and heading south down Broadway. To our good fortune, the parking place we'd found on Erik's street was still empty.

It took more than half an hour, and numerous trips to unload the car and haul all of our stuff up four flights of stairs, but despite my self-inflicted exhaustion, with Eric's help, I managed to accomplish it. It wasn't safe to leave anything in sight in the car, he said, because if it could be seen somebody would break out a window and take it. I now wondered what we were doing in New York in our shiny new car, which might no longer be ours come sunrise.

I now had been awake for more than 24 hours, and I couldn't recall when I last was in such a state of exhaustion—basic training at Ft. Jackson? Eric brought out a bottle of Irish whiskey and asked if I'd like a nip. I took it straight and, thankfully, it worked fast. Linda and I soon were sound asleep on the floor beside Erik's crib. At least for a while.

A few hours later, I was startled awake by what I thought was an explosion. It was only the drummer for a hard rock band warming up for the group's daily rehearsal in the loft of the adjoining building.

"Don't let it bother you," Eric mumbled from his cot across the way, "they only play until about noon." And he turned over and went back to sleep.

This turned out to be a very gray day and I had been all too keenly aware of a foul odor that seemed to follow us wherever we went. When I asked Eric about it, he had a two-word answer: garbage strike. Gray and smelly were never the combination for a good day as far as I was concerned. But we tried to make the best of it by taking the subway to Times Square and soaking in the bright lights, the crowds of tourists, the hawkers, preachers, dough-flying pizza makers, theaters, game rooms, going-out-of-business shops and porno palaces. At the corner of 42nd Street and 8th Avenue we encountered a small crowd exchanging insults with two Black Muslims who were promoting their beliefs. We lingered listening at the edge of the crowd.

Not far from us, a middle-aged man carrying two newspapers, with a gray jacket folded over one arm was threading his way through the assemblage when he suddenly grasped for his chest and collapsed on the sidewalk.

"Get a policeman," somebody yelled.

The angry arguments ceased as people began to realize what was happening. A cop came on the run, talking into his radio. Curiosity seekers were closing around the man.

"Get back!" the cop kept yelling.

I could hear a siren coming down 42nd St. More policemen arrived and began clearing people away. An ambulance pulled up. I couldn't help but notice that it was gray. A medic jumped out and started pounding on the man's chest. The crowd pushed closer. The ambulance driver brought out an oxygen tank.

"Get back! Give him some air," one cop kept telling the onlookers.

After a while, the attendant stopped pounding and shook his head.

"He's dead," somebody in the crowd said.

The body was lifted onto a stretcher, loaded into the ambulance and carried away. The two newspapers and the folded gray jacket still lay on the gray sidewalk. The cops formed a circle and began moving against the crowd.

"OK, break it up, move on," the cops were yelling. "Show's over."

A plump, white-haired woman expressed concern about the man's belongings to one of the cops.

"Mind your own business, lady," he told her.

Another cop scooped the newspapers and gray jacket off the sidewalk. One of the newspapers was the hefty Sunday edition of *The New York Times*, also known as the Gray Lady.

I suddenly felt overwhelmed by grayness.

After a superb dinner at a tiny basement restaurant in China Town, we returned to Erik's gray building for a gathering. An old buddy from B&VA, Tom Colt, a reporter in New Jersey at the time, showed up. So did three of Eric's relatives, a family of Ph.D psychologists, father, mother, and daughter, all of whom taught at Princeton. They were Eric's aunt, uncle and cousin, with whom he'd lived for a while when he first arrived to study at the Art Students League. They had come to say goodbye because they were moving on to teach as a family at the University of Wisconsin. They wanted to see Eric's latest paintings.

"Oh, that's pretty," the mother said of one. "This one's nice, too."

I could see that Eric was grimacing. He didn't paint for pretty and nice.

After they left, Eric explained why he had lived with them only for a short time.

"You have the feeling they're always analyzing you and everything you do," he said.

We got up the next morning not long after the band started playing, loaded up our prized car, which had managed to survive the streets of New York without vandalism or theft, and headed home. We took every toll road we encountered and couldn't have been happier when, in a reasonable length of time, we arrived back into the quiet, green hills of Randolph County, leaving behind the grayness, foul odors and frenzied streets of New York.

I, of course, couldn't resist writing about our trip. I wrote three articles and sent them by teletype to Smallwood.

The first was a self-deprecating humor piece about the frustrations of our drive to the city. The second was about grayness and our afternoon in Times Square, including the death we had witnessed. The third was about my friend Eric and our visit with him.

The series began on Sunday on the front of the "Cavalcade" section, in which the editorial pages appeared. The first article took up much of the bottom of the page and included another great cartoon by Bob Zschiesche. The second piece on Monday required less space on the front page but bore a headline that would prove to be overwhelmingly provocative: "N.Y. Looks Dull,

Smells Bad." It began and closed with grayness.

The reaction erupted that day with angry telephone calls. I had no idea how many New York lovers were readers of the *Daily News*, how sensitive they were about the subject, or how crude and nasty they actually could be. What I had written was nothing more than apt and true description, but they didn't want it to appear (although they did read it) and had no intention of tolerating it.

Letters came in dozens, not just to me, but to the "Public Pulse," as our letters-to-the-editor section was called. They accused me of ignorance and stupidity and called me all sorts of names. I took particular offense to one. It proclaimed me to be "a regionalistic intellectual hick."

I immediately fired off my own letter to the editor:

"I resent being called an 'intellectual hick' in the 'Public Pulse.' I have never been intellectual."

That prompted quite a few friendly calls from fellow hicks.

Although I had a great deal of fun in the High Point bureau, my time there also gave me a first-hand introduction to the most important story of the '60s—the struggle for civil rights.

15

DURING MY FIRST WEEK as chief of the High Point bureau, a minister dropped in to introduce himself. His name was Benjamin Elton Cox, although he preferred B. Elton when he signed his name, and friends called him Elton. Some who were familiar with his style of preaching referred to him as "Beltin' Elton," although I never would have suspected it because of his quiet demeanor.

He was 35 and a bit of a dandy. I can't recall ever seeing him when he wasn't wearing a suit with a thin, stylish bowtie, usually colorful, never a clip-on of the type I had worn to church as a child. His appearance was distinctive. He had light skin, a thin, precisely-maintained mustache and just a wisp of hair below the center of his bottom lip. His black hair was thick, wavy and appeared to be pomaded, although stray locks sometimes broke free, looking like cartoon question marks over his head. He joked about his hair, citing it as evidence of racial mingling somewhere along the line. If the weather was bad, a homburg with a bright band often was perched atop his distinctive hair.

Cox was the pastor of Pilgrim Congregational United Church of Christ in east High Point, an all-black church. (If there were any integrated churches in High Point at the time, I was unaware of them.). He also was a member of the Congress of Racial Equality (CORE), which he had served as state and national field secretary, and had emerged as the most prominent civil rights leader in High Point, although he was resented by some of the older leaders of the local NAACP.

During my 14 months in the High Point bureau, Cox would be my most frequent visitor. He usually came just to chat, joke and laugh, or to reveal some bit of interesting information he'd picked up. He never asked favors or pressed me in any way. Later, after some of his activities had made headlines and we'd gotten to know each other better, he would come for longer, more serious talks. Before Erik reached the toddling stage, Linda got a job at a downtown finance company, and I had to pick him up from childcare and keep him at the office for an hour or so until she got off work. Cox would sometimes come and play with him while I pounded deadline stories into the teletype machine. I took a photo of Erik wearing a diaper, pacifier firmly in mouth, sitting happily in Cox's lap.

Cox was serious about his religion and Gandhi-like in his dedication to non-violent protest. Born into a family of 16 children in Whiteville, Tennessee, a small cotton-processing town between Jackson and Memphis, he and his family moved to Illinois when he was five. He felt called to preach at 13. He was 15 when he took part in his first successful protest to get equal treatment. That was at an A&W Root Beer drive-in in Kankakee (whites could get their root beer in frosted mugs, blacks only in paper cups). His family lived 39 miles from Kankakee in Joliet, where he attended an integrated high school. But he had to drop out for more than a year, shining shoes to help support his family, and didn't finish high school until he was 19. After graduation he was accepted at Livingstone College in Salisbury, N.C., a black institution, connected with the AME Zion Church. He later studied at Howard University School of Divinity in Washington, earning his degree in theology in 1957. He was ordained a year later and came to Pilgrim Congregational Church in High Point in 1959.

Cox quickly got involved in civil rights activities and took a group of high school students from High Point to participate in the sit-ins at Woolworth's in Greensboro two weeks after they began in February, 1960. He was a modest man, never boastful about his accomplishments, and didn't restrict himself to local matters. It would be long after I left High Point before I learned that he had been one of the 13 original Freedom Riders and that just a year before I arrived at the High Point bureau, the U.S. Supreme Court had decided a landmark civil rights case based on one of his many arrests for protesting.

THE FREEDOM RIDERS, seven blacks and six whites, all trained in non-violent reaction, left Washington on Thursday, May 4, 1961, in two groups, one on a Trailways bus the other on Greyhound. Their purpose was to sit where they pleased in the buses, blacks and whites, side-by-side, use bus station facilities and be served at restaurants without regard to race. They had no problems at six stops in Virginia and three in North Carolina, but violence struck at Rock Hill, South Carolina.

When the first bus arrived, white teen-agers attacked John Lewis and two other riders, knocking Lewis to the ground and kicking him repeatedly before police intervened. When the Trailways bus, on which Cox was riding, arrived two hours later, the bus station had been shut down and ministers were waiting to pick them up.

Two riders were arrested the following day when they sat at a lunch counter in Winnsboro and refused to move. The rest continued on to Sumter, where a two-day rest stop was scheduled. Cox left the ride there and returned to High Point to deliver his sermon the following morning and remained to plan the church's big Mother's Day service the following Sunday. This caused him to miss the group's meeting with Martin Luther King Jr. and his father in Atlanta, but also to escape the violence lurking ahead.

Mother's Day turned into a bloody day for the Freedom Riders. That was the day the Greyhound bus was attacked and burned outside Anniston, Alabama. The Trailways bus made it to Birmingham where the riders were savagely beaten by a waiting mob which had been given a free hand by Birmingham's police commissioner Eugene "Bull" Connor. Cox rejoined the riders there but bus drivers refused to carry them farther. Federal officials arranged to fly them to New Orleans, their eventual destination. But Diane Nash, a young Nashville civil rights leader, brought a group of Fisk University students to Birmingham to continue the rides. John Lewis, who had left the original group in Rock Hill, joined this group that went on to be beaten in Montgomery on Armed Forces Day, which evolved into an almost disastrous situation later that night, causing the National Guard to be called out.

After arriving in New Orleans, Cox went on to be involved in numerous demonstrations in Baton Rouge, Louisiana's capital, causing him to be arrested a dozen times and spend 100 days in jail. One of those arrests would go all the way to the U.S. Supreme Court.

During a demonstration led by Cox to integrate restaurants in Baton Rouge shortly before Christmas in 1961, 23 university students were arrested and jailed. On the following day, Cox led nearly 2,000 students on a peaceful march in the rain to protest at the courthouse where the students were being held. As the demonstration was ending, a tear gas canister bounced across the pavement spewing sickening fumes. Several others quickly followed, one hitting Cox, chipping a bone in his ankle. The demonstrators scattered, many running toward the Capitol, yelling, gagging and crying. Cox later said he thought the first canister had been set off accidentally, causing the law enforcement officers to panic. The following day he was arrested on three charges from the incident and ended up spending Christmas in jail. The charges were disturbing the peace, blocking public passage and picketing a courthouse. He was found guilty of all three and the convictions were upheld by the Louisiana Supreme Court. But the U.S. Supreme Court overturned them, ruling that they were violations of Cox's first and fourteenth amendment rights under the constitution.

WHEN I ARRIVED IN High Point it had been nearly three years since the city had suffered lengthy demonstrations to desegregate restaurants and theaters.

That had taken place while Jesse Jackson, Cox's fellow CORE member, was leading similar demonstrations in Greensboro and one of the instigators and leaders of the troubles in High Point was Cox. Those demonstrations, which turned out to be successful, also had brought great animosity and resentment to Cox, not to mention threats to his life. He kept a list of those threats, which eventually would number 87.

I had no doubt that Cox was courting me because he needed *The Greensboro Daily News* with its wide circulation to report accurately and fully about whatever activities he might have in mind. The locally owned newspaper, *The High Point Enterprise*, was a defender of the establishment, which was not in favor of black causes or demonstrators. The editor of the *Enterprise*, Holt McPherson, who used his position to enrich himself, was a booster and blowhard, not a journalist. And he was no fan of Cox or his mission.

My first opportunity to write about Cox came a little over three months after I met him. That was just before the spring furniture market opened on Friday, April 22. Cox had tipped me that a plan might be afoot to hold protest demonstrations during the market with its thousands of visitors. He appeared before a city council meeting the day before the market opening to chastise the city for failing to respond to a list of grievances that the black ministerial fellowship had presented more than a year earlier. It was at this meeting that he announced plans for demonstrations beginning the following day. The all-white council clearly was displeased.

Cox told me later that day that he intended to have hundreds of protesters demonstrating, at 4 p.m., just before all the opening-day parties began.

"Whites downtown have always asked us not to march during the market because it will hurt the city," he said. "We always gave in, but we're not giving in anymore. When we march tomorrow, some of those people are going to get back in their Cadillacs and Oldsmobiles and hit the road."

The people in charge of the furniture market were outraged by this prospect, and city council was called into an emergency, but unofficial, session the following morning at 10, just as the market was opening. At that meeting Cox recited a list of grievances including unpaved streets, overflowing creeks and lack of street lights in black communities. But chief among them was that black police officers were too few in number, not allowed to patrol outside black areas or to arrest whites and had little chance to rise to command positions (only one had reached the rank of lieutenant). Beyond that were longstanding concerns about discrimination in employment and especially in education because integration had barely begun in High Point schools and black schools were second-rate.

Irving Hamilton, a white banker and chairman of the Human Relations Commission, which essentially was inactive and without sufficient members to function, suggested that ministers postpone demonstrations for two weeks to give the council a chance to act on their complaints. After most ministers accepted his proposal, another meeting was set for May 5, following the market, to disclose what those actions would be.

THE AGREEMENT BROUGHT IMMENSE relief to furniture officials but it didn't remove race from the spring market. Usually blacks were seen at the furniture shows only in service jobs, but that changed at this one. Two blacks showed up and signed in as buyers, a first for the market. They were the new owners of the largest furniture store in Harlem and market leaders thought they saw a chance to benefit by exploiting their presence and displaying that they were welcome. They called a press conference for the two on Monday, three days after the market opened.

"Negro" was the descriptive term that newspapers and others, including blacks, favored in those days, and the buyers said that while they thought that more Negroes should be in sales and management positions with furniture manufacturers, they weren't civil rights leaders, just businessmen, and that was why they were there.

"I must be frank, and admit that I came to High Point expecting to see a backward Southern town," said one of the buyers, Kenneth Sherwood. "But this is a splendid city. I think it's a compliment to the city and its public officials that race relations are so harmonious here. We have seen no signs of hostility, no signs of anything that made us feel uncomfortable. This has been a pleasant surprise, this city...."

Market officials were beaming about how well this had gone. But less than an hour later both buyers were angrily ejected from the showroom of a Chicago manufacturing company by its president. The company said this was just a business dispute, not racial, but local black ministers who got word of it considered it news, and I felt obligated to report it. Leo Herr, the director of the Southern Furniture Exposition Building was so incensed when I asked him about it that he called my editors trying to have me removed from High Point, and when that didn't work, called Frank Batten in Norfolk hoping to get me fired, still to no avail.

I found it interesting that while the two Harlem buyers were in High Point, they were guests in the home of Bob Brown, one of the city's new wave of civil rights leaders, albeit a low-keyed one, working mainly behind the scenes. A former High Point cop and U.S. Treasury agent, Brown had started B&C Associates, which would become one of the largest minority-owned public relations companies in the country, working with many major corporations. After Richard Nixon was elected President in 1968, he hired Brown as a White House special assistant, a job he held for five years. Later, President Ronald Reagan wanted to name him ambassador to South Africa. I suspected that Brown's hand was behind the press conference for the two black buyers, winning points with white leaders for him, and that he was as shocked as market officials by what happened quickly afterward.

THE CITY COUNCIL MEETING to hash out the problems raised by Cox and the other ministers did not go well for black leaders. Mayor Carson Stout, who had started building furniture in his garage in 1944 and turned that enterprise into a prosperous company manufacturing high-end upholstered chairs and sofas, made quick business of their concerns. He denied any discrimination in the police department and said the ministers should take their other complaints to the school board and Human Relations Commission. Cox was not surprised at this response but had no intention to accept it.

Representatives of four different black groups gathered after the meeting to plan a course of action, and Cox emerged as spokesman for the consortium. He announced their intention to get Martin Luther King Jr. to come to High Point and add it to his list of "target cities" to attract national attention. The group also announced a mass meeting for Sunday night, three days hence, at First Baptist Church on Washington Street (there were two First Baptists in High Point, one white, one black) so that citizens could express their grievances. It would be closed to the press, Cox said, to encourage people to speak without fear of recriminations.

Attendance at that meeting no doubt was greatly increased by the anger that swept through the black community that Sunday because of Holt McPherson's "Good Morning" column in the *Enterprise*.

McPherson called Cox a "troubled, shouting, self-appointed spokesman" and said that High Point was tired of "trouble-making, blackmailing, racketeering operations in the name of race."

"Truth is, B. Elton Cox has about run his course as a trouble maker in a field in which he has created far more ills than he has cured.... He is angered at his inability to rouse a citizenry which so questions his tactics and spirits that he seeks now to ride Dr. King's coattails to support his questionable purposes."

McPherson went on to accuse Cox of "spreading unduly the poison of racial hate on which he thrives."

"Elton Cox's usefulness, if ever he had any here, long since was outlived," he wrote.

Ensuing developments not only would prove McPherson wrong but would show him to be the one responsible for spreading lies and hatred and helping to foment a demonstration that led to violence.

Some 200 people showed up for the Sunday night meeting at First Baptist, and after it ended, Sammie Chess, a young lawyer, emerged to speak with waiting reporters. He said that those attending supported a sustained drive to open jobs for blacks, particularly in government, and that no plans had been made for street marches, but the assemblage had agreed to take "whatever action is necessary" to achieve its goals.

Chess made a special point that those present agreed that Cox "speaks for the Negro in High Point."

"We wanted to kill the myth that Reverend Cox stood alone," Chess said, a direct renunciation of McPherson's column that morning.

This gathering had enthusiastically received the news that Martin Luther King Jr. had tentatively agreed to come to High Point on May 20. They also were pleased that King's chief aide and close friend, Ralph David Abernathy, would be speaking at another rally at the church a week away on May 15.

Cox had told me about King's tentative agreement off the record two days earlier, and I was excited about it, because he assured me that he would arrange for me to have a private interview with King. He said he also would see that I got to meet with Abernathy, too.

Abernathy, who for 10 years was pastor of the black First Baptist Church in Montgomery, had been at the center of most of King's civil rights activities. The two had organized the Montgomery bus boycott. King also had come to Montgomery on the day the Freedom Riders had been beaten to support the riders who had taken refuge at Abernathy's church, where they were besieged by white rioters.

Abernathy left his church later that year to work with King, and the two conceived the Birmingham Campaign in the spring of 1963, during which King was arrested and wrote his famous "Letter from Birmingham Jail." The demonstrations attracted worldwide attention on May 3 when "Bull" Connor turned fire hoses and police dogs on 2,500 young black marchers, prompting the President to intervene.

NOBODY WAS EXPECTING TROUBLE from Abernathy's arrival in High Point, but trouble beat him there. Three days before his arrival, students at the black high school, William Penn, circulated mimeographed notes through the school. "We quietly walk you know where," the notes said. "We protest together, all at once, forever. Segregation never, freedom now. Read and pass on."

When classes ended, students began gathering on Washington Street in front of the school. Cox and a minister from Thomasville, W.E. Banks, were waiting there to offer advice. More than 200 students turned out, and the mood was light with chatter and laughter as they began to march. Police, too, had been alerted. They were present but keeping their distance and maintaining a low profile. Over the first few blocks, which took them through the small black business district, the marchers were applauded and encouraged. It was after they reached Main Street that trouble began. A city bus packed with white students passed, many of them yelling and giving the finger to the marchers. A few wrote "KKK" on sheets of notebook paper and held them to windows.

"Oh, boy," said a shoe store clerk who had stepped outside to see what was happening, "there's going to be trouble now. I can guarantee you that."

He was right.

As the lead marchers turned back toward the high school on Washington Street, they fell silent and slowed so that those behind could catch up. Police officers trailing on foot began speaking into hand radios. At the intersection with Hamilton Street, where police earlier had stopped traffic to allow them to pass, the students began spilling into the streets, blocking traffic in all directions. An officer jumped out of a police car parked near where I was standing, and I heard a call over his radio for more cars.

"No emergency lights or sirens," the dispatcher ordered.

Impatient motorists were honking their horns, and officers began blowing whistles and telling marchers to clear the intersection. The students moved reluctantly and sullenly, gradually opening the two streets to traffic again.

At the Centennial Avenue intersection, where the black district began, the marchers flooded into the streets again, and this time they had no intention of leaving. Many were carrying umbrellas, protective devices against nightsticks instead of rain. More police vehicles began arriving.

One stout female student had taken a firm stand in front of a maroon Chevrolet driven by a young white woman with a female child in the seat beside her. The student had her left hand on the hood of the car and in her right hand she clutched an umbrella from the end opposite the handle, as if it were a club. When the car eased slightly forward, the student screamed. The frightened driver hit the brake as the student began beating the hood with her umbrella. Other students rushed to her aid, yelling, kicking the car, beating it with fists and umbrellas.

Half a dozen cops moved on the female student, grabbing her from behind, pulling her away. I was standing beside the driver's door and managed to get a close-up shot with my twin-lens reflex as the cops began forcing her away. A melee erupted as a wedge of cops holding night sticks at arms length moved into the group. A bystander broke through the police line, swinging at officers, and was quickly taken down and hauled to a squad car. More yelling erupted as students resisted the advancing officers. Umbrellas were swung. Beer bottles from a nearby pool hall began flying, popping on the pavement. I managed to get one clear shot of the cops pushing into this crowd before I found myself the object of the cops' attention.

A big cop suddenly took position directly in front of me, face-to-face, toe-to-toe. Another fell in behind me. I could feel his gut against my back. Neither said a word, but when I moved, they moved too. We were a dance trio, although not a graceful one. The cops' objective was to stop me from getting photos. I had to hold the camera high above my head and snap where the action seemed to be occurring, then bring the camera down to wind the film and try again. There was no way to focus and all of these shots came out blurred and unusable.

The melee ended quickly. Cox got out of a car with a megaphone and began urging students to leave. "Go on to the church," he kept repeating, but the angered students, some still yelling insults at the cops, retreated slowly.

A headlight was broken on the car containing the woman and child, and dents were left in the hood, door and fender. The driver, still tense and pale with fright, her child in tears, looked immensely relieved when officers let her move her car out of the intersection. They wouldn't allow me to get close enough to talk to her. Several officers had been hit with fists and umbrellas and two had their ties ripped off, although none had been injured. No students had been hurt either.

The intersection was sealed off and traffic was detoured. Blue helmeted riot officers arrived and took up stations. The students lingered in the street in front of First Baptist Church, still within sight, but police kept their distance.

I had to get back to the office and start writing. I turned out two lengthy pieces which got big display the following morning along with my two clear photos.

The clash between students and police had a bigger effect than city officials expected. Governor Dan K. Moore sent the chairman of his Good Neighbor Council, D.S. Coltrane, and Moore's top aide, Charles Dunn, to High Point Friday morning to confer with city officials. They met with black leaders in the afternoon. Coltrane and Mayor Stout announced that a public meeting for government and community leaders would be held that night in the council chambers. After classes ended at William Penn, word reached Coltrane and Stout that students were gathering to march again. Cox was asked to talk them out of it and invite them to the meeting that night.

The chamber was filled, almost entirely by blacks, including many students. Coltrane began by asking for "a cooling off period"

"Give us a little time," he said. "I think progress can be made. Something is going to be worked out. I hope we can have a quiet weekend in High Point."

An indignant student stood to say that a cooling off period wasn't good enough.

"They're always asking for more time," he said, before sitting down in frustration.

Another student rose to say that he and his fellow students had been inspired to march out of anger about Holt McPherson's column, but it should be clear that they had far more than that to be angry about.

After Cox detailed the problems, other leaders began coming forward to challenge the city's claim that discrimination wasn't happening.

"I've been a Negro thirty-some years," Sammie Chess said. "We know what it's all about. We know discrimination exists and it's all because of the color of a man's skin."

Dr. Perry Little, a dentist and the only black member of the school board, brought up problems in the schools, claiming that the superintendent resented doing anything for black schools and made threatening remarks to black teachers' groups.

"Our superintendent, Dr. Pruette, is definitely a segregationist if you ever saw one," he said. "It's true."

A black member of the Human Relations Commission said the reason blacks no longer brought complaints to the group was because nothing was done about them. "You might as well take the Human Relations Commission and throw it out the back door," he said.

Frustration was apparent from every speaker, but no attempt was made to settle any issues, and none of the blacks leaving the meeting seemed to be in a mood for cooling off.

A rally and demonstration by black students had been planned for Saturday night, beginning at Chavis YMCA. But when I drove by there Saturday afternoon, a hand-lettered poster taped to the door said the rally had been postponed—the first indication that negotiations might be underway because the students clearly wanted to keep marching.

I wrote a summary of the grievances expressed by black leaders and what they wanted done about them, and it was stripped across all eight columns at the top of the front page Sunday morning. Although I arrived early at First Baptist Church that evening in the hope of getting to talk privately with Rev. Abernathy, so many people already were gathering that I had to park well up the street at the high school.

An hour before the service was to begin, the pews in the sanctuary already were filled and people were still arriving by the score. I wandered in search of Cox and finally found him in a crowded hallway. He took me to a noisy room which appeared to contain almost every prominent black person in High Point. Abernathy was somewhere in the middle of it. We eventually worked our way to him and chatted briefly, but it was apparent that I wouldn't have a chance to interview him privately.

I never had attended a service in a black church, and wasn't sure what to expect. The event this night was a combination prayer meeting and political rally, and the church never had seen such a crowd. Every pew was jammed, all walls lined, the vestibule packed. Many people could not get in and crowded on the sidewalk outside. It was estimated that more than 500 people showed up. All those bodies so close produced a lot of heat, and many people were flicking funeral home cardboard fans to cool themselves.

There was a lot of preaching, a lot of praying, and a lot of singing, a joyous occasion. When the congregation sang "We Shall Overcome" early in the service, it was deeply moving and powerful.

What I hadn't anticipated was that this event would go on for hours, building momentum all the way. Cox teased the audience with a "progress report" about meetings black leaders had been holding with state and city officials, saying that by agreement he couldn't reveal details, but that announcements would be coming at another mass rally Tuesday night, following a special city council meeting. He encouraged everybody to attend that rally.

The gist of Abernathy's combined sermon and speech turned out to be a warning about what might happen if city officials didn't choose to deal with the issues that black leaders had raised.

"If the furniture people don't do something about this," he said, "we're going to have to call for a nationwide strike and stop buying their furniture. We're not going to hit you with a brick, we're going to hit exactly where it hurts the most—right in the pocketbook."

He, Martin Luther King Jr. and the SCLC stood ready to come to High Point, he promised.

"And if we come, we're going to march and we're going to stay here until the walls of segregation come down."

The crowd roared so loudly and so long that I was sure it could have been heard blocks away. The event didn't end after Abernathy spoke either. The crowd was having too good a time and it just kept going. I had to wiggle out and run to my car to meet my deadline.

B. Elton Cox was smiling when Tuesday's city council meeting began. Mayor Carson Stout read a lengthy statement acknowledging that the "council recognizes that it has a responsibility to all the citizens of High Point to establish sound non-discriminatory policies and to see that these policies are administered without regard to race, color, or creed, fairly and impartially, without fear or favor." He and the council intended to do just that, he said.

The appointment of three new members to the Human Relations Commission was announced, and the council voted unanimously to require the commission to meet monthly and deal quickly and fairly with all problems brought to it.

More than 200 people turned out for the rally that night, many high school students. Black leaders were beaming about the results of their private negotiations with city leaders. Bob Brown, the former High Point cop, reported that a directive had been issued that all officers are required to arrest all law violators without regard to race, and that for the first time a black officer had been assigned to the traffic division and would patrol city-wide, not just in the black community. A black officer also would be promoted to a policy-making position soon and black women would be hired as meter maids. Other developments would be forthcoming.

Rumors had swept through the city that a big march would be held on this night and groups of young white males had gathered along Main Street in hopes of disrupting it. Police had been dispatched to keep them under observation.

Brown, however, said that demonstrations no longer were necessary.

"The only reason to demonstrate is to accomplish something," he said. "We are accomplishing things that have never happened in High Point before."

He advised the students to go home in an orderly manner and not linger on the streets. Some seemed disgruntled about this, and Cox attempted to reassure them.

"The day that the city power structure decides they can't move any farther toward freedom, I'll be the first to march."

Not all blacks were happy about these developments. John Langford, a long-time lawyer and president of the local NAACP denounced them and personally attacked Cox and other black leaders claiming that they didn't represent the black community and their motives were only to gain "power and self-advancement."

His claims were largely dismissed as the complaints of an aging and fading leader who resented achievements that he had not been able to accomplish.

New developments continued to flow. In June the city school board voted to completely integrate High Point schools within two years, which would require closing William Penn High.

In July, a new police chief was hired. His name was Laurie Pritchett. He had been police chief of Albany, Georgia, where at the end of 1961 Martin Luther King Jr., with his new aide Abernathy, focused his first campaign. It did not go well, and King considered it a failure, but one from which he learned much.

Pritchett was primarily responsible for that outcome. He treated King and all demonstrators with courtesy and respect and without physical contact. He kept the KKK out of the city and tried to suppress any actions that might lead to trouble. When King and Abernathy were arrested, white community leaders posted their bonds so they would be quickly released.

Without the presence of anger and violence the national news media largely ignored the Albany campaign and King cancelled it after seven months. During this period King and Pritchett became friends, and Pritchett visited him during the Birmingham campaign and on other occasions. Robert F. Kennedy invited both to Washington for the signing of the Civil Rights Act, and Pritchett assured Kennedy that the law would be enforced in Albany.

Pritchett, who was 39, had a military bearing and a firm manner. When he was sworn in on the first day of August he told his men that he would not tolerate brutality in any form. Under his direction, he said, the department would provide "honest, efficient law enforcement...without favor or reward... regardless of position, wealth or color."

"I won't be satisfied with anything but the best," he said.

Pritchett kept his word. He was wary of me, however, and did all he could to avoid me, no doubt having been warned about me by officials who didn't like what I was reporting. I didn't get to know him until long after I left High Point.

While I was covering these matters, I got a call from a guy who wouldn't identify himself. He was angry about one of the articles I had written and ranted on and on about it.

"Wait a minute," I said, attempting to challenge one of his claims, "are you sure that's what I wrote? Read that part to me."

"I ain't read the trashy thing," he snapped. "Somebody told me about it."

He then informed me that I had better watch myself because he belonged to a group that was going to "git" me.

"Places has been blowed up, you know," he said, and slammed down the receiver.

One thing was certain. I didn't want to be got. And I surely didn't want to be anywhere that was about to be "blowed up." But I wasn't certain what to do. Should I call the police? Would they just laugh at me?

I decided I'd better consult my editors. I sat down at the teletype, wrote everything that just had happened and asked for advice.

About five minutes later, my teletype sprang to life. I hurried to it and found this brief message from Chuck Hauser: "If he shows up, try to sell him a subscription."

Later that year, I got a Christmas card from the High Point chapter of the Ku Klux Klan. On the front was a tranquil winter scene. The message inside was traditional: "May all your Christmases be white."

THE CONGRESS OF RACIAL EQUALITY underwent radical change in 1966, and it bothered B. Elton Cox deeply. At the beginning of the year, Floyd McKissick was elected as CORE's director, replacing James Farmer. McKissick, an

Asheville native, was the first black to be admitted to the University of North Carolina law school in 1951. He later set up practice in Durham and became involved in civil rights causes. He had handled a lot of CORE's legal matters. He also was an advocate of black power and a supporter and friend of Stokely Carmichael, a leader of that movement.

I learned about this when Cox came by the office for one of his visits. He had been told that letters were on their way to CORE chapters informing them that all white leaders would have to be removed. The chapters in High Point, Greensboro and Winston-Salem all had white members, and all were opposed to this move. The Winston-Salem chapter was considering withdrawing from CORE, Cox told me. Cox no longer was a national leader of the group, but he still was on its speakers' panel.

"I believe in racial equality in the total sense of the word," he told me.

To him, purging white leaders was nothing more than racial discrimination, the very thing he'd spent much of his life fighting.

McKissick stuck to his plan, and nearly three months later, Cox and other black leaders in High Point held a press conference to denounce black power and appeal to the community to oppose it.

Cox read a statement in which he said that he and the other black leaders who stood with him were "unalterably opposed to black or white power" and sought only to "make democracy real for persons of all races."

"Our urgent call goes out to every good American, black and white, rich and poor, to speak out against all forms of violence and hate," Cox said. "This is not a time for silence."

Questioned by reporters about why he was taking this action Cox said, "As a Christian, I cannot support such a movement. We in High Point feel we have made a lot of racial progress through many sacrifices and we are not going to sit down and let this cry creep up louder and louder until it's too late."

Cox and the other leaders went on to commend the mayor, city council, police chief and school board for "the role they are not only accepting, but the role they are playing to make democracy real."

"Our city is moving ahead of others," Bob Brown said.

"The time of racial unrest in High Point is a thing of the past," Dr. Otis Tillman added. "I think we'll never again have cause to take to the streets."

This would be the last article I wrote about civil rights in High Point.

On the last day of December, 1966, Cox gave up his membership in CORE.

Floyd McKissick resigned as CORE's director two years later to carry out a grand scheme to build a black city of the future on 5,000 acres in rural eastern North Carolina. Funded by the U.S. Department of Housing and Urban Development, it was to be called Soul City. It turned into a grand disaster stretching over many years and costing taxpayers many millions of dollars.

Not long after McKissick began work on Soul City, Cox left his church in High Point and moved his young family to Illinois, where he had grown up. He taught in public schools, became chaplain at the Veterans Affairs Hospital in Danville and later was a program director at Parkland Community College in nearby Champaign. He remained in Illinois for 30 years before moving in 1998 to Jackson, Tennessee, not far from where he had been born.

I deeply admired Cox for his character, his courage, his commitment, his sense of reason. He was willing to risk his life and suffer for a just and necessary cause, and he did it without desire or expectation of personal reward or recognition. In my view, he epitomized the best of the civil rights movement and I was blessed to have known him.

Although I had felt close with Cox and enjoyed his visits during the 14 months I was in High Point, I never saw him again after I left. That's the nature of journalism. Each day new stories and new people enter your life, leaving little time for earlier ones, and eventually they fade away. After I learned that Cox had moved to Jackson, a city I sometimes passed through in my travels, I intended to look him up someday so we could recall old times. But when I finally got around to that, the first thing I found was his obituary. He died in June, 2011, at 79.

Cox was right about many things, and one of them was his fear about the dark forces that were forming within and without the civil rights movement and the deadly violence they might bring. Unfortunately, I would be caught in the midst of far more of that than I could have imagined.

16

My plan to use "High Point Notebook" to land a job as columnist worked. After I had been in the bureau for 14 months, Hauser and Smallwood agreed to give me a shot at it. At the beginning of March, 1967, I was assigned to the newsroom in Greensboro. I would have to spend two months on the police beat and two more covering city hall to acquaint myself with the city. After that I would become a general assignment reporter and be allowed to write a column once a week to see if it might catch attention.

The police and city hall beats required a lot of mundane work, but during that time Smallwood also handed me some choice assignments. I was sent to the airport to greet Bob Hope as he arrived to play at the Greater Greensboro Open golf tournament. That meant a lot to me because Hope had produced the one bright spot in my final days in the Army when he brought his USO holiday show to Okinawa.

I also spent an entire afternoon in the midst of a major forest fire in Rockingham County and was honored to interview former editor Slim Kendall on his last day at work and be the first to see his desk completely cleared of the mounds of debris that had cloaked it for decades.

Another assignment I got during this period created a controversy involving some of the city's most prominent citizens, who had no reticence in expressing their displeasure. I was to cover the Greensboro Beautiful annual awards luncheon and the dedication of a new, supposedly highly beautified welcome sign on the eastern edge of the city.

The dedication was first. The governor was supposed to be present, but apparently had more important matters to attend. Joe Hunt, a local resident who was chairman of the State Highway Commission, was to participate, along with the mayor, Carson Bain, city council members, and leaders of the consortium of garden clubs that had taken on the project. Scores of garden club members gathered to listen and watch, almost all wearing hats adorned with enough colorful artificial flowers to make a cemetery envious.

The problem I was having was trying to figure out why this ceremony was taking place, because there was no welcome sign, just a huge stack of bricks still bound with metal bands, and no beautification of any type unless weeds, which filled most of the field, were considered to be nature's idea of beautification.

Apparently being the only person present who saw anything unusual about this, I had the audacity to seek an explanation after the ceremony. It was this: weather and other problems had delayed construction of the sign, and there would be no point in beautifying the area until that was completed because workmen and their machines would just destroy it.

That made sense, I thought. But why not just delay the dedication until the project actually existed?

Well, I was told, it had been scheduled to coincide with the Greensboro Beautiful awards luncheon, for which Joe Hunt had agreed to be the keynote speaker as well as participating in the dedication, and the luncheon date could not be changed. Therefore, we were dedicating a field of weeds as a significant beautification project.

After the ceremony, a caravan was formed to take the group to a hotel near downtown, the Voyager Inn, where I would find myself undertaking an epicurean voyage. The exalted leaders of various garden clubs were riding in a black Cadillac limousine provided by a local funeral home. Two police cars were present. One led the caravan with emergency lights flashing. The other raced ahead, blocking traffic at intersections with stoplights so that this speciously important procession could pass unimpeded. More than 20 cars made up this cavalcade, and I fell in line behind Joe Hunt's flashy new sports car. As we made our way along Lee Street through the black community I noticed that approaching vehicles were pulling over as we passed, and a few older male pedestrians were removing their hats and holding them over their hearts, obviously thinking this was a funeral procession. Later, I'm sure, some of the garden club ladies would be wishing that it had been and that I was the corpse on the way to a well-deserved planting.

The dull luncheon speeches and handing out of scores of awards seemed to go on forever, but it was the food that became a challenge to me, primarily because I was expected to eat it.

The first course was a small cup of tepid chalky white stuff with green vegetative bits in it.

"What's that?" I asked the waiter.

"Vichyssoise," he said, with his nose slightly in the air.

"Vishy what?" I asked.

"Tater soup," he replied coldly.

The main course was colorfully spectacular—half a fancifully carved cantaloupe containing a scoop of melting raspberry sherbet, perhaps the reason the cavalcade had been in such a rush. Alongside it were five red grapes, half a canned pear, six stewed prunes, two baked figs, a pair of tiny crust-less triangular sandwiches with thin and gooey unidentifiable contents, and a puddle of something mushy and green, the likes of which I never had encountered.

When I finally made it back to the office famished, I sat down and wrote a Dear Boss memo to Smallwood, telling him about all that had gone on and how I obviously was not the appropriate person to be covering such an uneventful event.

"I'll try to knock out some kind of story," I wrote, "but right now I've got to go get something to eat."

The following morning I found my "memo" on the front page under this headline: "Dear Boss: What It Was Was Beautiful" (a take-off of Andy Griffith's break-through comedy record "What It Was Was Football"). The sub-head: "Pretty Highway, Pretty Hats, Pretty Hungry."

When I got to work, Fleta, the receptionist and switchboard operator in the lobby, was looking overworked and abused.

"Well, you've done it this time," she said. "I can't remember when the switchboard was lit up like it has been this morning."

I hadn't been at my desk long when a messenger arrived carrying a brown paper bag, with a note attached from "Chamber of Commerce Man." I opened it to find a container of stewed prunes decorated with a sprig of wilted parsley, apparently a take-out from the luncheon. Not long after that a Highway Patrolman entered the newsroom carrying a beautifully wrapped gift box from Joe Hunt. It looked as if it might contain a fifth, as indeed it did—of Pepto Bismol, beautifully pink but sickeningly tasting diarrheal relief.

A short time later, the phone rang. It was Fleta.

"Jerry," she said, "I just want to give you a little heads up. There are some really angry ladies in really fancy hats down here, and they've got a TV crew with them."

I did what any sensible reporter would do. I went to the men's room, locked myself in a stall and didn't come out until I was convinced the coast was clear. As soon as I sat down at my desk another messenger appeared, this a welcomed one. He was carrying a huge sack of McDonald's burgers. A big note on the bag said, "Compliments of the Garden Clubs of Greensboro to a hungry reporter." I knew it hadn't come from the garden club ladies. It had been sent by the mayor, who had a great sense of humor and whom I liked very much. The TV crew found its way to the newsroom to film this blessing, and I made my first TV appearance on Channel 2 that evening, chomping happily on a burger.

The angry garden club ladies didn't show up for this, or I would have offered them something fit to eat. They were otherwise occupied downstairs in

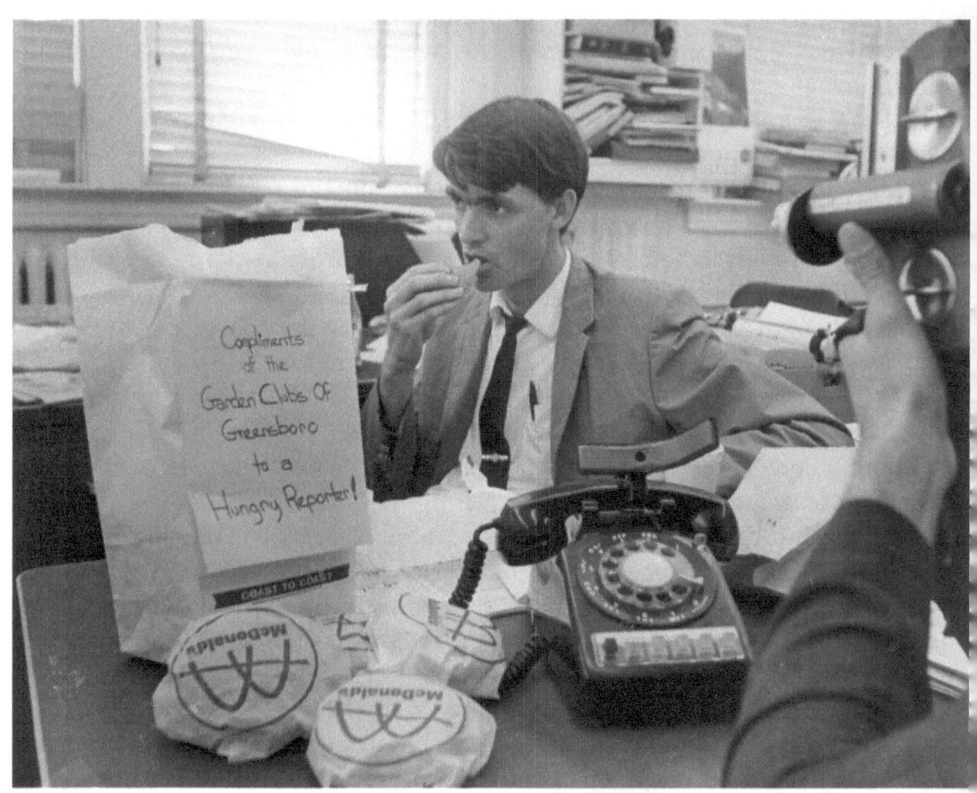

Munching away on McDonald's burgers

the office of General Manager Pete Bush hoping to get me canned. Smallwood later told me that Bush had asked them what damage my effort had wrought.

"For one thing," one of the ladies replied indignantly, "he messed up our scrapbook."

ON JULY 1, LAUNCH day for my new column finally arrived.

Columns had to have titles in those days and I had settled on "Meandering Me" for reasons I no longer can recall, although I did favor alliteration. It would appear on the local front every Saturday. It received no advance promotion, showing up as a horizontal interloper at the bottom of the page. A smiling thumbnail photo appeared beside my name. The headline, "Ol' Mr. Catfish Sniffing Around," set up a slice-of-life piece.

My dad and I had gone fishing on the huge rocks at the base of the dam that held back High Rock Lake in Davidson County, where we had fished for many years. It was a good spot for catching crappie and smallmouth bass, but on this hot Saturday afternoon nothing was biting.

Nearby, within easy hearing range, two women were fishing, one tiny, old and gnarled, the other much younger, grossly fat in tight and bulging pink pants. The old woman sat close by the water on a small, folding canvas stool in the blazing sun. The other lounged in the shade of a nearby tree, far from her bamboo fishing pole. The heat became the topic of conversation. The old woman said it reminded her of the day she had her stroke.

"Hot, I reckon," she said.

The younger woman expressed shock that a woman who had suffered a stroke would be sitting in the sun. She asked when the stroke had occurred and the old woman embarked on a lengthy tale about it.

"I believe I had a stroke," the younger woman said when she had finished. "I'd been drinking some ol' wine one night, was feeling pretty good, and all of a sudden I got to feeling real funny in my head. Had to lay down. Was that the way you felt?"

"Yeah, kind of," said the old lady, "real funny. Couldn't get out of bed."

"Well, I guess I had one then. Must've been a light one. I got all right."

Just then the float on the old woman's line bobbed, then disappeared. She yanked on the pole and out of the water popped a small blue catfish, flopping frantically.

"Ol' Mr. Catfish," the woman said, "I knowed you'd come sniffing around."

I don't recall getting any reaction to this column, either from readers or colleagues, but I tried not to let it bother me. I just hoped it might make a few people look for the next one.

I SOON WOULD GET more reaction than I could have imagined, and much more than the newspaper wanted, almost all of it unfavorable, some of it so mean that I had trouble comprehending the nature of it, considering its sources. It wasn't a column that provoked this outpouring but another assignment. The Monkees, the hottest rock group in the country, were coming to town for a concert at the coliseum on Wednesday, July 12. I was assigned not only to cover the event but to attempt to interview the group, a goal producing ultimate frustration.

The Monkees had been created as a fictional ensemble for a TV situation comedy about a teen rock band in southern California struggling to achieve success. The show, which hoped to cash in on the success the Beatles were enjoying, began appearing on NBC the previous September and became a quick hit. It would win an Emmy for best situation comedy for its first season. I hadn't seen a single episode.

In just a few months the Monkees became a real band whose records reportedly were outselling those of the Beatles and the Rolling Stones combined. Their big hit was "Last Train to Clarksville," a song about a soldier talking to his girlfriend on a train station pay phone in Clarksville, Tennessee, just outside Ft. Campbell, Kentucky, begging her to come for one last night together before he leaves for Vietnam. Most of these record sales were to 13- and 14-year-old girls, teenyboppers, as they were called, who were the overwhelming core of the Monkees' fan base.

The Monkees were built around Davey Jones, a British performer and former jockey who had appeared on Broadway in *Oliver* as well as on *The Ed Sullivan Show* on the same night the Beatles debuted on national TV. Fans would refer to him as "the cute one." The other three—Peter Tork, Mike Nesmith, Mickey Dolenz—had been chosen from casting calls. With their show a huge success, the group scheduled a 26-city tour beginning in early July and ending just before the series began its second season in September.

On June 9, these corporate-fabricated new stars, who ironically didn't have to struggle in the least to achieve stardom as rock stars, did a warm-up concert at the Hollywood Bowl. They then spent two weeks recording their second album before flying to Paris to film a show for the coming season. At the end of June, they stopped in London to put on five concerts over three days at an arena called Wembley Empire Pool, and partied with British rock stars, including the Beatles.

The U.S. tour began in Jacksonville, Florida, on Saturday, July 8. Miami was the next night, followed by a one-day break. Charlotte was Tuesday, July 11, Greensboro the day after.

The handlers of the Monkees seemed intent on protecting them from the press, perhaps because they feared they might be portrayed as they actually were instead of the way the network powers wanted them to be perceived. They also wanted to keep their whereabouts secret. Days before they were to arrive, Jim McAllister, who had become entertainment editor, and I had been doing everything possible to find out when they would be arriving, where they would be staying, and how we could line up interviews. We called all the major hotels and motels. None would admit to having reservations for the Monkees. McAllister put in calls to contacts at NBC in New York, to the record producer, the TV production company in California.

Even Bob Kent, the coliseum manager, was in the dark.

We knew from news reports that the Monkees, their handlers and road crew were traveling in two chartered, propeller-driven DC6s. Kent said all he had been told was that he needed to have five limousines and a truck at the airport at midnight, and another truck at two a.m. for the second plane which was carrying gear. Two hours later, Kent called to say he now had been informed there would be no need for the limos and the trucks. He'd been offered no explanation. Apparently the Monkees would be depending on land transportation to make the 90 miles from Charlotte.

Not until I got to work the next day did I learn where the Monkees were. A radio disc jockey revealed that they had arrived after midnight in a chartered bus at the Oaks Motel, a drive-to-your-door, family-owned accommodation behind a grove of oak trees on Summit Avenue, only a mile and a half from the newspaper building. It was not the kind of place you'd expect to find a hot rock band. They had rented 22 rooms. Word of their whereabouts had spread long before I got there, and hundreds of teenyboppers had gathered under the oaks on the motel's expansive, grassy lawn. A couple squadrons of police officers were present to keep them safely away from their idols.

When I arrived, the teenyboppers were enthralled and concentrated on the kidney shaped swimming pool because an actual Monkee, Davey, the cute one, was sitting in a lounge chair by the pool wearing nothing but swim trunks and a sullen look. One group of girls was discussing the possibility of swarming the pool on the theory that if enough of them took part a few might make it to Davey, even though a stern and vigilant cop was standing directly behind him.

While this was going on, a squeal erupted from another section of Monkees watchers. A second Monkee, Mickey Dolenz, emerged from a distant room wearing a flowery, puffed-sleeved blouse and a pair of faded cut-off jeans. He was headed toward the pool. He turned, smiled and waved when the squeal erupted, prompting the girls to break into a run toward him, leading him to almost walk into a tree before the cops intervened.

A woman was sitting beside Davey Jones and appeared to be talking to him intently. She was wearing a polka-dot bikini that her body was not molded to accommodate and some parts appeared on the verge of escape. When I asked a cop if he had any idea who that woman was, he said, "I think they said she's the press agent."

"Marilyn Schlossberger!" I said.

She was the person McAllister and I had been trying to reach for days without any success.

The cop seemed impressed that I knew her name. I asked if he'd let me speak to her, but he said he couldn't do that. After a bit of cajoling, he agreed to ask her himself. She looked irritated when he approached, and after only a few words between them, he beat a hasty retreat.

"She said they don't have time to talk to anybody," he told me.

I knew there was no point in hanging around hoping to see another Monkee from a distance. I went back to the newsroom and wrote an apologetic piece directed personally to the teenyboppers. I told them about all the effort we'd committed to trying to find out everything they wanted to know about the Monkees.

"Man, we were going to really lay it on you. All that good inside stuff. What Peter Tork is really like. What kind of girls Davey Jones goes for. What Mike Nesmith had for supper. The color of Mickey Dolenz' toothbrush."

Alas, I had to report, we'd failed miserably. All I could offer was what I had witnessed at the motel with their fellow teenyboppers.

"That's about it, gang," I wrote. "All we got. Now you know why those movie magazines fake all those 'exclusive interviews' and make up all those stories.

"Hey, baby, why not....?

"In an exclusive interview Wednesday, the *Daily News* Monkees team learned: Peter Tork is a grouch. Davey Jones loves a locker and can't stand girls. Mickey Dolenz never brushes his teeth. And Mike Nesmith eats sauerkraut."

I didn't think teenyboppers read the newspaper but I thought this might amuse their moms. I would be proven wrong on both counts.

I wasn't really looking forward to the concert that night and didn't know what to expect. I never had attended an event of any type in such a large forum. The coliseum had 7,100 seats at the time (now 23,000) and all were sold. I didn't have one. Bob Kent issued me a free-roaming press pass that gave me access to every part of the building, with the exception of female restrooms and dressing rooms for the stars unless I was invited.

What I hadn't expected was the unbearable decibel levels of high-amp rock speakers and thousands of screaming pre-pubescent girls, along with the shock of explosive psychedelic lighting and matching sound effects, a first for Greensboro.

I had to write a story about the concert for the first edition, which meant I'd have to leave before it ended so I could get back to the newsroom without being trapped in departing traffic jams and get it written in time to meet my deadline.

The din of the concert was still rattling my brain when I wrote the piece. It began this way:

"How do you explain a Monkees concert?

"It was the sinking of the Titanic...the bombing of London...a bad trip on LSD....Not recommended for people with heart conditions or nervous disorders."

Eighty cops were on hand to keep screaming girls from swarming the stage, I reported. In the seating areas coliseum employees waved pin lights attempting to get the frenzied fans to sit down.

"It was like trying to mow a field of wild oats with fingernail clippers," I noted.

Photos from the concert and the motel pool, along with my two articles, took up much of the local front page the next morning. The most prominently displayed piece with a big headline and sub-headline was my apology for failing to get the desired goods on the Monkees. The package attracted far more attention than I imagined.

Fleta gave me an angry glare when I passed the switchboard as she frantically patched in lines that morning. My phone was ringing when I got to my desk. I actually answered some of the calls, only to hear angry insults, unintelligible comments wrapped in sobs and quick hang-ups. I didn't realize teenyboppers knew such words. After that, I left the receiver off the hook for most of the rest of the day. Another reporter told me that a deejay at one of the area rock stations was attacking me on air and urging Monkees' fans to call in protest.

I scribbled down what gushed from one caller as I held the receiver for another reporter to listen. The girl sounded to be maybe 11 or 12 and apparently had rehearsed what she intended to say: "I hate you. I hope you fall off a cliff and break all your bones. I hope you die slow so I can watch and clap and cheer. You stink."

I didn't get a chance to thank her for calling. She slammed down the receiver.

The following day, Friday, brought stacks of letters. I used a few of these for my third "Meandering Me" column in the next day's paper. This was one of the kinder ones:

"I think your articles about the Monkees are sickening, untrue, and just plain trash....If they are supposed to be jokes, they aren't funny. They are nauseating, insinuating and not fit to be printed."

"I guess you know about the bombing of the Titanic," began another. "You were probably there! You probably went home and told your parents a pack of lies then."

One writer had second thoughts after finishing her letter. She once had liked me but now despised me, she wrote, and I'd never be even one-millionth as important as a Monkee. She signed it "An Enormous Monkee Lover," but scratched through "enormous."

On the same day this column appeared, July 15, my 26th birthday, the first outraged letter-to-the-editor also was published. Others would continue for five days. One contained a line with which I couldn't help agreeing: "Just because pansy-colored pants are different doesn't mean a life and death crime was committed..."

Only one letter was favorable. It appeared on the fifth day and was from an adult. She wrote: "Mr. Bledsoe was as kind as he could be."

This letter was followed by an editor's note: "Our correspondence on Mr. Bledsoe's coverage of the Monkees is herewith terminated."

Our editorial department was too high brow for this type of thing to be taking up so much of its precious space. Later, one of the editors sent me a letter that arrived a couple of days after that notice. If the editors had any truly sound judgment, it said, they should be terminating me. I wasn't sure whether that meant depriving me of my job or my life, but I didn't think I would find either outcome agreeable.

My attendance at the Monkees' concert brought an unexpected encounter that would provide material for my fourth "Meandering Me" 10 days later. I was standing by the stage watching the last of the audience trickling in, making a few notes. An attractive young woman approached and asked if I was with the newspaper. I cautiously admitted it.

"What are you planning to write?" she asked.

"Mostly about the audience, I guess. I wanted to write about the Monkees, but nobody would talk to me."

"That's because they don't need publicity. They're already famous and they're hot, but they won't last long. You should be writing about the opening act. He needs the attention."

"I didn't know there was an opening act," I said. "Who is it?"

"His name is Jimi Hendrix," she said, although I was picturing the first name as Jimmy.

"Never heard of him."

"Not many people have, at least not in this country, not yet," she said. "But they're going to. He's hot in England, but he's going to be big. Super big. Everywhere. I guarantee it."

"Is he from England?" I asked.

"No, he's just been living there. He's from Seattle."

"Are you his publicist?"

"I guess you could say that..." she said, and paused, "...among other things. I can arrange for you to talk with him if you'd like."

"Sure," I said.

"You need to see him perform first. He's getting ready to go on now. He can talk to you after his set. Why don't you come back and watch it with us. You'll get a close-up view."

It was close-up indeed. And unlike anything I'd ever witnessed. The road crew and everybody else connected with the show gathered just off stage to watch. They'd done the same at all three previous shows.

Hendrix, a tall, slim left-handed electric guitar player with a thin, spotty mustache curving around his mouth, was not appearing alone. He was the leader of a three-man band called The Jimi Hendrix Experience, which, as I soon was to discover, was an apt description, for it was an experience unlike any other. The two band members performing with him were British, bass guitarist Noel Redding and drummer Mitch Mitchell. The group had been formed in London in the fall of 1966 by Chas Chandler, former bassist for the disintegrating rock group The Animals. Chandler had become Hendrix's manager. Small though the band was, it could make a hell of a lot of noise.

All three band members had similar hairdos, puffed, round and frizzy, their heads from a distance resembling huge bowling balls with faces. Their costumes were all different, psychedelic, frilly, lacy, silky splashes of brilliant colors. Their velvet trousers were tight with big bell bottoms. Hendrix wore strands of love beads hanging almost to his waist. His fingers were adorned with heavy ornamental rings, and a red and blue bandana was tied around his head, tucked under his hair on his forehead. He opened with a tune called "Purple Haze," which he had written the previous fall. It had been released as a single in the U.S. just three weeks earlier, after his appearance at the Monterey Pop Festival in California attracted a lot of attention. It would become a Billboard Top 100 tune a month after Hendrix passed through Greensboro and later would be the opening song on his first album, *Are You Experienced*? Many fans considered it a song inspired by a drug vision, and the lyrics certainly could be read that way, hardly the kind of message that mothers would want to bring their 13- and 14-year-old daughters to absorb. The song received a tepid, uncertain response from the audience, along with plaintive calls of "We want Davey," a complaint that would increase.

Hendrix forged on with eight more tunes, the final one a version of "Wild Thing" that is unlikely ever to be topped. The song had been written just two years earlier by a writer who called himself Chip Taylor, although his real name was James Voight, brother of the actor, Jon. The song was first recorded by The Wild Ones, a New York band that lasted only a couple of years. In 1966 it became a number-one hit for a British rock band called The Troggs. Hendrix liked it enough to make it his own. He closed with it at Monterey, then set his guitar on fire and beat it into shreds that he tossed to the audience. A photo of Hendrix and that flaming guitar made the cover of *Rolling Stone*.

On this night he swept through the tune playing the guitar in every way it could be manipulated, switching early on from his left hand to his teeth, creating sounds I didn't know a guitar could make and causing me to wonder how many teeth he still could call his own. Shifting from his teeth, he played his abused Fender Stratocaster upside-down and backwards, over his head, behind his back, between his legs. He even got down on the floor and plucked it with his toes. At one point, back on his feet, he appeared to be having sex with it. As he neared climax, he began swinging his instrument in the air, slammed it to the floor and jumped up and down on it. He seemed upset that he wasn't inflicting enough damage, and as his fellow band members continued playing furiously, he picked up the guitar by its neck, swung it around knocking down microphone stands and began beating it on the floor until pieces started flying. He didn't set it on fire, perhaps because it might have gotten him arrested in Greensboro, because flames weren't allowed in coliseum performances.

Hendrix strutted off stage sweating profusely. The audience seemed stunned, uncertain how to respond. As he passed our group of applauding and smiling admirers, he muttered, "Let 'em fuckin' little Monkees top that!"

I didn't know it at the time, but Hendrix didn't hold in high regard the stars for whom he was opening. He had publicly called their music "dishwater," although later reports would indicate that he got along with them well enough on a personal basis.

The young woman who had brought me backstage told me that we needed to give him a little time to catch his breath and cool down before talking with him. When we got to the dressing room, his bandmates were half dressed and opening bottles of Champale. Hendrix had removed his frilly shirt and psychedelic jacket and was sitting on a folding metal chair with a mangy, hip-length mink coat draped around his shoulders.

He neither stood for our introduction nor offered a handshake. I took a folding chair a few feet across from him, reporter's notebook and ballpoint pen in hand. Knowing nothing about him, I wasn't certain where to begin. I often started interviews by noting something I observed or was wondering about, hoping to establish some personal contact.

"Where'd you get the fur coat?" I asked.

"Some little old lady," he said.

That didn't get me far.

I couldn't help but notice that his knees had burst through both legs of his tight, black velvet pants, so I stuck to the garment theme onto which I'd grasped.

"Does that happen often?" I asked, pointing to his exposed knees.

"Just every damn performance," he said.

I was getting the feeling that he didn't think much of my feeble questions and had little interest in continuing this conversation.

"Well, that was a hell of a performance," I told him. "I've never seen anything like it. Was that typical?"

By this time, his manager, Chas Chandler, whom I'd met earlier, had pulled up a chair with us.

"We have to consider the age range of the audience," Chandler interjected, hoping, I suspected, to keep his star from saying something inappropriate.

"Yeah," said Hendrix, grinning, "we toned it down a lot."

'I'm not sure I'd want to see what a performance you didn't tone down might do to your britches," I said, and he laughed.

I'd broken through.

I asked when he started playing guitar. He was 15, living with his daddy in Seattle, he said. He bought a cheap acoustic guitar and dedicated himself to learning to play it. It didn't take him long to realize that he was better suited to the more vibrant and far louder electric version. From the time he got that first guitar he'd played every moment he could, he said, except for four miserable months when he'd been totally deprived while undergoing basic and advanced infantry training at Ft. Ord, California.

That shocked me. I couldn't quite picture him as a soldier toting an M1 instead of an electric guitar.

"When were you in the Army?" I asked.

"I went in on the last day of May, 1961. It wasn't exactly my intention."

A judge, it turned out, had given him the choice of jail or the Army and he had foolishly taken the wrong option. He was 19 at the time and known as James Marshall Hendrix. After Ft. Ord, he was stationed at Ft. Campbell, Kentucky, home of the 101st Airborne, where he was a supply clerk in a maintenance battalion. I told him I'd been in the Army at the same time, but in Okinawa.

"How did you get along in that situation?" I asked.

"Not good," he said. "I hated every fuckin' minute of it."

"Well, we've got that much in common," I told him.

The first thing he did after arriving at Ft. Campbell was call his girlfriend in Seattle and ask her to ship him the guitar he'd left with her. He turned out to be more devoted to the guitar than to her. He was practicing at a service club on base when he met a fellow soldier, Billy Cox, a bass guitarist from West Virginia. They began playing in bars and clubs in towns near Ft. Campbell, causing Hendrix to miss bed check enough to get reduced in rank to Private E-1, the lowest grade. He never rose again above that rank because he had other problems as well—sleeping on the job, for one—and was honorably discharged after only 13 months, nearly two years short of his enlistment.

"How did you manage that?" I asked.

"They just didn't want to have to deal with me anymore. They said I was unsuitable and they were right."

"You got out of the Army by being unsuitable? Why didn't somebody tell me that was possible?"

"Maybe you just weren't unsuitable enough," he said.

After his discharge, intent on making a living playing music, he went to Nashville, which was only 50 miles away.

"You didn't play country, did you?" I asked with obvious incredulity.

He laughed. "No, man. I played the Chitlin' Circuit, R&B, black clubs."

After Billy Cox got his discharge, they played together, and for a while they lived in Clarksville, the town the Monkees were singing about in their big hit, only about 10 miles from Ft. Campbell, which straddles the Tennessee-Kentucky border.

After a year and a half on the Chitlin' Circuit, Hendrix left Cox behind and moved to Harlem, where he played that club circuit as well as the Apollo Theater before landing jobs with the bands of the Isley Brothers, Sam Cooke, Wilson Pickett and Little Richard, among others. After getting fired by Little Richard's manager for supposedly upstaging his boss, which might seem impossible, he returned to New York and began playing at the Cafe Wha? in Greenwich Village, where Bob Dylan and Bruce Springsteen also appeared. But it was at another club where the girlfriend of Keith Richards saw him and was so impressed that she told Chandler about him. Now Chandler was leading him down the road to super stardom.

The interview had gone on for about 20 minutes at this point, and I could tell that Hendrix wanted to get on to other interests. By this time the Monkees were into their act and the speakers and screaming of the teenyboppers were drowning us out. I thanked him and returned to the audience to suffer out my assignment.

Hendrix remained with the Monkees for only four more days and three more shows. All of those concerts were at Forest Hills Stadium in New York, after which he never again had to hear "We want Davey" when he started playing. Some reports claimed that at the third show he gave the audience a middle finger before stalking off the stage after "Wild Thing." That could be apocryphal but I suspect it was true.

He would go on to become the super star I was promised he'd be. Just three years and two months after my conversation with him, he died in a London hotel at 27, choking on vomit after a night of swilling a mixture of red wine and ale and topping it off with a handful of his girlfriend's sleeping pills. He would become an even bigger star after his death. It would be a long time before I realized that my encounter with him was the equivalent of getting to interview Elvis when he appeared in the auditorium of Main Street School in Thomasville, just a block from my house, on September 17, 1955, when I was starting the eighth grade there, although I was unaware of him or his music then, as were most people. Still, I can always truthfully claim that I appeared on the same stage as Elvis because I had a minor role in a fifth grade play there without speaking a word.

ON A WEEKEND IN September, Linda and I drove to Augusta, Georgia, to visit another Jimmy who was more conventional in spelling his name. That was Jimmy Jarrett, an old high school buddy. Our destination was Ft. Gordon, just southwest of Augusta, home of the Signal Corps. It would be my first visit to a military base since my discharge nearly five years earlier and I wasn't really looking forward to it, partly because our visit was to be at the post hospital.

I had been surprised the previous December when Jarrett saw my name and picture in the newspaper and called me. I hadn't heard from him in seven and a half years. We got together for a great visit, catching up, joking, laughing, sipping rum punch. Jarrett was one of the smarter people I'd known in high school and had a great sense of humor. We immediately began recalling our time in Lydia Stronach's second-year Latin class where we had so much fun, primarily because Miss Stronach, who was well into her 60s, appeared to still be abiding in Rome in the reign of Julius Caesar and seemed utterly unaware of our antics and disruptions.

Unlike me, Jarrett had gone to college, gotten his degree, and was thinking of becoming a high school history teacher when the government cut short that plan by drafting him. In basic training, like me, he had been offered the opportunity to attend OCS and become an officer, and much to his later regret he accepted it, causing his two years in the Army to be expanded to three. He eventually was promoted to first lieutenant and became commanding officer of a rag-tag company at the Army Language School at the Presidio in Monterey, California. San Francisco, the wine country and Big Sur were within easy reach on weekends. He met a nurse named Heidi, and they were planning to marry. He had only eight months left to serve when the Army upset not only those plans but the rest of his life. It was sending him to Vietnam as a Christmas present. He had come home to see his parents before he left.

In a few days my friend would be in the middle of a war, leading a 54-man reconnaissance platoon for an infantry brigade. He'd be the guy out front, hunting the enemy. Being a reporter, I felt obligated to ask a question for which the answer was obvious.

Was he afraid?

"You must be kidding," he said.

It was hard to picture this gentle and funny Latin-class cut-up leading 54 men he hadn't yet met into combat.

"It's them I worry about," he told me.

Over the three years that he had been in office, President Lyndon Johnson had radically escalated the war in Vietnam. By the time Jarrett arrived, 385,000 U.S. service members were assigned there, with another 60,000 offshore on Navy vessels. More than 6,000 Americans had been killed in 1966 alone, with another 30,000 wounded. The odds of becoming a casualty were high for infantry platoon leaders, especially for those in reconnaissance platoons, poking relentlessly into enemy territory.

The hospital at Ft. Gordon was a dreary concentration of long and narrow World War II era single-story wooden buildings painted white and spreading in a myriad of angular directions, resembling one of those cornfield mazes that later would become popular in the South and Midwest. Ward A-24 was our destination, somewhere near the center of the maze. It was an orthopedics ward for officers, one of nine regimentally like it, all of them filled with company commanders, platoon leaders and helicopter pilots from Vietnam. A small day room was at one end of the ward. It offered the distractions of paperback books and a large screen TV. A young man in blue army pajamas and both legs in casts leaned on crutches watching a baseball game. Nearby, another officer with one leg missing, his pajama leg neatly folded and pinned, lay on his stomach on a sofa, paying marginal attention to the ball game.

On the right side of the ward leading from the day room was a row of tiny rooms, each barely big enough for a hospital bed. These were for patients recovering from surgery or with open infected wounds. In the first room was a patient just out of surgery. One leg was in a cast from waist to knee, the other, also in a cast, was in a grotesque position that made it impossible for him to move. Just down the hall, we'd see a captain with both legs and one arm gone.

My friend Jimmy was in the second room. He was so gaunt that I barely recognized him. He'd lost more than 30 pounds but still had both arms and one good leg. The other leg, his right one, was mush from knee to ankle, deeply infected, the pain so great that it made his whole body quiver. He'd been in this condition for two months, and only in recent days had the fevers begun to subside. The date for his discharge had come and gone six weeks earlier, and doctors couldn't give him an estimate when he might be well enough to leave the hospital and the Army—could be six months, maybe a year.

Despite all of this, his sense of humor remained intact, and he still was able to joke and laugh, even as he winced in pain.

Jarrett had been sent to the Mekong Delta as soon as he arrived in Vietnam a week before Christmas. He had spent seven months fighting the heat, muck and mosquitoes, chasing Viet Cong who rarely stood and fought. He led patrols every day through jungle, rice paddies, murky streams, saw men lost to snipers and booby traps, set up ambushes every night. On June 20, he, three other officers, and several enlisted men in his platoon piled into a helicopter to check out an area they were about to enter. They were drawing small arms fire, but as the helicopter set down and the men began piling out, explosions began.

Jarrett thought they were being mortared. As he ran, an explosion sent him airborne and he remembered seeing his foot hit him in the face. He landed bleeding, feeling as if he were on fire and began crawling toward a dike, dragging his right leg. When he reached the dike, he took off his shirt to try to stop the gushing blood, then used his belt as a tourniquet. The men who had been in the helicopter lay all around him. Two officers were dead. He, seven others, and a dog were seriously wounded. The helicopter was knocked out.

Medevac Hueys soon arrived to haul away the dead and wounded. Only later did the survivors learn that the shells falling around them were U.S. Army artillery shells. An officer in a spotter plane called in wrong coordinates. "The cruelest joke of all," as Jarrett called it. He had been the person closest to the shell that did most of the damage, only 15 feet away, and was amazed that he had survived.

"I'm the luckiest guy alive," he told us.

This had happened just one week before he was to be pulled out of the field and brought back to Saigon, where he would prepare for his return home and his discharge from the Army. At first he was bitter about it, he said, but he realized he had to let that go and face life one day at a time. The doctors had told him that if the infection could be controlled they might be able to save his leg, but he'd still have to wear a brace.

He glanced at the leg with its bulky cast, made a face, and laughed.

"And I had wanted to run in the Olympics," he said.

I left that hospital realizing that if I had been able to go to college and had done so, I might at this moment be in the same shape, or worse, than my buddy. It was all a matter of timing. That war was just beginning when I got out of the Army and it started building rapidly when Jarrett finished college facing the draft, evidence, I suppose, that sometimes a failure to gain formal education pays. I left, too, with a new sense of futility about the war. Just two months earlier, I had reported about the first public protest in Greensboro prompted by the war. Thirty-two members of the American Friends Service Committee gathered on a downtown corner for a silent peace vigil. Now I had a better, more personal idea of their purpose, and I had little doubt that the anti-war movement soon would grow much bigger.

It would be a long time before I could put the Vietnam War behind me, because my youngest brother, Phil, eventually would take part in it on an aircraft carrier off the coast, but another unexpected event soon would bring important change to my life.

17

In November, 1967, four months after "Meandering Me" was introduced, I was allowed to begin writing two columns weekly, adding Thursday to my Saturday schedule, although "Me" got dropped from the title. I was greatly pleased by this, because it meant that Irwin Smallwood and Chuck Hauser approved of what I was doing, even if Monkees lovers didn't. But I also had to continue turning out general assignment stories. One of those would have a big effect on my future.

On Thursday, December 7, the Greensboro Chamber of Commerce held its 90th annual dinner, the biggest ever, attended by more than 2,000 guests, at the coliseum because no other place could handle feeding so many people. Joe Hunt, chairman of the State Highway Commission, was to receive the Distinguished Citizen Award, perhaps for his willingness to dedicate beautification projects that didn't yet exist and eat the indiscernible to impress garden club ladies.

Celebrities also were to be on hand, and a reception was held at the Statler-Hilton Inn for specially invited guests before dinner. A press pass allowed me to attend the reception to write about the celebrities. They included the actor Sidney Blackmer from Salisbury, who had won a Tony for best actor in the William Inge play *Come Back, Little Sheba* on Broadway in 1950, and had appeared in more than 100 films. He was wearing dark glasses and was surrounded by so many people that I didn't get a chance to talk with him. Also present was Mickey Spillane, the so-called "hard-boiled" crime novelist who created Detective Mike Hammer, with whom I spoke only briefly but later would get to know.

This night, I focused on two dead famous men who were being honored. More precisely, I concentrated on their wives, both of whom were present. Those men were Carl Sandburg, the peoples' poet, and Edward R. Murrow, the CBS broadcaster who became famous for his radio broadcasts from London during World War II and later was named director of the U.S. Information Agency by

JFK. Murrow had interviewed Sandburg on his *See It Now* show on CBS in October, 1955, during which Sandburg played his guitar and sang the Southern folk song "Goober Peas." The two men and their wives became friends.

Murrow, who smoked even in televised interviews, had died of lung cancer two years and seven months earlier, two days after his 58th birthday. He had been born near Polecat Creek in Guilford County south of Greensboro, but his family moved to the timberlands of Washington when he was five. He had many relatives in Guilford County and came to visit them when he had a chance. It was one such visit that brought a major development to his life.

I got to chat briefly with Mrs. Murrow, whose maiden name was Janet Brewster. She told me she was happy to be in Greensboro because this was where she first laid eyes on Ed. It was 35 years ago almost to this date in 1932, she said. She was a senior in college on a train making her first trip south of Washington and had been asleep.

"When I awoke it was about 6:30 in the morning and the train had stopped in Greensboro. I raised my blind. It was a dreary morning and there was only one person standing on the station platform. It was Ed Murrow."

Murrow, who had graduated from Washington State University in 1930, had become president of the National Student Federation and had been on his way to Atlanta to preside over a conference, but stopped off in Greensboro to visit relatives. Brewster was a member of that group as well, and on her way to the same conference. They met on the train and married two years and three months later.

On the following day, Mrs. Murrow would be attending the dedication of a new, four-lane boulevard, only a half-mile long, which was to be named for her husband.

Carl Sandburg had no connection to Greensboro, but he had been one of North Carolina's most famous citizens for 22 years, and had died four months earlier at 89 at his home in Flat Rock, south of Asheville. That and his remarkable career, which brought him three Pulitzer Prizes and great fame, was why the Chamber wanted to honor him. It had hired an artist to sculpt a bust. His wife, Paula, was to accept it at the dinner. She also was supposed to be at the reception, but I kept trying to find her without luck.

Most of those present, like myself, had no idea what she looked like. Finally, a buzz started in one section of the room and I heard somebody say, "That's Mrs. Sandburg." At 84, she was tiny, slightly stooped, with a kind face and blue eyes that smiled through thick glasses. Her white hair was wiry and unruly, stretched into a small bun at the nape of her neck. A Chamber person rushed to greet her and guided her to a reserved empty table near the bar.

I quickly made my way to the table, introduced myself and was invited to join her. A waiter appeared, carrying a glass of ginger ale and a small saucer of snacks. She sipped the ginger ale, apologizing for being late. She was napping, she said, and overslept.

She was very happy that people in Greensboro wanted to honor her husband, she told me. He loved North Carolina, she said, especially their home at Flat Rock.

A small crowd had gathered around us, leaning in to hear her, and somebody interrupted to ask about her goats. I didn't know she had goats. She seemed delighted by the query and said she had sold the entire herd after her husband died because it had become too much for her to handle. The conversation ended quickly with the announcement that the guests needed to proceed to the coliseum for dinner, and Mrs. Sandburg was whisked away.

At the dedication ceremony for Murrow Boulevard the following morning, the speakers barely could be heard because of roaring buses and trucks and the relentless rumble of a long freight train passing nearby. After the ceremony, Mrs. Sandburg spotted me and came over to say hello. Again she was apologetic. She was concerned that she might have made a bad impression at the dinner. She had been so moved by the presentation of the bust, which looked so much like her husband, she said, that she had difficulty responding.

"All those people there and I just couldn't say much. I don't know what I said. I think I said, 'I just can't talk.'"

I assured her that she had been fine.

"Do you know who's supposed to take me home?" she asked.

"No," I told her, "but I'll try to find out."

I asked the driver who had brought her. His job was to take her back to the hotel, he said, and he didn't know how she was to get back to Flat Rock. I asked several others, even the mayor, but nobody knew. Mrs. Sandburg looked forlorn when I informed her.

"What am I supposed to do?" she asked.

"I'll take you home," I said.

"Oh, that's so sweet of you."

Her driver was ready to deliver her back to the hotel.

"You go ahead and get your bags, and I'll pick you up," I told her.

I rushed back to the newsroom, told Irwin Smallwood that I was going to take Mrs. Sandburg home and needed a staff car. I was certain I'd get a great story from it. He gave his approval. I called Linda to tell her that I'd need a change of clothing and some overnight toiletries.

The trip to Flat Rock stretched out for nearly five hours, and during that time I got a deeply personalized summary of Carl Sandburg's life and career.

"He was a newspaperman, you know," she told me early on. "I wish you could have met him."

Mr. Sandburg, as she frequently called him, had been born in Galesburg,

Illinois, one of seven children of Swedish immigrants. He had to leave school after eighth grade to help support his family, and later became a hobo riding freight trains around the west. At 20, he volunteered to serve in the Spanish-American War and was stationed in Puerto Rico without seeing battle. He returned to Galesburg and enrolled at Lombard College, but left without receiving a degree. After an appointment to West Point was throttled because he failed entrance exams in math and grammar, he began writing for the local newspaper, and in 1902 his first published poem, "The Thistle," appeared in a college literary magazine.

He was working as an organizer for the Social-Democratic Party of Wisconsin in 1907, when Lillian Steichen met him at party headquarters in Milwaukee. She was a Michigan native, the daughter of immigrants from Luxembourg, a Phi-Beta Kappa graduate of the University of Chicago. She had been teaching high school for four years. Her older brother, Edward, a year younger than Sandburg, already was on his way to becoming a world-renowned photographer and artist. She and Sandburg began writing to one another and the relationship became romantic. They married in 1908. Sandburg began calling her Paula, a name she would adopt.

After his marriage, Sandburg worked as an advertising copy writer and reporter in Milwaukee before becoming secretary to Milwaukee's Socialist mayor, a position he'd hold for two years. The Sandburgs' first child, Margaret, was born in 1911. They lost a daughter, Madeline, at birth two years later. Two more daughters would complete their family, Janet in 1916, Helga in 1918.

In 1912, the Sandburgs moved to Chicago where he wrote for various publications over the next four years, including newly created *Poetry* magazine. His book *Chicago Poems* would be published in 1916, setting him on his march to fame at age 38. The following year he became a reporter for *The Chicago Daily News*, a newspaper where he would work for the next 16 years.

The family moved to Elmhurst, a Chicago suburb. During the nine years they lived there, Sandburg published *Rootabaga Stories* that he had written for his daughters, as well as the first two volumes of his biography of Abraham Lincoln. In 1928, the family moved into a house that Paula Sandburg designed on the dunes of Lake Michigan near her hometown of Harbart. They would live there until 1945 when the harsh winters drove them southward, looking for a warmer place and greener pastures for Mrs. Sandburg's champion goats.

They would find their new home on a 243-acre farm at Flat Rock. It was called Connemara. The big white house was imposing. It had been built on the side of Big Glassy Mountain, completed in 1839, as the summer home of Christopher Memminger, a Charleston lawyer and politician who became the first Secretary of the Treasury of the Confederacy. It had three stories and a spacious front porch with small white columns and an impressive stairway.

Mrs. Sandburg recalled the first time she and her husband climbed that stairway. He leaned against the porch railing taking in the magnificent view of the mountains to the west.

"This is the place," he told her. "We will look no further."

Years afterward, she told me, they would sit on that porch and he would spread his arms wide and say, "Look at all the sky we bought."

Darkness was settling when we turned off Little River Road up the long driveway lined by 100-year-old white pines, hemlocks, spruces and rhododendron. Mrs. Sandburg was clearly tired. We had talked most of the way and she had promised me that she would devote the entire next day to telling me more and showing me the home she loved but soon would be leaving.

At 8 a.m., I joined Mrs. Sandburg and two of her daughters, Margaret and Janet, who lived with her, for a breakfast of coffee, toast, jam and grapefruit halves. Her granddaughter, Paula, daughter of Helga, an accomplished writer who now lived with her third husband in Cleveland, had been staying with her grandmother since her grandfather's death, but was not yet up to join us. Helga and her two children, Paula and John Carl, had lived for eight years with her parents when they first moved to Flat Rock, and Paula was finishing a book about the Connemara years. The dining room had a row of broad windows without curtains where dozens of birds of many varieties chattered and hopped about on a huge, freshly filled feeder where peanut butter was the most popular treat. This was a foggy, misty morning, with rain predicted for the afternoon, and Mrs. Sandburg suggested we might want to do our outdoor exploring first.

That trek began at the big red barn which had housed the goats for so many years. At one time the herd, which she called Chikaming, had numbered more than 200, including Nubians, Toggenburgs and Saanens, but it was down to only 60 when she sold it in September. There was a real sense of loneliness about the barn, which long had been such an active place, and I could tell it affected her. The prize-winning herd hadn't been just a business but a primary focus of her life, leading her to become a nationally known breeder and authority in the field.

Her youngest daughter was responsible for leading her to that situation. As a child, Helga began begging her daddy to get a cow.

"'Why do you want a big old cow?' he said. 'Why not a nice little goat?' First we bought two, then we bought two more when he said, 'Why not get four, enough for our own butter?'"

Later, she would show me a photo of Sandburg with those first two goats.

"He loved the kids. That was the reason, too, why we always brought the kids to the house," she said before switching to present tense without realizing it, I suspected. "As soon as they are born, if Mr. Sandburg is awake, I bring the kids to him, because he wants to see what color they are. He was always interested in seeing them when they are tiny. We'd bring them in the dining room. By that time, they'd hop up in the air and kind of dance around."

Laughing, she held out her arms and twirled in imitation. "As cute as they could be. He loved to see that. So while he was eating dinner, I'd bring the kids in and they would play around the dining room. He was always close to them from the time they were born."

After inspecting the barn and the dairy building from which Mrs. Sandburg had sold milk over a wide area in two states, we headed upward behind the house to a big clearing, where the mountain exposed its rocky gray innards, now carpeted with moss, lichens and pine needles. A chair typical of the mountains, constructed of saplings, was there. It had wide arms and a rounded back. A similar little table sat beside it. When the weather was nice, Sandburg often could be found at this spot with pads and pencils. He had written much of his autobiography, *Always the Young Strangers*, here.

"Nobody but the dogs came near him," she said.

From this spot, we took a trail to the top of Big Glassy so that I could sense the scope of Connemara and take in the magnificent view. This hike would turn out to be nearly three miles, up and back. Only one spot was steep enough to provoke heavy breathing, but it didn't slow Mrs. Sandburg much. She was disappointed when we reached the top because fog and low-hanging clouds obscured most of the view.

Just a couple of months earlier, Mrs. Sandburg had made this same climb with U.S. Secretary of the Interior Stewart Udall and his entourage. It was a sunny day and the view was magnificent, she said. The purpose of that visit was to assess the property so that the National Park Service could fulfill Mrs. Sandburg's desire to turn it into a historic site. Udall was delighted with the plan. A bill already had been introduced in Congress. There was no doubt that it would pass, and President Lyndon Johnson already had acknowledged that he would sign it.

"It will make a great park for the people," she told me with a glow on her face.

By the time we got back down the mountain, the rain had begun, and we hurried inside to warm ourselves with bowls of soup. Afterward we began our interior tour in her business office just off the dining room. The walls were lined with family photos and red and blue ribbons awarded to her goats. Photos of her husband were throughout the house, many by her famous brother.

In the living room, Sandburg's guitar lay in a case atop the piano. He loved strumming it, and for many years had performed with it before audiences, especially when he was working on his extensive collection of folk songs, *The American Songbook*, published in 1927. Some considered him America's original nationally recognized folk singer.

In the front study, an array of yellow, fan-shaped Ginkgo tree leaves were spread across a desk top.

"Mr. Sandburg always used to pick up some of them to keep for the winter. He really loved to pick little things. Now not all men feel like picking a few flowers, but he was always picking. You see different things around here, you'd think it would be maybe one of our kids that did it but he always brought things in."

I was impressed with the number of books in the house. Nearly every room had bookshelves jammed tight. When I commented about it, Mrs. Sandburg smiled and said I hadn't seen anything yet. She led me to the basement, where one large section had been set aside with row after row of double-sided bookshelves, all heavily loaded. These clearly were books that had been read and used. Many bristled with bookmarks and some were not in the best condition.

Mrs. Sandburg saw that I'd taken note of that.

"When we used to go from Elmhurst to Chicago, he tore books up," she said. "People said that was terrible, a man who loved books so much. He'd actually tear the book up so that he'd take a small section with him and put it in his pocket, and he'd read it. That's the way he got his reading done.

"He didn't want to carry a great big book into town. He was a reporter. He had to have some little thing that was inconspicuous. So many people said it was very peculiar that a man who loved books, you know, there'd be so many of his books that were all torn up.

"The main thing is to get what's in the book into your head. There are some people that really a library is something to show off. And there are wealthy people who have beautiful libraries, all the best editions and everything, hardly ever look at any of them. Carl had just the opposite idea. With Carl a book was something to read, not something to look at. And if he had to tear it to pieces to read it, he would do it."

Sandburg's bedroom and adjoining work room were on the top floor of the house on the west side.

"'You can't sell me an eastern exposure,' he said," Mrs. Sandburg recalled.

That was because he often worked through the night and didn't want the morning sun disturbing him. She never knew when he might be getting up, she said, so she always brought his breakfast—fruit and a Thermos of coffee—on a tray and left it outside his door.

Both of these rooms were just as he had left them. In the bedroom, part of Sandburg's collection of handmade walking sticks rested against the window sill. Books he treasured were crammed in shelves floor to ceiling. On a bedside table were more books, magazines, a Regency beer can filled with sharpened pencils, a small figure of a hippopotamus, packs of Chiclets, a box of Havana cigars, a blue muffler, and a tin can filled with buckeyes from a tree up the mountain.

"Oh, he loved the buckeyes," Mrs. Sandburg said. "We'd stop along there, and there usually weren't many of them lying there, you know. We'd look just a little. He'd fill his pockets full of buckeyes."

Buckeyes had been talismans of good fortune of many types for many cultures over centuries, she noted, and her husband held them in the same regard.

Sandburg called the adjoining room where he worked "a dizzy corner, kind of a crazy corner, because I don't pretend it's organized."

Although the room was chilly, a Dixie Flyer woodstove with a dent in its side had provided heat for it while Sandburg worked. The typewriter on which he had written so much had developed problems and been temporarily replaced by a portable on a small table. Next to it an upended wooden orange crate served as a work bench.

"He said it's just a handy size," she said of the crate. "When we had our first home we had one of those."

Notes in Sandburg's heavy-handed, unreadable scrawl were pinned on a board. Cigar boxes were stuffed with reference materials. Cardboard boxes that had borne cans of pork-and-beans, cranberry sauce and green peas were filled with articles, photos, jokes, poems, comic strips (mainly *Pogo*, his favorite), and whatever else had attracted his attention that he considered worth saving. Old, unrecognizable machinery parts served as weights for papers that hadn't yet made it to refuge in the boxes.

"He preferred something like that to something fancy," Mrs. Sandburg said. "He was always interested in machinery. He knew nothing about machinery but he was always interested. He'd be in a factory, you know, he'd see something like that where they were lying around. He'd say, 'Do you need these things?'"

I lingered in this room where he had written so much, examining its contents, perhaps hoping to absorb some of the energy and creativity that might still be lurking there.

"I really do like to come up here and sit," she said. "I feel closer to him here."

After he had suffered a heart attack, developed other problems, grown weaker and become bedridden he occupied her big bedroom at the front of the house on the main floor. When we left his work room and started down the stairway, Mrs. Sandburg suddenly stopped.

"One of the last things he tried to do, he tried to walk up these stairs one day," she said, her voice quavering. For a long moment she was unable to go on. I realized that she was seeing him there at the foot of the stairs, weak and pulling at the railing, struggling to get back to his work.

In a whisper, she said, "He couldn't make it."

Later, at the dining room table, with her granddaughter present, she began to recall his last days. By this time she had grown hoarse from talking so much.

"He always had a feeling that...I think, that's why at the last, when he couldn't anymore, when he couldn't even, you know, take solid food, it was... he really had some bad weeks there, and that's the reason I was so resigned to his death, because to prolong that, to have more of that was..." She paused.

"I didn't expect him to die though. I spoke to him at one o'clock in the morning. I came into his room, you know, and I bent over his bed there, and you see we had a nurse staying right with him, and he looked at me and said, 'Paula.' You know, he was so happy to see me. I said, 'Now you'll want to sleep, won't you,' and then he fell back.

"And the nurse, you know, said that from then on he began breathing less, not such a vigorous breath, and so she was worried about him. Wasn't anything she could do about it though. Then another nurse came on in the morning, and the other nurse said she noticed it too, that he wasn't breathing so deeply. So they called the doctor and then the doctor came. He said, 'Well, there's nothing we can do.' And they were trying to give him artificial respiration. He said, 'There's no use in that,' because he felt, you know, his heart had stopped.

"Really, the tears that I shed were before that when he wasn't able really to enjoy life anymore. I was only thankful that it was an easy passing. You know, that he just breathed away. Everything had been very, you know...death is always difficult, but to have it come this way, so easily, just breathing away.

"He used to joke about his going to, you know, how long he was going to live and all that. But he wasn't frightened of death. Any man that has written all the poems he did about death—'Finish,' you know, let it come easy, and not too much ceremony either, he said."

She laughed.

"He had written many poems about it. He knew he left enough behind him that he was really here when he was gone.

"I think of everything about him. But it doesn't make me feel sad. I think really, if he had died in a different way, if he had been suddenly cut down, that would have been different. But he suffered so much I'm just glad that he's dead, that's all I can say. I would hate to think that he had to keep on living. I know how he suffered there for those days, so I just think that it's wonderful that he's relieved from it, that that's over and he didn't suffer any more. And he's left himself. If anyone ever left himself still here on earth, it's he with his books. Especially to me with his poetry.

"He seems, I don't know, there's something about a man like my husband that put so much of himself into everything, that I really don't feel lonely. I just feel as though—and I don't have any superstitions about it—I know that he's gone, but at the same time his spirit is with us, and he's going to live for America hundreds of years. There are many people who are going to feel he's still around, you know, a man who has put himself the way he has into books. He's really going to be around all the time. And there's so much of himself here."

The following morning, Mrs. Sandburg gave me a copy of *Life* magazine's February 21, 1938 edition with her husband's portrait on the cover, cigar in hand. On page 43, she had signed and dated a photo of the two of them looking out a window at their Michigan home. As I was preparing to leave, she asked me to walk down the long driveway with her.

"Normally, I don't talk much," she said, her voice still hoarse. "But when the subject is my husband, then naturally I am voluble. We had a wonderful life together, so it's all been good."

When we reached Little River Road we stood looking up the mountain at the house. The moment they first turned into this driveway, she said, she knew this was where she was supposed to be.

"This is what I fell in love with," she said. "This is really where my heart is...look at that stonework and the ivy growing on it. We put in these small hemlocks...."

When she came up with the idea of turning Connemara into a historic site, she said, she thought that she and her daughters would move back to Michigan.

"When I began to think of going away, I thought who wants to go away from so lovely a place?"

A year from now this no longer would be her home, and she was planning to begin looking for a furnished place in Asheville, a city her famous brother favored.

"It'll be sort of a slower breaking away," she said.

It also would allow her to see how the National Park Service was handling the transformation.

"I won't be spying on them," she said, "but I want to see how it's run. And then when we feel lonesome for this place—you know, we have so many ties to it—we won't have any trouble getting here. I decided this was the best place for Carl to live out his years, and I think this may be the best place for me to live out my years too."

When we got back to the house, Mrs. Sandburg's granddaughter pulled me aside and thanked me for my visit. This was the first time her grandmother had opened up about her grandfather's death, she said, and she thought it was going to be good for her.

When we said our goodbyes and I hugged Mrs. Sandburg, she slipped a buckeye into my hand.

After Mrs. Sandburg and her daughters settled in Asheville, nearly six years passed before the home she loved was opened as a national historic site in May, 1974. By then she was too ill to attend. She died February 18, 1977, at 94. Her ashes were placed with her husband's at Remembrance Rock at his birthplace in Galesburg, Illinois.

I spent several weeks working on my story about my visit with Mrs. Sandburg. When I finished I thought it probably was the best thing I had written so far. It, along with beautiful photographs taken by Larry Tucker, took up the entire front of the "Cavalcade" section and much of an inside page on Sunday, January 21, 1968. "The Final Winter at Connemara" it was called.

After the story appeared, I typed up a copy and sent it to *The Atlanta Journal-Constitution Magazine*. Five days later I got a call from the editor, George Hatcher. He wanted to use the piece, he said, but he also had another matter to talk about. The magazine had an opening for a writer. Would I be interested? I would, I told him.

The following week I took a day off and drove to Atlanta. I was impressed with Hatcher. We talked for nearly an hour. One of the magazine's writers, Andrew Sparks, who later would become editor, took me to lunch with his wife, Olive Ann Burns, who also had been a writer and columnist for the magazine, but now was free-lancing. She later would write a bestselling novel, *Cold Sassy Tree*. They told me that Margaret Mitchell, author of *Gone with the Wind*, also had worked at the magazine in the 1920s, although she had been known as Peggy then. They also convinced me that this was an opportunity I shouldn't turn down. Before I left, Hatcher told me the job was mine if I wanted it. I told him I'd think about it and call him back.

When I got home and discussed this with Linda, she said she would have no problem with the move if that was what I wanted. Although I had enjoyed my time in New York and Tokyo, I wasn't sure that I wanted to live in a big city. But this would remove me from the daily stress of news coverage, allow me to concentrate on writing, and provide me a much wider audience. I called Hatcher and accepted the job. We set a starting date for a month hence, giving me time to serve my notice and hopefully to find a pleasant place to live.

I dreaded having to tell Irwin Smallwood about this. He had done so much for me. I held him in high esteem and had deep affection for him. The same was true for Chuck Hauser. Smallwood seemed taken aback when I built up courage enough to give my notice.

"What would it take to keep you here?" he asked.

I told him my starting date already was set and I was looking forward to the challenges.

"What if I made you full-time columnist?" he asked.

Now I was the one taken aback.

"I'd have to think about that," I said.

"Why don't you do that?"

This was quite a dilemma. My dream of becoming a full-time columnist could now be real. Yet writing longer and fewer pieces for a much wider audience was enticing.

After a couple of days of struggle, I called Hatcher, explained the situation, and told him I'd changed my mind. He was understanding. He still would be happy to publish any pieces I sent him that were appropriate for the magazine, he said. I could have it both ways.

But as I started my expanded job as columnist, supposedly freed from having to cover whatever news events might pop up, I couldn't have imagined that I soon would be back in the streets during the darkest hours of the civil rights movement.

18

The concerns that B. Elton Cox expressed about the black power movement—that it was another form of racism that likely would stir anger and lead to violence—didn't take long to materialize. The arrest of black power leader Stokely Carmichael for inciting a riot in Atlanta in September, 1966, sparked growth of the movement, and the year to come would see racial uprisings producing devastation and death in numerous American cities.

The month of July, 1967, brought a rash of rioting, hitting cities including Durham, just 54 miles from Greensboro; Cairo, Illinois; Cambridge, Maryland; as well as larger cities, Cincinnati, Milwaukee, Minneapolis, and Memphis. The worst of these took place in Newark and Detroit.

The Newark looting and burning began on July 12, after a black taxi driver was stopped on a traffic violation, engaged in a scuffle with police and was hauled to a precinct house. A crowd gathered outside and exploded into violence when a false rumor spread that the taxi driver had died. The mob began attacking the precinct station and police officers. The upheaval continued for five days, leaving 26 dead, more than 700 injured, 1,500 arrested, and millions in damages to businesses looted and burned.

The Detroit riots began a week after the eruptions in Newark were quelled, when police raided an unlicensed bar in a black neighborhood. These riots, too, continued for five days, leaving 43 dead and nearly 1,200 injured. Two thousand buildings were destroyed, and more than 7,000 arrests occurred. President Lyndon Johnson had to send in Army troops to back up the National Guard before the violence was contained.

As similar disturbances continued to spread, I figured the odds were good that I'd be caught in one. That happened on November 2, 1967, in Winston–Salem, 20 miles from Greensboro.

On the morning of October 15, two white police officers had attempted to arrest a 32-year-old black man, James Eller, for public drunkenness. Eller resisted and was pepper sprayed. As officers were trying to put him in a jail cell, an altercation erupted. One of the officers struck Eller in the head with a blackjack. He died from a fractured skull 13 days later.

Following Eller's funeral, angry young black males began gathering downtown after dark. They soon began breaking store windows, setting fires in trashcans, and throwing rocks and bottles. Police Chief Justus Tucker summoned every officer to duty and called for assistance from the Highway Patrol.

As soon as word came about the troubles, police reporter Kent Pollock and I struck out for Winston-Salem in the only aged staff car that had a functioning police radio. The violence had intensified by the time we arrived. Cars and trucks were being overturned, stores looted. Some officers were carrying shotguns and sporadically firing them into the air.

Pollock headed for the action and I went to City Hall to find out what the authorities were doing and try to establish a base from which we could call in reports.

The area of violence included six blocks at that point. Traffic had been halted, but that wasn't stopping more rioters from infiltrating, keeping police on the run. City hall was within the zone of turmoil, but a large number of cops and highway patrol officers were protecting it.

The Mayor, M.C. Benton, was in his office with the police chief and had no time for reporters. One of the reporters present was city editor of *The Winston-Salem Journal*. He had been hit in the back of the head and slugged several times when he attempted to talk to some of the rioters.

A rumor soon swept through City Hall that black power leader H. Rap Brown was on his way to Winston-Salem on a flight from Atlanta. Brown had succeeded Stokely Carmichael as chairman of the Student Non-Violent Coordinating Committee. He had been arrested for inciting a riot in Cambridge, Maryland, three months earlier when he stood on the trunk of a car and shouted, "If America don't come around, we're gonna burn it down…Don't be trying to love that honkey to death. Shoot him to death! Shoot him to death, brother…." The ensuing riot had left much of Cambridge's black district a smoldering ruin after constant sniper fire kept firemen out of the area.

The police chief sent two detectives to the regional airport near Greensboro to intercept Brown, only to learn that the sole passenger with that last name was a startled businessman on his way home.

At 9:22, the mayor asked Governor Dan K. Moore to send the National Guard. Troops began arriving within an hour, a second group from Greensboro a couple of hours later, bringing the total to 200 men. They spread out downtown. Meanwhile a white-owned furniture store in the black section outside the riot area was firebombed, and police had to protect the three fire companies that were fighting the blaze from a taunting and rock-throwing crowd. The store was destroyed.

The mayor, haggard and sullen, finally came out to talk with reporters after the National Guard deployed. He said he'd just spoken with the governor and told him that things were improving.

"It's quieted down," he said. "This appears to be a greatly disorganized bunch of hoodlums who seized the opportunity to destroy property and harass the police and in general create disorder."

THE MAYOR LEFT ON "a quick trip home" after telling reporters that he would be touring the city in the morning to assess the damage and try to prevent further violence. It turned out that his claim that things had quieted down applied only to downtown.

By midnight, the action had spread to other parts of the city and was growing worse. A gas station in Waughtown, south of downtown, was set ablaze, and the police radio bristled with reports of sniper fire, much of it in the mostly black eastern section. One police car was riddled with bullets, although the officer at the wheel escaped injury. Others weren't so lucky. Forty-seven people were injured on this night and taken to hospitals for treatment. Eleven were admitted, 10 of those with gunshot wounds, three of them police officers. Eighty arrests were made and damages were estimated to be hundreds of thousands of dollars.

Pollock and I hit some of the hot spots after meeting our deadlines, including a housing project where scores of people were in the street. After we were spotted we had to make a hasty departure.

Irwin Smallwood became concerned about our safety and bought two construction hard hats for us to wear the following night. There was one problem with them. They were silver in color and would make us stand-out targets. A can of black spray paint reduced those chances, and the hats actually would come in handy because we would be dodging rocks and other dangerous missiles throughout the night.

The governor had toured the riot areas during the day, expressing his dismay at the destruction. The number of National Guardsmen in the city had been raised to 800. They were equipped with jeeps, trucks and armored personnel carriers with .50-caliber machine guns. Nearly 100 highway patrolmen had been assigned to assist the police. This show of force apparently had given the city council a feeling of security. In an emergency meeting that afternoon it voted against a curfew.

But as dusk began to settle a group of more than 100 blacks formed on the edge of downtown, and their intentions clearly were not peaceful. Forty officers in riot gear rushed to the area, formed a wedge and began moving against the angry crowd with shotguns firing into the air. The crowd dispersed, but so did the violence.

This prompted the mayor to call a press conference and announce an immediate night-long curfew for downtown.

While the mayor was speaking, the first fire call came in. It was at a white-owned grocery in the eastern part of the city and Pollock and I headed toward it in our feeble staff car. We didn't know Winston-Salem streets and it took longer than we expected to find it. By the time we arrived, the building was fully enveloped and police cars had created a semi-circle around the front to protect the firemen from a large crowd that was taunting and cursing them. Pollock pulled up behind one of the police cars and soon we not only were among the taunted and cursed but were dodging thrown objects for the first time that night.

More police and guardsmen arrived with shotguns, M14s and tear gas before the crowd could be controlled enough for us to make a get-away. By this time mayhem was breaking over wide areas—buildings firebombed, many more looted, shootouts taking place. Some business owners had armed themselves and were defending their property. We arrived at one shopping center to find eight young black men lined up with legs spread wide and hands on a brick wall, guarded by several cops and two civilians with hunting rifles whose stores had been looted. A paddy wagon was on the way.

Soon after this, we heard over the radio about a gun battle on Patterson Avenue. We found the street but weren't certain about the location. Snipers had been firing from the roof of a two-story building, and police and guardsmen had been exchanging shots with them. Pollock was driving, and suddenly I realized that we might be there. I could tell this because we were passing cops crouched behind their cars clutching handguns, guardsmen with rifles behind a wall. We had driven into the firing line and the cops began yelling at us, concerned for our safety, but not nearly as concerned as I just had become. I slipped so low in the seat that my knees were the only portion of me visible from the outside, and I was wishing I had two more hard hats to protect them, although I doubted they'd offer much resistance to bullets.

Pollock hit the gas. So startled was our arthritic staff car by this unexpected surge of energy that it quivered briefly, then leapt forward as if it had rediscovered younger, more energetic days. The building where the snipers were hiding was on a corner, and that intersection had a stoplight. It turned red. Out of instinct or habit, Pollock hit the brake, setting tires squealing and slamming my scrawny knees into the dashboard.

"Kent," I said, my hard hat knocked sideways by the force of the sudden stop, "this is no time to be concerned about a traffic ticket."

"You don't have as many speeding tickets as I do," he said, bashing the steering wheel with his right hand and recovering his senses enough to allow our startled and confused conveyance to take flight like an old man hobbling in fear. We doubled back on another street and got out to talk with the cops and guardsmen, who began laughing about our respect for red lights. They were waiting for an armored personnel carrier to shield them before attempting to flush out the snipers. Six men, a woman and child eventually were brought out of the building, but no weapons were found. The snipers had fled. This was an unseasonably cold night and cops and guardsmen were dressed appropriately. A bullet had passed through a guardsman's field jacket without even grazing him. He showed us the holes, expressing amazement at his close call.

After more than four hours of running from hot spot to hot spot, periodically stopping at phone booths that looked safe enough to allow us to report to editors, Pollock and I returned to city hall to scribble our stories and dictate them before deadline. By this time the mayor had declared a city-wide curfew and called for more National Guardsmen.

I wrote a first-person piece that began with this paragraph: "Never before have I felt I was in a foreign country while I was in North Carolina, but Friday night I did."

I went on to describe some of our experiences and the story appeared on page one in the final Saturday edition.

The night's violence had not yet been squelched, and we tried to get to some of it, but got stopped at almost every turn. Orders had gone out to clear the city's streets of vehicles, leaving open only major highways, and news vehicles were allowed no special privileges. We headed home unscathed, feeling lucky that we had passed through battle zone after battle zone shielded by spray-painted hard hats.

On Saturday, 1,200 guardsmen in combat gear were stationed through the troubled sections of the city and officials thought it safe enough to allow Wake Forest's homecoming football game with the University of South Carolina to proceed that evening. Two nights of violence didn't keep the crowd away. Nearly 13,000 fans showed up. But at one point a group of young blacks began throwing rocks at cars waiting to get into Bowman Gray Stadium, damaging 10 and forcing the occupants to take shelter behind them as police swarmed the area prompting the assailants to flee. Downtown was under curfew again and peaceful that night. A few reports of gunfire at police and guardsmen came from other areas. One roving sniper was arrested and his weapons seized.

National Guard groups began withdrawing Sunday. Pollock and I were relieved that we no longer would be dodging rocks, bottles and bullets and could hang up our trusty hard hats, but not for long.

APRIL FOOLS' DAY FELL on Monday in 1968. It also marked the beginning of my new job as full-time columnist. I took that fluke as a license for foolery. This also was the week for the Greater Greensboro Open at Sedgefield Country Club. The tournament was a big deal for Greensboro as well as the newspaper, bringing a flood of money to both, attracting thousands of visitors from many states and more ads and readers for the paper. It also captured national TV attention, prompting lots of preening by its Jaycee sponsors and portraying Greensboro as the tranquil and beautiful haven it was in early spring. Nobody dared make fun of the GGO, and that presented a challenge to me.

I never had attended a golf tournament and didn't care much for the game.

My intention was to find enough material to write a couple of amusing columns. The pro-am began on Wednesday, and it always had a big-name celebrity as well as a selection of lesser ones. This year the featured celebrity was Pat Boone, one of the top teen idols of the '50s He was playing with Arnold Palmer, and I followed them for a while through off-and-on rain without coming across anything funny.

I had prepared a Thursday column in advance, so I was under no pressure to meet a deadline. That was to my benefit, because I ended up with nothing to write about. When the tournament began on Thursday, a cloudy day, I was there again, this time focusing on the nature of the game and the onlookers, not the players. I was able to gather enough material to build a column around that, and I planned to come back the next day to enlist in Arnie's Army, as the largely shoe-tasseled mob that followed Palmer was tagged. I hoped this would provide material for a second column. Palmer was starting early Friday, giving me time to get back to the newsroom and write my Saturday column.

Spending nine hours roaming a golf course was tiring, and I was relieved to get home, have a drink and sit down for dinner. It must have been about 8:30 when regular programming on Channel 2 was interrupted by a CBS News Special Report. A somber Dan Rather in New York announced that Martin Luther King Jr. had been shot to death by an assassin in Memphis. The scene switched to the emergency room at the hospital where King had died an hour after he was shot. A reporter from a local TV station was talking to Andrew Young, one of King's assistants. Young said that he and others were outside the motel where they were staying, waiting to go to dinner with King when he came out of his second floor room and leaned over the balcony rail to speak to somebody in the parking lot. They heard a loud pop.

"We thought a fire cracker had gone off," Young said.

I was suddenly overcome with the same shock and sorrow I'd felt when I heard Walter Cronkite's announcement of President Kennedy's death. But I also felt a sudden sense of dread for what seemed inevitable.

"I've got to get back to the newsroom," I told Linda.

Chuck Hauser and Irwin Smallwood, who normally didn't work at night, already were there when I arrived. They were ripping apart the earlier plan for the morning paper and trying to prepare for what might come. By this time the wires were bringing early reports of violence in Memphis, Washington and other cities and there was great concern that it could erupt in Greensboro, too.

The city had two black colleges, Bennett for women and N.C. Agricultural and Technical, which recently had become a university. Both were a mile or so east of the newspaper building and both had played major roles in Civil Rights accomplishments in the city: the sit-ins at Woolworth's in 1960; and the lengthy demonstrations in 1963 that led to desegregation of cafeterias, theaters and other facilities. On this night a testimonial dinner was being held at A&T for its retiring president, Dr. Louis Dowdy. As word of King's murder spread, groups of students began gathering on campus. As their numbers grew, they spilled into Massey Street adjoining the campus.

Word reached police commanders that A&T students were organizing to march downtown and students at Bennett were planning to join them. Kent Pollock already was on the scene, trying to assess the situation. I hurried two blocks to City Hall to see what was going on. Mayor Carson Bain usually was jovial and joking, but this night he was worried and more serious than I ever had seen him. He was keeping close touch with Police Chief Paul Calhoun, who already had called some officers back to duty. At the police department I saw a large group of officers being outfitted with riot gear.

A little before 11 word came that A&T students were headed downtown on Friendly Avenue. Their numbers were estimated at about 250. At Murrow Boulevard, some broke away, running into the sales lot of a car dealer, smashing windows and kicking doors and fenders. Word of this brought dismay to the mayor.

The three-story *Daily News* building sat at the northeast corner of Friendly and Davie, facing Davie. The marchers would pass right by it, just as hundreds had during the demonstrations of 1963, and any who glanced up at the well-lighted newsroom windows on the third floor could see curious editors peering down at them.

After the vandalism at the car lot, a group of about three dozen officers in riot gear with billy clubs and tear gas gathered at Friendly and Elm near City Hall at the center of downtown. As the marchers started uphill toward Davie, the officers proceeded in a wedge toward them. Traffic was halted, and it looked as if a standoff was about to take place, conveniently by the newspaper building. The police stopped on one side of Davie, the marchers on the other. Captain Conrad Wade approached leaders of the march and began a conversation. He soon walked back to the line of officers, directed them to fall back, and allowed the march to continue. Wade later said that the marchers told him they intended to hold a brief memorial service at the county courthouse, and assured him that their purpose was peaceful.

The marchers turned left on Elm and at Market Street, the city center, were joined by nearly 100 Bennett students. Some began clapping and chanting "black power" as the combined group continued westward on Market to the courthouse a block and a half away. The chanting stopped when leaders mounted the courthouse steps to speak briefly about the loss of King before calling for a silent prayer.

After the reverent silence, the students seemed uncertain what to do next. Most started back down Market toward Bennett and A&T, some chanting, "We shall march and we shall change white society." But at Elm groups cut off in both directions into the business district and soon began smashing store windows. One group surrounded a car driven by a white male, breaking its windows and trying to pull the driver out before officers in riot gear came to his rescue and began attempting to disperse the crowd. Other officers closed off all streets into downtown. When the marchers reached another car dealership at Murrow many more cars were damaged.

As soon as the mayor got word of the violence, he called the governor requesting National Guard assistance. Considering what was happening elsewhere in the country, he told me, he couldn't take the risk of waiting to see if the situation grew worse. But it would be couple of hours before the first troops deployed.

I returned to the newsroom to write what I had seen for the front-page story that was being patched together. A little after midnight, word came by police radio that young black males were looting Murchison Grocery on East Market Street. Police arriving at the scene were met by an angry crowd, cursing and throwing bricks and rocks. Officers used tear gas to break up the crowd. Pollock was on the scene and called in a brief report before deadline for the final edition. I didn't wait to see what else might develop. I was too tired. I headed home to bed.

The GGO proceeded as scheduled Friday morning, and as planned, I showed up to become a private in Arnie's Army. This was a gloomy morning with sporadic rain but it didn't inhibit Palmer's massive army. It was a sea of umbrellas of many colors, often making it difficult even to see the commanding general. On the seventh hole, Palmer laid his tee shot within a couple feet of the hole, prompting much applause and cheering by the troops.

As he walked onto the green he seemed surprised at finding his ball so close to the hole. He turned to the crowd looking almost angry.

"Oh, I missed it again, dammit," he said to uproarious laughter.

By the ninth hole I was drenched, sodden-shoed, falling behind and unable to get close enough even to see the green. I was no happier in Arnie's Army than I'd been in the U.S. Army. To put it in Army terms, I went over the hill, deserted, returned home for dry shoes and clothes and went to the office to write my first GGO column deploring golf as a sport that was more strenuous and difficult for spectators than it was for players, and extremely boring on top of that. As a televised sport, in my estimation, it ranked in excitement right along with bowling. Much heavier rain would cause this day's play to be cancelled at 3 p.m., wiping out all scores, including Palmer's 67 as well at the 68 of Billy Casper, who would go on to win the most beleaguered and delayed GGO in history.

Memorial services for King were held at Bennett and A&T on Friday, and late in the morning Bennett students began a march that had been coordinated with police and the National Guard. It circled through the A&T campus, picking up many more marchers, eventually numbering more than 400. They kept to the sidewalks, clapped and chanted, but as the students headed back to their campuses cries of "black power!" erupted with fists thrust into the air.

At one o'clock Mayor Bain, the Rev. Cecil Bishop, the black chairman of the Human Relations Commission, and the presidents of A&T and Bennett, Louis Dowdy and Isaac Miller, went on Channel 2 for a special broadcast praising King and appealing for calm. They were all too aware of what was going on in more than 100 other cities, but particularly in Washington.

The rioting and looting that had occurred in the nation's capital on Thursday night, laying waste to a prominent business district, had erupted anew after Stokely Carmichael proclaimed at a press conference Friday morning that "White America has declared war on black people, and today the final showdown is coming." By mid-afternoon much of Washington was aflame and in gridlock as panicked government and private employees attempted to escape to the suburbs. At one time the rioting almost reached the White House. Exhausted and outnumbered police no longer could contain it. Once again President Johnson would be called upon to send troops to American cities, 5,000 to Chicago, 5,000 to Baltimore and 13,800 to Washington, the largest number of troops occupying an American city since the Civil War. Marines set up machine guns on the Capitol steps, hardly a proper homage to the dream that King so eloquently expressed not far from those steps less than five years earlier.

Yet Greensboro remained calm. As night fell, Louis Dowdy announced that he was closing A&T five days ahead of Easter break. This was presented as a decision to honor King, but actually was a safety move encouraged by the city. Most of the dorm students, however, wouldn't be leaving until Saturday. At about the same time, 400 more National Guardsmen from Hickory arrived at the coliseum which had become the billet and command center for the Guard, bringing the number of troops in the city to 900.

In the newsroom, preparations had been made in case violence did break out. Pollock and I would take to the streets again, since we were experienced in such matters. Our hard hats had been brought out of storage, and Smallwood had gone to the trouble of borrowing high-end walkie-talkies from Bob Kent at the coliseum so we could communicate as needed.

After I finished my column, Jim McAllister and I went to eat at a favorite spot called IPD. When we got back to the newsroom, a problem developed. Our city editor was a tippler. He kept a bottle in his bottom desk drawer, and now and then he would bend over and take a nip, apparently thinking he wasn't being noticed, although everybody in the newsroom had long been aware of his disappearing dips, which increased as deadline pressures grew. On this night, he went for one nip too many and fell out in the floor. We had to get him to the cot in the women's restroom and call his wife to come and get him.

"Can you fill in for him?" Smallwood asked me.

I started trying to figure out what he'd been working on and puzzling over what to do about it. The police radio sat on an adjoining desk. The mundane traffic on the radio suddenly was interrupted by the excited voice of a patrol officer: "Shot fired at A&T!"

Nobody had to tell Pollock to get moving. He grabbed his hard hat and walkie-talkie and was out the door. I snatched a legal pad and began taking notes from the radio. The shot had come from a white station wagon occupied by two white males. It was aimed at a group of A&T students on Market Street. I already could hear sirens headed that way, but the good news so far was that no call was made for an ambulance.

Not long after all of this took place, my walkie-talkie crackled to life.

"Pollock to newsroom, Pollock to newsroom."

I picked it up and pressed the send button.

"Go ahead, Kent. What you got?"

"Right now I've got a door knob in my hand."

"What?"

"A door knob. I had to make a stop. I'm locked in the men's room on the second floor and I can't get out. The damn door knob came off in my hand."

We had to send a rescue crew to free him. If Smallwood hadn't had the foresight to borrow the walkie-talkies, Pollock might have been stranded there all night and we might have thought him missing in action.

Within 10 minutes, calls of shots fired began coming in a stream. This time the shots were from the campus, aimed at police and guardsmen. Reinforcements were rushed to the area, including guardsmen in an armored personnel carrier. Fires were set at a construction site and an apartment complex not far from the campus. Firemen arriving to fight the blazes had to take cover from snipers. Over the next two hours the campus would become a battle zone. Three police officers were shot, two hit in the head and face with shotgun pellets, creating wounds that were bloody and painful but not serious. A Juvenile

Division officer took a full shotgun blast in the back and was admitted to the hospital. He would survive. Another policeman and a guardsman were injured by thrown bricks.

On two occasions, police and guardsmen used tear gas attempting to disperse hostile crowds only to have the gas canisters thrown back at them. Students stood on dorm ledges watching and sometimes cheering the violence. Nobody knew how many snipers were firing, but shots were coming from several different spots. National Guard sharpshooters were brought in to return fire but the sniping continued.

I was taking down all of this information from Pollock over the walkie-talkie, typing it in paragraphs and passing it to the copy desk where the main story was being pieced together. I even was able to get the identities of the wounded police officers from Major Ed Wynn before final deadline. An hour after the shooting began, police stopped a white station wagon and arrested the two men who had started this melee with a single stupid shot. They were next-door neighbors. Wynn provided us their names, ages, addresses and the multiple charges filed against them.

As midnight approached, police and guardsmen who had entered the campus were pinned down by gunfire. More guardsmen were brought in and a plan was conceived to assault Hodgin Hall, which housed the School of Education, from which most of the shots had been coming. The guardsmen would divide into two groups and attack the building from different directions, using armored personnel carriers. As one unit approached the building three students with hands held high emerged from a corner of the building. One was singing a Beatles song, "Lucy in the Sky with Diamonds." All were pulled out of line of fire, questioned and released.

The building wasn't officially cleared until after our deadline, but the assault was successful and no more injuries occurred.

The GGO went ahead as scheduled on Saturday, as A&T was evacuating all of its students and shutting down. The City Council met in emergency session that afternoon. It unanimously approved Mayor Bain's request for a city-wide curfew from 7 p.m. to 6 a.m. for as long as the mayor deemed necessary. It made all marches and demonstrations illegal and forbade the sale of alcohol, guns, ammunition, and explosives of any type. Gas could be purchased only if it was pumped into the tanks of vehicles. Traffic would be allowed only on major highways during curfew hours, but entrance and exit roads would be blocked. Inter-city buses would be allowed to proceed to the bus station, but any passengers disembarking would have to remain in the waiting room until the curfew expired. People going to essential jobs would be escorted. Anybody else seen outside of buildings anywhere in the city during curfew hours would be arrested. Laws would be enforced with whatever strength was required.

"We're not playing around," the mayor told reporters. "We mean business."

The mayor also requested that churches use their Sunday services to honor Dr. King. President Johnson already had declared Sunday a national day of mourning.

The curfew was a major financial blow on one of Greensboro's busiest weekends each year. Restaurants, nightclubs, theaters, and other entertainment venues suffered heavy losses. Hotels and motels were filled because of the GGO, but when the tournament shut down on Sunday to honor the President's request, rescheduling the final two rounds for Monday, most of the out-of-town fans went home. The curfew remained in effect until Wednesday morning, the day after King's funeral in Atlanta. During those four days, Greensboro's crime rate was reduced almost to zero, although several hundred people were arrested and fined for violating curfew.

On the day of King's funeral, as curfew was nearing, McAllister and I went to a poolroom a few doors up the street from the newspaper, as we often did. This had been a day of church services honoring King all over the country, including many in Greensboro, some attended by blacks and whites together, a rare occurrence.

I was bent over aiming at an eight ball when a funny thought struck me. Black people and white people didn't attend church together in Greensboro, as throughout the rest of North Carolina, but here they did shoot pool together. The makeup of regulars at this distinguished establishment was about equally divided between blacks and whites. We shot against one another, the losers often handing over dollar bills. There were some rough and scraggly characters, but everybody got along. We joked. We laughed. We kidded. We even had some meaningful discussions. But not once had I heard a racial slur, or seen a racial incident, not even when disagreements occurred.

An idea for a column hit me. It appeared on Thursday, a week after King's assassination. I contrasted segregated church congregations to my experiences with the regulars at the poolroom. The column began with me bent over, taking aim at the eight ball. This is how I closed it:

"That's the way it is at the poolroom. A man is respected for what he is, for what he can do. And, after all, isn't that what it's all about?

"But who would dare stand up and say it's time we started getting more people out of churches and into the poolrooms?

"I laugh and slam a good one into that old eight ball, the black one. It bounces all over the table, but it doesn't drop."

FOR A YEAR BEFORE his assassination, Martin Luther King Jr. had been rethinking his civil rights campaign to include improving economic conditions not only for blacks but for poor whites, Mexican-Americans, Puerto Ricans, Native-Americans, and any others who resided in poverty. To him the War on Poverty declared by Lyndon Johnson in 1964 wasn't fulfilling its purpose. This decision would lead to his death. He was killed while trying to improve pay and job conditions for garbage workers in Memphis.

In November, 1967, at a retreat for the Southern Christian Leadership Conference in Frogmore, South Carolina, King announced a plan for a campaign that would include a march on Washington to encourage the federal government to do more for the poor. Soon after King's assassination, the SCLC, decided to move forward with that plan.

Seven bus caravans of poor people originating in different parts of the country would wind in erratic paths through city after city holding marches and rallies before descending on Washington. There 3,000 marchers would encamp in tents and plywood lean-tos on the Mall near the Lincoln Memorial Reflecting Pool to attempt to pressure Congress and the White House. The encampment would be called Resurrection City.

The southern caravan began in Edwards, Mississippi, on May 5, with about 120 marchers. Their first demonstration would be to walk across Edmund Pettus Bridge in Selma, Alabama, where in 1965 state troopers had attacked and beaten marchers seeking voting rights, sparking a campaign that would leave three civil rights workers dead. In Selma the number of participants in the Poor Peoples March nearly quadrupled before moving on to Montgomery. The Montgomery march by choice was small and ceremonial because Governor Lurleen Wallace, a victim of cancer and wife of George Wallace, was lying in state in the Capitol. But a big rally was held at Dexter Street Baptist Church, the second-oldest black church in the city, where King had kept an office while conducting the bus boycott. In Birmingham, the marchers were treated to a huge fund-raising rally and concert featuring Harry Belafonte, the Supremes, the Temptations and other acts, attracting more than 13,000 people. For many marchers, some of whom never had been out of their small hometowns, this was considered an experience of a lifetime.

Next stop was Atlanta, where the highlight was a visit to King's grave. The caravan moved on to Macon and Savannah, then Charleston and Greenville in South Carolina. North Carolina would have three stops—Charlotte, Greensboro, Durham. Kent Pollock and I would cover this leg of the journey. He'd turn out news stories. I'd write columns. A week earlier, I'd made arrangements with SCLC to ride one of the buses on the Charlotte-to-Greensboro run.

The caravan that arrived in Charlotte at 12:35 p.m. on Tuesday, May 14, consisted of nine chartered Greyhound Sceni-Cruisers carrying 420 marchers, three rental trucks loaded with equipment and supplies, and a string of cars. It was an hour and a half late. A crowd of about 600 was waiting when the buses arrived at a vacant lot in downtown Charlotte. It included three busloads of students from Johnson C. Smith University, founded as a black college in 1867, 200 students from a nearby elementary school, and a lot of church members, the vast majority black. The crowd cheered and applauded as marchers streamed off the buses.

A local black minister, the Rev. R.L. Shirley, was in charge of this reception. He was decked out in crisp, spanking new overalls, his idea of poor folks' attire, and he climbed onto a car to get the marchers' attention.

"Everybody here's your friend," he called out. "Nobody's going to take anything from you. Put your luggage here and get yourself something to eat."

"Another leader," mumbled a marcher standing near me. "Every time you turn around, somebody else is standing on top a car running his mouth."

When all the baggage was removed from the Sceni-Cruisers and clumped into a huge pile to be loaded onto trucks, the big buses departed, not to be seen again until the following day. While some marchers visited Jiffy Johnnies, church ladies began serving sandwiches, potato chips, cookies, soft drinks. Young black men wearing denim jackets with red and green armbands scurried about with walkie-talkies. They had been trained as marshals. They rode the buses, maintained order, attended to details, answered questions and solved problems. A drawn little man in a baggy, double-breasted suit walked silently through the crowd holding a self-made sign in palsied hands: "The brute killed the dreamer, but it didn't stop the dream."

When the march finally began at 2:05, so did a light rain. An old woman looked up at the sky.

"I declare," she said, "sometimes it looks like the Lord just naturally works against the poor folks. But He knows best. Yes, He knows best."

The previous day's march in Greenville had to be halted because of a stormy downpour, but this one would proceed despite the rain, accompanied by police cars and motorcycle officers and trailed by trucks, an ambulance and two church buses to pick up dropouts. As the procession turned onto Tryon, downtown Charlotte's Main Street, the participants grew more spirited. They strutted, sang hymns, clapped and chanted.

"We got the fever. We hot. We can't be stopped."

The destination, the Charlotte Coliseum, was nearly five miles away, and after leaving downtown the planned route meandered through low-income residential areas, black and white. By this time, rain was falling harder, and few of the marchers had umbrellas. Some marshals took off their jackets and gave them to older people. All along the way, the marchers called out to spectators on front porches and under shelters.

"Come on brother, come on sister. Join the poor people."

Some did. At one intersection in a black community, a shiny late-model

Lincoln Continental had been stopped by the march. A rear door opened, and a woman dressed in maid's attire jumped out and ran to join the parade. On seeing this, a woman far too fat to march let out a high, shrill "Whee-ooo-eee."

"I always wanted to holler like that," she cried. "Ain't nobody gonna say nothing to me now."

The person leading this march was Robert Henson, who was 27, from Birmingham, an unemployed upholstery worker. Childhood polio had left him with one shriveled, useless leg. He could walk only with crutches. But he was keeping such a good pace that some were falling behind. He had a big smile and a bigger laugh, and he was filled with enthusiasm and hope for this campaign. I walked with him for a while.

"Are you going to be able to keep up this pace the entire distance?" I asked.

"I'm good for 10 miles," he said with a laugh, and picked up the pace even more.

The rain kept coming. Shoes squished. Hair and clothing were plastered to bodies, mine included. Rain dripped from ears and noses. Not all marchers could abide it. A young boy, maybe eight or 10, was taken to the ambulance, shaking from chill. An older male marcher in shabby clothing sat on a curb, pulled off a worn shoe and sock. Every toe was blistered. A marshal led him to one of the church buses.

But most kept on, displaying no loss of spirit.

"We ain't going to let a little rain stop us," one woman cried out, and others began yelling, "Ain't no rain going to stop us. We going to Washington. We going to see the head man."

The pace picked up when the coliseum finally hove into view, and as the marchers began streaming inside, a tapestry of Martin Luther King Jr. was unfurled overhead. Church ladies with towels and steaming cups of coffee welcomed all. Hot showers awaited, and marchers could pick what they wanted from piles of used clothing, clean, and comfortingly dry.

For the first time the marchers would be sleeping in a group on thick foam pads with sheets and blankets on the coliseum floor. In other cities they'd slept in private homes, church and college facilities. But much lay ahead before sleeping spots could be picked.

After drying myself as best I could, I flopped into a folding chair, one of many that had been spread out for marchers. A young woman wearing wrinkled clothing she'd picked from one of the piles was sitting in a chair in front of me. She was holding a child, a boy not quite the age of my son Erik, who was not yet three. From where I was sitting, I could see only the child's bare legs, which seemed not much bigger than broomsticks. One bore a festering sore. The woman was waiting for her husband and two other sons, the eldest perhaps school age, who were changing clothes in a restroom. These were the only whites I'd seen among the marchers so far, and the whole family was gaunt and pale. When I tried to talk with them, they shied away.

Later I learned that the family had been with the march since it began in Mississippi. The father had been unable to find work, and the family had been evicted from the place where they were living. They carried all their belongings in cardboard boxes and paper bags.

"They came with us," a marcher named Orville Hoffman told me, "because they had nowhere else to go."

We were standing near a table heavily laden with dishes prepared by local church ladies when the supper call was announced. I saw the young family getting into line.

Hoffman looked across this vast spread of food.

"Some of these people," he said, "are living the best right now they've ever lived in their lives."

Supper was followed by a rally attended by about 3,500 supporters. The featured speaker was the Rev. Hosea Williams, a close friend and colleague of King. He had flown from Washington, where he had been working to ready Resurrection City. He stirred the crowd to a chorus of "Amen, Amen, Amen." He praised God, stressed the importance of King's non-violent approach to change, and warned against violence.

"We can get one million people into Washington," he shouted, "but if one single person is stupid enough to throw a single brick, the trouble is going to start and white society is going to keep us in slavery."

THE NEXT MORNING, I discovered that the Poor Peoples' March had one thing in common with the Army: hurry up and wait. I learned that when I climbed aboard Sceni-Cruiser Number 8, to which I had been assigned. It was called the medical bus because that was where the aspirin, rubbing alcohol and first-aid kits were kept. It also was where the caravan's two nurses, a mother and daughter team, rode.

At the time I boarded all but a few seats in the back were occupied. I took a seat near the nurse everybody called Mama. She actually was a retired nurse. She was 68, from Atlanta, white, gray-haired, grandmotherly, a veteran of many civil rights campaigns throughout the South. She also was an organic vegetarian, rarely seen without her familiar can of sunflower seeds. She offered me some. Her son and daughter sat across the aisle from her. The son had shoulder-length hair. A victim of birth defects, including blindness, he wore sunglasses, a hearing aid and never spoke on this trip. Mama seemed to be beloved by everybody on the bus, and we chatted as we waited, and waited, and waited.

Departure time had been set for 10. We finally got rolling at 11:15. Just before that a final passenger climbed aboard. That was Pee-Wee, one of the most popular people on the march, a funny little guy, a black version of Marty Allen, a popular big-eyed, frizzy-haired TV comic at the time. Passengers called out to him, kidding him as he made his way down the aisle, hoping to stir a humorous reaction, but he was in no mood for that. He had spent the morning loading trucks and part of the night standing guard over the sleeping marchers. He took a seat at the back and soon was snoozing.

The passengers didn't have to worry about entertainment though. They still had Indian Joe. He had come aboard just before Pee Wee and stood at the front talking to the driver. Indian Joe was what the other marchers called Orville Hoffman, whom I had met the day before. He began working the aisle when the bus started moving. I knew that Indian Joe loved to talk. Nobody was a stranger to him. He talked to anybody who would listen, hugged every woman who would allow it and some he caught by surprise. If TV cameras were in range, he was maneuvering to get in front of them.

As best I could determine, Indian Joe was the only Indian, as Native Americans called themselves at the time, among the marchers, 100% Cherokee, or so he claimed. But then he claimed many things.

He had a master's degree in theology, and once was pastor of a church he never named in a place he never mentioned. He had spent most of his life in show business playing drums and bongos, had worked with Lionel Hampton.

"Music?" he said. "I read, write and arrange. And then I'm a licensed mortician, too."

He had a tiny mustache, slick, black, thinning hair, and a huge, grotesquely shaped belly he claimed to be the mangled result of wounds suffered during World War II. He had to take leave from a veterans hospital to attend the march, he said. He felt obligated to do that, he said, because he'd been a friend and follower of Dr. King long before the rest of the world had heard of him.

As he worked his way down the aisle, a discussion about politics developed, this being a presidential election year. A woman announced that she intended to vote for comedian Dick Gregory for President. Indian Joe was standing not far from me at that point, leaning against the side of a seat back. When he heard that comment, he seized on it. It reminded him of a story, he announced, although the story he began had no connection to Dick Gregory or presidential politics. Perhaps Gregory's bond to humor was the tenuous instigator.

"I remember the last humorous story Dr. King told," Indian Joe said. "I was with him when he was killed, standing right below the balcony. But he came in the room that night and told a story about Dexter, his little boy. He said he told Dexter to go out and get the paper but it was dark and Dexter was scared. So Dr. King told him, 'Son, there's nothing to be afraid of. God's out there. He'll look after you.' So Dexter went to the door and he peeked out and he said, 'Lord, if you're out there, would you please hand me the paper.'"

Indian Joe began laughing hard but nobody else did. Suddenly his mood changed.

"Dexter was the littlest one," he said. "I'll never forget when we got back to Atlanta in that plane. You know who sent that plane, don't you? Bobby Kennedy. And Dexter came on with his mother and he asked her where his daddy was, and she said he was back there sleeping. Ain't that pitiful? And then at the cemetery Dexter said, 'I don't like this place, Mama.'"

Tears were running down Indian Joe's face, and he began dabbing his eyes with a towel draped around his neck.

"That man was closer to me than my own daddy," he said, and took a seat nearby. He fell silent and spent the rest of the trip looking out the window at the passing scene, keeping his thoughts to himself.

One thing was certain about Indian Joe. He could tell a story, but he left everybody wondering what his own story really was.

Just outside Greensboro, the motorcade began pulling onto the shoulder of I-85 and came to a halt. More waiting. Nobody on Bus 8 knew what the problem was, and not until later would we learn that the supply truck leading the caravan had been pulled over by a state trooper and warned about speeding. Just another delay.

Greensboro Police cars were waiting at the city limits to escort the caravan to Windsor Community Center on Lee Street in the black section of East Greensboro. We finally arrived at 1:45, nearly two hours late. A huge welcoming throng was waiting, estimated at about 900, many students from nearby A&T and Bennett, others from church groups.

The marchers on the buses were hungry and expecting lunch. Many became disgruntled when they disembarked and learned that lunch was at the coliseum, the destination of their march and, as things would turn out, two hours away.

The Greensboro march would be proclaimed the biggest and best so far by organizers. It would be rain-free and shorter than Charlotte's, only 3.2 miles, a straight shot along Lee Street. Police had closed the west-bound lanes to accommodate it, and police cars stopped traffic at intersections as it passed. More than 400 locals joined the march, although not all would complete it. Just after it began a group of A&T students began shouting "black power!" Organizers drowned them out with "We Shall Overcome," as marshals removed the students.

Greensboro would bring even longer delays for the traveling marchers. Organizers spent much of the following morning dealing with two problems. Eighteen bus riders were ejected for reasons including drinking and homosexual activities. A rider who joined in Charlotte was found to be a strident black militant with a lengthy criminal record and a history of mental illness, and he too was culled. The second problem was that organizers in Durham had failed to find adequate sleeping accommodations for the marchers. After a frantic morning of calling and cajoling by organizers and SCLC leaders, five churches in Chapel Hill agreed to take in the bulk of the riders.

It was 1:45 p.m. before the caravan finally left Greensboro, the buses again loaded with lunch-deprived riders. Just beyond Burlington five buses peeled off, headed to Chapel Hill, where a rally would be held but no march. The other four continued on to Durham, a city embroiled in racial conflict, for a depleted and hours-delayed march in which the bus riders, numbering only about 180, upset and discouraged by these unexpected developments, would display little of the spirit and enthusiasm they had shown in Charlotte and Greensboro.

The Southern caravan had only two more stops after Durham—Norfolk and Richmond—before arriving for a month-long stay at Resurrection City. I couldn't help wondering how the people I'd met on the bus and at the marches and rallies would feel about their time there, especially after it became apparent that Resurrection City was becoming a disaster.

Heavy rains fell throughout its existence, turning the entire encampment into a muddy bog that at one point was five inches deep in water. Tensions arose. Disputes and fights erupted. Crime, including vandalism, theft, robbery and sexual assault, became a growing problem.

Just over two weeks after Southern cavalcade riders took up residence, Resurrection City, like the rest of the country, was stunned by the assassination of Robert F. Kennedy as he campaigned for President in Los Angeles. He had been a supporter of the Poor Peoples' March from its inception. His family altered the route of his funeral procession to pass by Resurrection City where its inhabitants lined the street in homage.

Worsening living conditions, combined with the failure of leaders to obtain any concessions from Congress or the Johnson Administration, created disappointment and a sense of hopelessness among the encamped demonstrators. Some gave up and left for home. The flight would continue.

The highlight of the Poor Peoples' campaign was to be Solidarity Day at which King's widow, Coretta Scott King would speak at the Lincoln Memorial. Organizers hoped to attract as many as 100,000 people. Originally scheduled for May 30, problems and complications created delays. It finally took place on June 19th, called Juneteenth, an observance of the date in 1865 when slaves in Texas first learned that the Civil War had ended and they were free. It was estimated that more than 50,000 people attended, many white. The line-up of speakers included Democratic Presidential hopefuls Eugene McCarthy and Hubert Humphrey. Coretta Scott King used the occasion to speak out against the Vietnam War, another of her husband's worries.

The following day, police employed tear gas at Resurrection City after rocks and a Molotov cocktail were thrown at them. The National Park Service permit allowing the encampment expired on June 23, but the remaining inhabitants, numbering about 500, refused to leave. On June 24, 1,000 police officers encircled Resurrection City and began eviction. Residents who refused were arrested. They numbered 288, including Ralph David Abernathy.

That night blacks protesting the eviction began attacking police and rampaging in the same downtown area where riots had erupted after King's assassination. Windows were smashed, fires set. An emergency curfew was declared and 450 National Guardsmen were called out. Sadly, the outcome of the Poor Peoples' March, King's final non-violent campaign, only was more violence.

Jerry Bledsoe | DO-GOOD BOY

19

As frightening and dismaying as 1968 was turning out to be, it also would be a tumultuous year politically. Vietnam was a major cause of that. At the end of January, North Vietnamese troops and Viet Cong launched the Tet Offensive attacking nearly every town and city in South Vietnam. It dragged on for months, costing tens of thousands of lives and devastating both sides. It left the Pentagon and President Lyndon Johnson appearing to be confused, uncertain, indecisive, and turned many more Americans against the war.

It also would change the Presidential race. In the first primary in New Hampshire in February, Johnson barely eked out a victory against his challenger Eugene McCarthy, an anti–war Senator from Minnesota. That outcome also drew into the race New York Senator Robert F. Kennedy, who previously had declined to run against Johnson.

The two challengers and developments in Vietnam led the President to address the nation on March 31, announcing that he would not seek re-election. That brought into the race Vice-President Hubert Humphrey, a former Minnesota Senator who twice had run unsuccessfully for President. Kennedy's assassination in June mournfully clouded the entire process.

It seemed likely that the Republican candidate would be former Vice President and Presidential candidate Richard Nixon, who had decided not to run against Johnson in 1964, leaving his own party to suffer a devastating defeat with Arizona Senator Barry Goldwater as its candidate.

A complicating factor for both parties, however, was George Wallace, Alabama's feisty segregationist former governor. He had first run for the presidency as a Democrat in 1964, entering primaries in Wisconsin, Indiana and Maryland, shocking party leaders with the number of votes he received. In 1968, he decided to run as a third-party candidate, creating the American Independent Party.

On Thursday, August 8, as expected, the Republican Convention in Miami

Beach chose Nixon as its candidate and Maryland Governor Spiro Agnew as his running mate. A day after it ended I learned that Wallace was going to be in Greensboro the following day. I normally didn't work Saturdays but I thought it might be interesting to meet Wallace. He wasn't coming for a public appearance, no speeches or crowds. He would be recording a TV interview at WFMY. I had to suffer a lot of rigmarole to be permitted in his presence, and when I finally made it past guards into the TV station I learned he was in make-up, so I sat watching TV.

I was surprised when I looked up and saw him standing in the doorway. He was shorter than I expected. His dark hair was slicked back in a swirl, and the makeup artist had plastered on enough cosmetics to make him resemble a corpse. I could tell he wasn't dead because he was smoking a fat, green cigar. I couldn't abide cigar smoke. It gave me headaches, but I'd just suffer the consequences.

I also was surprised that a child was with him, and when I introduced myself, he introduced her. She was the youngest of his three daughters, named Janie Lee, supposedly for Robert E. Lee, and called Lee. She was seven, with big blue eyes and short blonde hair. She had a Band-Aid on one ankle and was holding a small doll. She smiled shyly, clinging to her father's pants leg, and as we chatted he tousled her hair.

"Scratch my back, Daddy," she said. "Scratch my back right there."

Daddy scratched.

"Down, down, down," she said.

Daddy scratched lower.

Only then did it hit me that she had lost her mother only three months earlier, and no doubt needed all the fatherly attention she could get.

Wallace and I chatted about Greensboro and my year in Alabama. I told him that a photo of me had appeared in *The Montgomery Advertiser* standing at the spot at the State Capitol where he later had been sworn in as governor, a site he had chosen because it was where Jefferson Davis had been sworn in as President of the Confederacy. A friend and I had gone to Montgomery one weekend in our dress uniforms and a newspaper photographer snapped a shot of us. I'd never heard of Wallace at the time.

Although I was not one of his admirers, I was impressed by how friendly and charming he was, especially since I was of the news media he regularly demeaned. Our chat was interrupted for the taping of the show, which I was invited to watch.

"I was about to jump up and cheer when you said that you were going to eliminate almost all federal taxes when you became President," I told him after the interview, which was to be shown the following day. "But then you had to go on and say all that money should be going to the states. I guess when it comes to government there's always a catch."

"But some catches are better than others," he said with a smile and a twinkle in his eye.

"Maybe for governors," I said. "If you don't become President are you going to run for Governor again?"

"I intend to become President," he said, and was whisked away by aides to another TV taping in Winston-Salem, which I also attended, continuing our conversation.

As nice as Wallace had been to me, I couldn't help poking fun at him in a column. In speeches he frequently maintained that one of the gravest threats to the American way of life was "pseudo-intellectual, briefcase toting, pointy-headed professors who couldn't park a bicycle straight."

Greensboro being a city of five colleges and universities I thought it shouldn't be a problem finding such a professor and giving him an opportunity to respond. It didn't take long. I found him right in my brain. He was middle-aged, wearing a tweed blazer with leather elbow patches and a small brimmed hat with a feather in the band. He was muttering to himself and trying to park a bicycle with a briefcase in the basket.

"You wouldn't know anything about parking one of these contraptions, would you?" he asked.

"Sorry," I said. "I don't know a thing about machinery."

"I just can't seem to get it straight," he said.

"Could I ask what you teach, sir?"

"Students."

"I mean the subject."

"Ornithology. You know. Birds. Right now I'm writing a book titled *The Irrational Irritability of the Southern Redneck When Confronted With the Free-Flying Ordinary Blackbird.*"

He wheeled the bike around, kicked at the kickstand.

"How's that look?" he asked.

"The front seems a little too much to the left," I told him.

"I guess you're right," he said, shaking his head. He took off his hat to wipe the sweat from his brow. I must have looked startled. His head came to a point.

"I can't help but notice that your head is pointed," I said.

"Everybody notices that," he replied. "I was born like that, don't know what caused it."

"That must have been hard on you growing up," I said sympathetically.

"Oh, it was. All the big kids used to wrap a rope around my feet, turn me upside-down and spin me like a top."

The column went on in that vein, and closed this way:

"I guess you know that George Wallace says it's you and your kind who're driving this country right into the hands of the communists," I said.

"Not I," he snapped indignantly. "I don't have a license. That's the reason I ride this damn bicycle."

"What do you think of Mr. Wallace?" I asked.

"I don't know. Can he park a bicycle straight?"

I doubt that Wallace ever saw this column, but if he did I hoped he might at least have smiled about it.

This wouldn't be my last encounter with Wallace, however. The next wouldn't be quite as pleasant as the first.

JUST A FEW WEEKS after Hubert Humphrey became the Democratic nominee in Chicago as anti-war demonstrators were bloodied in the streets by Mayor Richard Daley's cops on live TV, I got a call from my friend Eric Alberts in New York.

"Tom Colt and I are going to Cape Canaveral next month to see Apollo 7 blast off," he told me. "You want to join us?"

"What brought this on?" I asked.

"Well, we both wanted to see a space shot and Tom's father is an old friend of the commander of the Cape Canaveral Air Force Station. This is going to be the last shot from there, and Tom said this would be our only chance to go and get first-class treatment."

Tom's father, Tom Colt Jr., had been a Marine fighter pilot in World War II and had fought in the battle for Okinawa. Before becoming a war hero, he organized the Virginia Museum of Fine Arts in Richmond in 1935 and became its first director. He returned to that position after the war before going on to become director of art museums in Portland, Oregon, and Dayton, Ohio. Perhaps I should mention at this point that his son was the great, great, great grandson on his mother's side of President Andrew Johnson, a North Carolina native who succeeded Lincoln and was the first President to face impeachment, winning acquittal by a single vote. The impeachment was a situation that Tom never was able to find acceptable, and friends had learned to avoid bringing up the topic lest he go on at plodding length about it.

"Count me in," I told Eric, "as long as nobody brings up Andrew Johnson."

"I won't mention him," he said. "I promise."

The shot was set for Friday, October 11. It would be the first manned space flight for the United States in nearly two years, the first on the mighty Saturn rocket designed to deliver humans to the moon. Apollo 7 actually would be Apollo 1-7. America's space program had suffered a drastic setback when the astronauts who were to pilot Apollo 1—Gus Grissom, Edward H. White, and Roger Chaffee—died in a capsule fire during a training session in January, 1967. Pressure for the success of this flight was intense. It would determine whether Apollo 8, scheduled just two months later, might meet President Kennedy's commitment for reaching the moon before decade's end.

Apollo 7 was to be commanded by one of the original Mercury 7 astronauts, Wally Schirra, an amiable but cool-headed and self-assertive Navy test pilot and aeronautical engineer whom I later would get to know. The other two crew members were Donn Eisele and Walter Cunningham, neither of whom had yet been in space.

The *Daily News*, like many newspapers of its size, had for reasons of prestige sent a reporter to earlier space flights. The same reporter had covered all of those and considered the space beat his alone. He was one of the paper's old hands, twice my age, not a fan of the new management, or of me. The paper already had agreed to send him to cover this flight.

When I told Irwin Smallwood that I wanted to get credentials to cover it, too, he had no objections, but informed me the paper couldn't pay my expenses. I intended to go anyway, although I knew I'd be on a very tight budget—so tight that I took a tent, camping gear, and cans of Beanee-Weenees when I set out for Cape Canaveral in my trusty Mustang. Trusty, that is, to that point.

I intended to drive all night and arrive at Cape Canaveral early Thursday morning. But a malfunctioning water pump left me stranded deep into South Carolina in the middle of the night. I finally made it to Cape Canaveral at mid-afternoon and managed to get my credentials in time to join the biggest mob of reporters I'd ever encounter for a press conference with the astronauts and flight officials. I was wandering around bewildered when I spotted Tom Colt talking to a man in uniform. I managed to thread my way to him.

"We were getting worried about you," he said.

He introduced me to the officer with whom he was speaking, his father's old friend, Colonel Tom McClure, a tall garrulous man with bright brown eyes and a big smile.

"If you guys want to," McClure said, "I'll take you back and let you meet Wernher von Braun before this thing gets going."

Von Braun, who had built rockets for Nazi Germany before seeing brighter horizons, was the head of the Marshall Space Flight Center in Alabama, the man who had made it possible to get to the moon by developing the mighty Saturn missile. The colonel introduced us. Von Braun asked if we'd been to a space shot before. A first for both, we told him.

"It's quite a spectacle close up," he assured us.

The colonel and von Braun chatted briefly before the two had to proceed into the crowded room for the press conference. Von Braun was in suit and tie, as were flight officials. The astronauts, however, were in casual attire, like most of the reporters, as if they might be heading to the golf course after this was over. The colonel followed von Braun into the room with Tom and myself tagging respectfully behind.

Nobody had a clue or a concern about who we might be. Except for one person. The *Daily News* science reporter, who was unaware that I would be attending the event. He had found a seat right on the front row. Seeing me coming out with von Braun was such a shock that he looked even more dumbfounded than usual. Later, he angrily called his editor complaining about my presence and questioning how I was allowed in von Braun's company. I should have been the one complaining. He had a nice motel room at company expense. I was going to be sleeping in a tent and dining on 15-cent slider burgers at Royal Castle when I ate out.

The blast-off was to be at 11 Friday morning from Complex 34. Tom and I were to watch it from Press Site 2, which was about two miles away. Eric couldn't get press credentials and would climb a palm tree to watch the shot. Before that, Tom and I got on a bus with a lot of other reporters and rode to a site by the Banana River where about 1,000 VIPs were to watch from bleachers. They included many top military brass in uniform, along with public figures, politicians, and a lot of finely dressed wives.

We were granted 20 minutes to interview whomever we deemed worthy. I didn't recognize anybody until I saw Curtis LeMay, a four-star general and World War II bombing master who had been U.S. Air Force Chief of Staff. He had retired three years earlier and now was George Wallace's running mate for Vice-President. Dressed in a blue suit, surrounded by Secret Service agents, he was smoking a big cigar and had a little shred of tobacco stuck on the right side of his bottom lip. I thought he looked surly, and so apparently did a fellow standing near me with his wife, who was carrying a Brownie camera.

"Go shake his hand," she told him, "so I can get a picture."

But he was reluctant, rightly so as it turned out.

A minute or so later, a *New York Times* reporter showed up carrying a reporter's notebook and strode right up to LeMay. I straggled along with him thinking it might impress LeMay if I told him that I had visited with his running mate just a few weeks earlier.

"General," the *Times* guy said, "I was wondering if...."

LeMay interrupted him.

"I've got nothing to say to either of you!"

He angrily jabbed his cigar into the right corner of his mouth and chomped down on it, as if to emphasize his response. Men who served under him had called him "The Big Cigar." I didn't think he made much of an impression as a political campaigner.

I recognized only one other person at the VIP area. That was comedian Bill Dana, who had created an astronaut character he called Jose Jimenez. The original astronauts loved the character and adopted Jose as one of their own. When Alan Sheppard blasted off to become the first American into space in May, 1961, the first words to him from Flight Control were "OK, Jose, you're on your way."

Alas, by the time I spotted Dana, our time with the VIPs had run out, and I was herded back onto the bus with little to write about.

The old sportswriters' adage, "No cheering in the press box," obviously didn't apply to reporters covering space shots. There was a hushed excitement at Press Site 2 as loudspeakers began the countdown. Everybody was on their feet.

A flash of orange appeared at the base of the rocket.

"There she goes," a formerly sedate male reporter yelled excitedly.

Dirty smoke and steam billowed around the rocket.

"We have liftoff," the loudspeakers proclaimed.

"Go, baby, go!" one of the few female reporters screamed.

The sound was incredible, unlike anything I'd ever experienced, waves I actually could feel.

As the rocket slowly rose, applause rippled through the press site, turning to cheering as it speeded up, quickly becoming a tiny point of flame in the blue sky, its path soon visible only by a white contrail arcing southward.

Wernher von Braun was right. From two miles away it was a hell of a spectacle.

The astronauts would remain in orbit for 11 days and be the first U.S. astronauts to develop colds in space, creating re-entry pressure problems that caused them to splash down in the Atlantic without donning their helmets.

NASA had set up a large press room at the Ramada Inn in Cocoa Beach that had free coffee, three big TVs, many typewriters, all the paper and carbon sheets needed, telephones for local and collect calls only, and speakers that conveniently broadcast every communication between the astronauts and Mission Control. Tom and I went there with quite a few other reporters that afternoon. He worked on a news story for his paper in New Jersey, *The Bergen Record*. I wrote my Saturday column about my tribulations getting to Cape Canaveral.

I returned to the press room Saturday to turn out my Sunday column about the previous day's events, and after I'd finished it, Tom, Eric and I knocked around on the beach for a while and took in some of the other local sights, including a bar or two.

Colonel McClure and his wife had invited us to their home on the base Sunday morning for a steak-and-eggs breakfast on their patio. Afterward, the colonel took us on a tour in his command staff car. Our first stop was a huge, stainless steel sculpture of a futuristic 7, commemorating the original Mercury 7 astronauts. He stopped so we could take photos.

A couple of hundred yards to the east we could see the orange tower that dominated Launch Complex 14. It was from this complex that four of the original astronauts had made their initial flights, beginning with John Glenn's first orbital flight for an American on February 20, 1962, making him the fifth person into space after orbital flights by Russians Yuri Gagarin and Gherman Titov, and sub-orbital flights by Alan Shepard and Gus Grissom.

When we got back into the car, the colonel rounded a curve and headed toward the launch pad.

"A bunch of people are trying to get me to make a monument out of it," he said. "We don't have the money to make a monument out of it."

The blockhouse, a big concrete igloo, lay to our left, used now for storage. Metal buildings to the right housed the 4th Detachment, 1318th Geodetic Survey Squadron.

The colonel drove past "No Entry" and "No Smoking" signs, through a gate, then swung right, pulling slowly up a ramp that led to the base of the gantry.

"Now they would pull the rockets right up here," he said.

He stopped and we got out, walking the rest of the way up the ramp passing signs saying "Hard Hat Area" that almost had faded away. This was the last of the A-frame Atlas gantries, 15 stories tall and badly rusting. Just over five years earlier, Gordon Cooper had made the last flight from it.

"Back in those days," the colonel said, as if he were talking of ancient history, ducking his head as we started to climb the gantry stairs, "the astronauts, they would use this elevator...You see the various lines and how they feed across...All of this would be pulled away and what you've got left is the service tower, the umbilical tower...You see, very simple, very crude. Now we've got sexy methods."

On the third level, a big writing spider had spun a web and caught a large moth on which it was feasting. Higher up, the colonel stopped for the view. Just to the north was Pad 34 where Apollo 7 had launched only two days earlier. Beyond that, but not on the Air Force base, stood the gleaming white Saturn 5 which would deliver three Americans on a trip around the moon just two months later.

"This stuff is so small compared to those," the colonel said as a flock of white herons swept past below us.

The higher we climbed the more bird poop we encountered. Finally we reached the white room, where John Glenn had been the first to enter the tight and primitive Mercury capsule from this gantry. Later, when I got to know Glenn, he would be impressed that I had stood at this spot, one of the last to do so.

As we descended the tower, the colonel shook his head.

"The historian would say great to restore this," he said, "but again, it's a function of bucks."

The gantry already was being advertised. It soon would be torn down and hauled away as salvage.

"It may have cost $5 million to build it," he said as we got back into the car, "and we may only get $25,000 to sell it for scrap, but that's the way it is."

TEN DAYS AFTER I returned from Cape Canaveral, George Wallace entered my life again. Thinking that he was leading the presidential race in North Carolina, he had made no campaign appearances in the state. His only rally was set for noon Thursday, October 24, just 12 days prior to the election, in, of all places, Durham. Not only was Durham a city with a large black population and long simmering racial problems, it also was the home of liberal Duke University and North Carolina College at Durham, a black institution that soon would become N.C. Central University. The University of North Carolina at Chapel Hill, where Wallace could claim few supporters but many enemies, was only 11 miles away.

The choice of Durham gave the appearance that Wallace might be looking for trouble to gain attention and stir his voters and others who might be leaning his way. Whether or not that was true, his choice of the rally site tended to indicate it. That was the parking lot of the Durham Police Department. He was to speak from the presumed safety of the department's elevated entrance plaza standing behind a bullet-proof podium that came almost to his shoulders.

Thinking that violence still could break out even with cops close at hand, Kent Pollock and I teamed up again to cover the event, minus our hard hats. The turnout was huge, estimated at about 10,000. Most were Wallace supporters, many of whom were wearing Wallace hats, Wallace badges and carrying Wallace signs on sticks. They congregated in the area nearest the podium. But several hundred demonstrators from Duke, Carolina and North Carolina College also showed up, gathering behind them.

I was amused to find among the demonstrators a man holding a sign that said: "Another Pointy-Headed Professor for Wallace." He wouldn't give me his name but said he was indeed a professor at Duke.

"We're not going to have a disruptive disturbance," he said, grinning with more than a hint of irony in his voice. "We're for Wallace."

The first disturbance occurred before Wallace arrived. A man wearing Wallace buttons got into a shouting match with a black female student and sprayed her in the face with a small gas canister hidden in the palm of his hand. She screamed and a shoving match began. A big, red-faced man in a blue suit removed a short strand of heavy chain from his coat pocket and began threatening demonstrators with it. He put it back in his pocket and slipped away when several police officers hurried to separate the two groups.

Wallace arrived to cheers and jeers. One group of students, mostly white, extended their right arms shouting, "Sieg Heil! Sieg Heil!"

"Pay no mind to them," Wallace told his supporters. "That's all they've managed to learn in college."

Wallace's speech was his standard campaign fare—local control of public schools, law and order, ending the Vietnam War, replacing the Supreme Court, which he branded as "sick." He also attacked Richard Nixon, a graduate of the Duke University Law School, for refusing to debate.

"He's afraid that we're going to find out that he talks one way in North Carolina and another way in the state of California."

He also couldn't leave out newspapers.

"I want to tell you liberal North Carolina papers, where you've misquoted me about what I said, when I become your President and I come to Winston-Salem or Durham or Raleigh and a group of anarchists lies in front of my automobile, I'm gonna wean 'em from lying in front of automobiles."

That brought a rousing cheer from his supporters.

Wallace hadn't been speaking long when violence broke out again. It erupted near me. I was at one side of the parking lot, near the dividing line between the Wallace supporters and the protesters. A black police lieutenant was standing not far from me. A man in khaki work clothes slipped up behind him and sprayed him in the face with a small gas canister. The startled cop grabbed the man's arm and his shirt collar, holding on as his assailant squirmed and yelled. At that point, three others suddenly surrounded the two. One of them was the big guy in the blue suit. He was swinging his heavy chain. Another had a thick section of rebar, a potentially deadly club, stuck in his belt.

I could see the fear in the lieutenant's eyes as they darted in search of other officers to help him, but none were nearby or even aware of what was happening. He chose to let the guy in khakis go but without his gas canister.

At this point, students were loudly jeering and taunting Wallace supporters, calling them "rednecks" and chanting, "Go back, go back, go back into the woods."

When two black male students attempted to go beneath the rope separating the two groups, a rotund man wearing a big Wallace badge kicked one in the neck, knocking him to the ground. An affray erupted and began to spread. A huge Wallace banner on two heavy wooden poles was toppled onto the protestors, the poles striking several. Wallace supporters picked up the poles and began using them as battering rams. Protestors grabbed onto the poles and tugs of war began. Some Wallace supporters broke the wooden sticks on the signs they were holding and began throwing them at the protestors, who began flinging them back. People on both sides were swinging wildly at one another.

The melee interrupted Wallace's speech.

"Let the police handle it," he called, as a formation of officers wearing riot helmets and carrying clubs moved swiftly into the crowd. "Let the police handle it."

He stepped away from the podium.

The officers began attempting to separate combatants, pushing the protesters back from the Wallace supporters and forming a line to hold them in place so Wallace could finish his speech. No arrests were made, no injuries requiring treatment reported.

Surprisingly to some, Wallace didn't carry North Carolina, losing to Richard Nixon by more than eight percentage points. In a state that previously had been solidly Democratic, Hubert Humphrey came in third with only 29% of the vote. Wallace did win five states, Alabama, Arkansas, Georgia, Louisiana, and Mississippi, but not enough electoral votes to leave the decision to the House of Representatives, as he had hoped.

The Wallace campaign stop was the last story I would cover with Kent Pollock. In September, he had replaced Nat Walker as chief of the High Point Bureau and four months later he would accept a job with *The Miami Herald*.

Sadly, this wasn't the only change about to take place at the *Daily News*. In November, Frank Batten moved Chuck Hauser to Norfolk to be vice president and general manager of *The Virginian-Pilot*. Although it was quite a promotion, it wasn't a good move for Hauser, because it took him away from news coverage, which he loved. Four years later, he became editor of *The Providence Journal* in Rhode Island, where he would remain for 16 years before returning to North Carolina to teach journalism at the University of North Carolina and Davidson College.

Not only was Hauser a great editor, he also was a courageous one. He stood with reporters, and in 1985 he drew national attention by defying a federal judge's order not to publish secret recordings in a case involving an organized crime boss. He was held in contempt and sentenced to 18 months in prison. The conviction was overturned on appeal and upheld by the Supreme Court, a resounding victory for free press.

Hauser died at 76 in Chapel Hill in 2005 from an infection that killed quickly. On the way to the hospital, he asked his wife, Jane, to stop so he could pick up a Sunday edition of Raleigh's *News & Observer*. He was a dedicated newspaper man right to the end, and it was my great fortune to have had him enter my life at such a crucial stage and care enough to attempt to guide it.

20

Howard Fuller was the first and only black power advocate I got to know. I met him in October, 1967, when I was assigned to cover a talk he made in Greensboro. He was addressing the Luncheon Group, made up of black businessmen and professionals, at Hayes-Taylor YMCA, the black Y.

Fuller, a community organizer for an anti-poverty group, had been in the state for only a couple of years, but it hadn't taken him long to stir controversy and break into the news, where he kept popping up, sometimes stirring virulent reaction. Most of his news making had taken place in Durham, where he lived. Only a few months earlier, during the nationwide summer of racial rioting, he had led a march in Durham that resulted in the National Guard being called out after violence erupted as the demonstration was ending.

I was surprised and amused by Fuller's audacity. He was six months older than I. We both were 26. But his youth didn't keep him from chiding his older and much more experienced male audience, declaring them to be among the most conservative people in the state. Many blacks who had attained a better living standard, he told them, had adopted this stance on the way up: "Man, if I can get away from here, I ain't ever going to look back."

But despite North Carolina's feigned "progressive" identity, Fuller claimed, 90% of blacks in the state remained in poverty, bound by an economic and political system that was designed to keep them there. These people, he said, put middle-class blacks "in the same boat as whitey."

Some who had managed to escape poverty, Fuller said, goading even deeper, had begun to believe that they no longer were black.

"But I'm here to tell you brother, you are."

This didn't go well with some in the audience. During a lengthy question session at the end of the talk, one club member stood and told Fuller, "You talk just like a Black Muslim." He accused Fuller of "stirring backlash," and even attacked his hairdo, which he called "bushman." But Fuller laughed it off, no doubt figuring his point just had been made.

What impressed me most was what Fuller told his audience about some of his beliefs just before he began taking questions. He described himself as "a black man who has no illusions about being black," who is "proud of being black," and "who just happens to be tired of seeing people kicked around because they are black."

He said he was not a communist, not seeking to overthrow the government, or working against democracy. Instead, he said, he was working for "the realization of democracy."

He went on to note that he believed in black power but described it differently than it was being perceived by many and practiced by its outspoken proponents. To him, he said, it meant economic and political power, along with a better self-image for blacks. Unlike Stokely Carmichael, H. Rap Brown and Black Panther Huey Newton, he denounced violence and said he didn't believe it was necessary to bring about racial change.

FULLER WAS AS IMPRESSIVE in appearance as he was at speaking. He was six-feet-four with a graceful, athletic body and eyes with an intensity that left no doubt of his commitment to his cause. Born in Louisiana, he grew up in Milwaukee, living nearly half of his early years in a housing project. He attended a Catholic school until switching to public schools in junior high. In high school, he was captain of his championship basketball team, ran cross country and played on the tennis team. In his senior year he was elected student body president. In 1958, he won a full basketball scholarship to Carroll College in Waukesha, Wisconsin, just 18 miles from Milwaukee, where he became one of the first black students. After graduation four years later, he won the Urban League's Whitney Young scholarship to attend graduate school. He chose Western Reserve University (later Case Western) in Cleveland because it offered a degree in a field that interested him: community organizing.

It was in Cleveland that he first became involved in civil rights struggles, and where he heard Malcolm X speak. He was transfixed by Malcolm X's message of fighting by any means the "white man's" oppression and degradation of blacks, which clearly conflicted with Fuller's later claims opposing violence.

After receiving his master's degree, Fuller was obligated to work a year for the Urban League in Chicago trying to place blacks in jobs formerly filled only by whites. As his year in Chicago was ending, he was offered a job by an anti-poverty program called the North Carolina Fund and moved to Durham to work in the city's poorest black neighborhoods. He was stunned by what he found.

Dirt streets were not uncommon. Dilapidated shotgun rental houses were the norm, some without running water. He began by getting to know the residents, going door-to-door, dropping in at pool halls, stores, restaurants, speaking in churches, seeking out potential community leaders. His first big move was a successful neighborhood clean-up, overcoming unsanitary conditions and helping to alleviate rats.

Within six months, Fuller had organized five neighborhood councils with strong leaders. The councils began pressuring city officials, politicians, slumlords and others for change. They also began organizing demonstrations and registering people to vote. Unsurprisingly, this stirred a lot of opposition and criticism of Fuller, especially after he began using the term "black power" in his public appearances.

At the beginning of 1967, Fuller became the Fund's Director of Community Development, allowing him to spread his activities statewide and making him the target of even more and stronger attacks by critics.

ONLY A COUPLE OF weeks after I met Fuller, he was back in Greensboro, this time as the star of a black power forum at the University of North Carolina Greensboro. Fuller worked the mostly black crowd of about 800 with the style and skill of accomplished black evangelists. He had them repeatedly leaping to their feet, cheering, whooping, waving their arms.

"The only way the black man in the ghetto can break out of the ghetto is to organize—organize for black power," he shouted. "If we don't organize we're not going to win this struggle. Why not vote in a bloc?"

Many in the audience rose, shouting, "Why not? Why not?"

Blacks who had been elected to public office weren't serving other blacks, he told the crowd.

"They're masquerading. They're black on the outside, but on the inside they've got a white heart."

The crowd cheered.

"Money?" Fuller asked. "We just ain't got none. When you go to the white man's store on the corner, your money goes in his pocket and you just don't see it no more."

Poor black folks were powerless, Fuller said, and something had to be done about it.

"We are faced now by a situation where conscienceless power meets powerless conscience, threatening the very foundation of our nation. The sounds of the powerless, the sounds of the ghetto ought to be us singing, with our heads held high, 'New Black Joe.'"

The three-day forum would reap criticism that the university was endorsing and promoting the deadly violence the black power movement had stirred across the nation. Although Fuller promoted no violence, the very words "black power" left that implication.

What I didn't realize at the time was that Fuller was beginning a radical transformation.

North Carolina Fund had come under assault by conservative Republican Congressman Jim Gardner, who was running for governor. That led to the group's downfall. But a new group, the Foundation for Community Development, emerged from it with all-black leadership. Fuller became Director of Community Development Training. Although he proudly proclaimed himself to be the most hated black man in North Carolina, he had no intention of altering his methods or his image. He was going to continue to raise hell, he said, and indeed he did.

Some of that hell raising took place in Greensboro, where he helped organize and train leaders for the Greensboro Association of Poor People. The group not only began holding rent strikes and filing slumlord lawsuits, but organized voter registration drives that would lead Greensboro to have the highest percentage of black voters in the state. And just as Fuller had urged in his sermon at the black power forum, they would vote in a bloc, changing Greensboro government and politics.

I didn't encounter Fuller again for nearly a year, but in the fall of 1968 I called and asked if he would grant me an interview. We sat on the edge of the front porch of his modest house in Durham and talked for nearly two hours. Four months later, I would encounter Fuller again. This time I would be peering into an open basement window at the back of the Allen Building at Duke University.

BEFORE DUKE UNIVERSITY GOT that name, it was Trinity College, a small Methodist school that began training ministers before the Civil War. It had been just up the road from our house in Randolph County. In 1892, Trinity College had been enticed to move to Durham by the generosity of Washington Duke, founder of American Tobacco Company. In 1924, Duke's son, James Buchanan, called "Buck," decided to turn the college into a university and build a new campus for it in a forest on the city's southwestern outskirts. It would take on the family name and become one of the country's most prominent and prestigious private universities.

For decades, Duke had a conservative board of trustees, along with a lot of wealthy and powerful alumni. It wasn't opposed to change but sought to implement it with due process. It was unaccustomed to demands by students, faculty and other employees.

Integration had come slowly at Duke. Four blacks were allowed into graduate programs in 1962. A year later five undergraduates were admitted. They became Duke's first black graduates in 1967. By the fall of 1967, 170 blacks were enrolled, and many were becoming discontented. Trouble was about to stir, and it was no coincidence that Howard Fuller often was seen on campus.

On November 10, 1967, four black students presented a list of demands to Duke President Douglas Knight. Three days later, 35 members of the Student Afro-American Society staged a seven-hour "study-in," blocking the entrance to Knight's office in the Allen Building.

Martin Luther King Jr.'s murder brought a longer siege. At noon on Friday, April 5, students began a vigil on the quadrant in front of the university's imposing Collegiate Gothic chapel. That evening, as the vigil grew, about 450 students, black and white, marched in a driving rain to the president's home, just off campus. Knight met them outside and invited them in to talk. About 250 accepted and the talks went on for hours.

When Knight told them he didn't have the authority to grant concessions on matters that the board of trustees had to decide, an impasse ensued, creating a sit-in.

On Saturday, after more failed discussions, Knight spoke at a memorial service for King in the chapel and fell ill afterward. He had suffered a severe bout with hepatitis eight months earlier and stress apparently brought on a relapse. He was hospitalized, and under doctor's orders, he took medical leave, removing him from further negotiations.

Meanwhile, more than 300 students from nearby all-black North Carolina College joined the vigil. Not until Sunday did the students at the president's home end the sit-in and move to the camp-out on the quadrant where more than 1,000 slept Sunday night. At times, when speeches were made, the vigil would number as many as 2,400. Total university enrollment was about 7,800, some of whom opposed the demonstration.

The vigil continued on Monday with boycotts of classes and cafeterias, prompting non-academic employees to go on strike and creating a crisis for the board of trustees.

Although Howard Fuller had been working with Duke's cafeteria employees and janitors to improve their situations, he was not involved with the sit-in, or the early stages of the vigil. He was occupied with other matters regarding King's death. But on Tuesday, the day before King's funeral, Fuller led students on a peaceful march on city hall to honor King, who had made at least four visits to Durham, preaching and protesting. After the marchers arrived at city hall, Mayor Wensell Grabarek, who had worked to end segregation in local facilities during demonstrations in 1963, addressed the gathering. He commended Fuller for preventing the rioting that was occurring in so many other cities. Durham would not be without troubles though. That night arsonists set 13 fires in the city, and a curfew was imposed.

The vigil ended two days after King's funeral when university officials conceded to the black students' demands. Some of the trustees surprisingly joined the closing of the vigil, singing "We Shall Overcome" with the participants.

That summer, the president of the Student Afro-American Society, Chuck Hopkins, worked as an intern for Howard Fuller. Only a few weeks after classes resumed, the group presented another list of demands to Knight, who had recovered from his hepatitis setback.

Black students wanted a black studies program, a black faculty adviser and a black recruiter to attract more black students. They wanted a substantial amount of the university's community contracts to go to black businesses, and they wanted Duke to support reforms in housing, welfare and other fields in Durham. As usual, the university moved at its own deliberate pace, angering black students and eventually stirring them to action.

ON THURSDAY, FEBRUARY 13TH, 1969, I wandered into the newsroom a little before noon. Moses Crutchfield, the assistant managing editor, waved me to his desk. He was holding an AP wire report. Black students had taken over the main administration building at Duke, where all of the university's records were stored, he told me. Reports were that they had carried in gasoline cans and matches and were threatening to burn records if their demands weren't met. I grabbed a yellow legal pad and a few pens and headed to Durham, just under an hour's drive away.

The main quad was filled with milling people when I arrived, including many reporters and photographers. Groups of students and faculty were engaged in discussions and sometimes fierce arguments.

I learned that about 60 students were inside the three-story Allen Building, more than a third of black enrollment. They had entered the building at 8 that morning before employees arrived. One exception was Bill Griffith, dean of student affairs. He had come into his first-floor office at 6, as usual. When he heard hammering in the hallway, he stepped out to see what was going on. He found black students nailing two-by-fours across the rear entrance double doorway and was politely escorted out of the building.

The black students had a spokesperson outside the main entrance. His name was Sandyles Person, a junior from Enoree, S.C.

"We just rented a U-Haul-it truck and brought a few people and sneaked them in," he told me. "That's all there is to it."

The U-Haul had carried the equipment and supplies the students needed. Person said they had enough food to last a week.

From an administration spokesman I learned that President Knight had flown to New York before the occupation that morning, ironically to see if he could raise funds for a black studies program. He had met with black students the evening before. An annual event called Black Culture Week was winding down. It had featured Mississippi civil rights hero Fannie Lou Hamer, singer James Brown and comedian Dick Gregory. Gregory had led black students on a march to Knight's house. Knight met with them for two hours without satisfying results. After his arrival in New York, Knight conferred with university officials and trustees by telephone while attempting to arrange a flight back.

At 2:30 about 500 supporters of the occupiers gathered in the chapel to try to decide a course of action. The white male student who served as moderator began by suggesting that the chapel was an inappropriate meeting place.

"I'm an atheist," he said. "I don't know who suggested we meet in the God Box."

Over the next hour, students and faculty members engaged in argument after argument. Some wanted a strike. Others thought white students should begin seizing buildings. At one point, the meeting turned into a shouting match. At another, the clearly distressed chaplain felt compelled to intervene. He cautioned that wearing hats, eating, drinking, smoking and cursing, all of which were taking place in ample excess, were not allowed in the chapel. As the meeting went on, students kept running in with dire warnings that police were gathering.

The only agreement that emerged from this meeting was that if the cops were called in, the students in the Allen Building likely would be "crunched," and it was the duty of all other students to protect them. They should disperse and prepare for battle, and that was what many did.

While this meeting was going on, Knight made the decision to allow police to recapture the building. At 3:30, as the meeting in the chapel was breaking up, the black students in the Allen Building, who actually were occupying only the first floor and basement, were given an ultimatum by Provost Marcus Hobbs. They had an hour to come out and begin peaceful discussions, or else. Their supporters began posting themselves around two sides of the Allen Building where the main entrances were. They brought towels, lemons and petroleum jelly to protect against tear gas. Some had helmets. It was a cold windy day, and female students handed out blankets to some defenders.

Hundreds of students had gathered on the quad to watch. A few started fires in barrels to warm themselves. Some hoped to see the police clear the building and bloody some heads.

"We're going to cheer when they start," one student who was warming his hands over a barrel fire told me.

The deadline came and passed with no police in sight. An emergency faculty meeting had been called on the east campus where Knight, who had made it back to Durham, showed up late. As he explained his decision, a group of professors who opposed it walked out in protest. Some came to confer with the white Liberation Front students who were protecting the Allen Building, now numbering about 100. They speculated that the police would wait for darkness before clearing the building, making it harder for TV cameras to record their activity.

I went to the back of the building, which had been built on a hillside. The basement was at ground level there. This was where runners came to pass supplies and provide news of developments to the students inside through an open, push-out bottom section of a basement window. Durham police and State Highway Patrol officers had been gathering in a parking lot at Sarah Duke Gardens not far away, and black students had them under watch.

"If they get in," one of the students inside was telling a runner, "we're going to fight."

He held up a heavy chain to show it off.

"I'll be down at the courthouse with the bail money," the runner said.

When the runners departed to gather more information, the students inside left the window. I peered through the open portion and saw Howard Fuller walking past an open door in the hallway.

"Howard!" I shouted.

He had disappeared from view, but he suddenly stepped backward, peering in my direction. He recognized me and strode to the window.

"What are you doing in there?" I asked.

"These kids don't know what the hell they're doing," he said. "I had to get over here and see if I could help them."

"Can I come in?"

He paused for a moment.

"Yeah," he said, "come on in."

I figured he was thinking it would be helpful to have an objective witness inside when police stormed the building, which he considered to be inevitable.

After I climbed through the window, Fuller told me he'd been unaware of the students' plan to seize the building. He was giving a luncheon speech at Bennett College in Greensboro when he got the news. He and one of his staff members, Nelson Johnson, a radical student leader at A&T State University, who only nine days earlier had staged an occupation of A&T's administrative building, left Bennett and drove hurriedly to Duke. They probably had arrived after I did. Fuller and Johnson climbed through a window, too.

The students, all male, had gathered in a room in the basement. Some were arguing. Others were noticeably quiet. A short time earlier, they had been informed that all now were suspended from Duke. Some, like the chain bearer, still were determined to stand and fight. Others had begun to worry about what their parents would think if their rash action got them thrown out of Duke and burdened with criminal records. Were they squandering a high-caliber education that few ever had a chance to achieve, not to mention their reputations and futures? Fuller was staying out of the arguments. He was available for advice but made no attempts to lead in either direction.

Arguments ceased when a student came to the door and shouted, "The cops are on the way." I looked at my watch. It was 6 p.m. and darkness was setting in. For a few moments nobody seemed to know what to do.

Finally, one of the leaders said, "Let's take a vote. All in favor of leaving say aye."

A loud burst of ayes erupted, making the next question unnecessary.

A jammed rush to the basement stairway ensued. Desks and other furniture had been piled in front of the two entrances to the first floor. Students climbed over the furniture at the rear entrance, which was on the side of the building facing the quad. This entrance was at the point where the quad began and the two-lane street leading to the chapel became dual streets lined with trees on each side of the grassy quad.

After the furniture had been moved out of the way, students began using claw hammers and a crow bar to pry away the two-by-fours they'd nailed across the double doors. When those had been tossed aside, the students discovered an unexpected complication. The doors were locked, as they had been from the time they entered through the front entrance. And nobody had a key, or any idea where one might be.

Beating the door handles and locks with hammers proved ineffective. Only brute force would work, and that required a lot of bruising effort, further splintering the doors and costing precious minutes. The students wanted their exit to look victorious. They had decided to depart thrusting fists into the air and shouting, "black power!"

When the first students burst through the doors, their supporters cheered. Others jeered. The black students ran down two short flights of stone steps and turned left onto the broad flagstone sidewalk, running away from the chapel. They veered onto the two-lane street, trotting in the traffic lanes. As the last students left the building, myself following, their supporters and other students fell in behind them. I didn't notice until a little later that Howard Fuller wasn't among them. He apparently had slipped away into the crowd. I didn't see him again that night.

The black students' victory lap didn't last long. When they were about halfway down this short street, a police car, emergency lights flashing, turned into it, headed straight toward them. Then came a second. And a third.

The students hesitated, uncertain what to do. The driver of the lead car slowed, then stopped just short of the students.

"Go ahead," ordered the driver of the second car over a loudspeaker.

The lead car began moving slowly into the students, brushing several aside. Screams and curses erupted. Students surrounded all three cars, forcing them to stop. They pounded on the doors and fenders, kicked them, smashed a side window in the lead car. Black student leaders hurriedly conferred and began calling for students to pull back to the quad. The group turned and began running the other way.

While this was going on, more police vehicles had arrived on a different street, just down the hill. They came to a halt at the back of the Allen building and began disgorging officers wearing riot helmets and gas masks. They were carrying long batons, fogging machines and tear gas launchers. Some entered the Allen Building through a heavy metal basement door, others began taking up positions around the building.

Students pressed against the officers outside, taunting them. Wads of paper were thrown. Then an unopened soft drink can flew through the air and a police officer dodged it. Bottles followed, then rocks.

I was standing with our photographer Larry Tucker and WFMY-TV videographer Eddie Dick. We were about 20 feet back from a line of cops near the rear entrance of the building, with students all around us. Dick had been talking about what a rough day he was having. He'd been cursed, threatened and shoved by students who didn't want to be filmed.

Moments after he said that, the cops, numbering 120, including highway patrolmen and Durham reserve officers, got the order to move out.

One turned on a fogging machine and headed for us. Another launched a tear gas canister straight at Tucker. He got a photo of it in mid-flight. It barely missed him. When Dick raised his camera to start filming, a cop came up behind him with his nightstick in the air and struck a strong blow across his back and right shoulder where his camera nestled. The blow almost knocked Dick down, but he regained his footing and started running through the fumes with Tucker, me and nearby students.

"If the students don't get you," Dick later quipped, "the cops will."

To make things worse, Dick would get back to the TV station that night with the battle film he'd shot only to have the processing machine break down and ruin it.

I'd experienced tear gas before, but never to this extent. My eyes burned, my vision was blurred, tears streaming. I soon was joining the choruses of violent retching that were breaking out all over the quad.

The cops were wildly swinging extended riot batons at anybody in their paths and frequently connecting. Some students fled into the chapel seeking sanctuary but cops even followed them there.

I had no doubt that the officers were deliberately targeting reporters and press photographers. Kathy Cross, who was reporting for *The New York Times*, was gassed on the steps leading to the chapel, then clubbed in the head knocking her down and leaving her bloodied. Six stitches would be required to close the wound.

A heavy-set cop began chasing me on the chapel plaza. With my long legs, I knew I could outrun him, but I quickly ran out of running room. I darted behind a huge shrub next to the Divinity School building and the cop came after me. When he moved one way, I went the other. We danced religiously round and round before he gave up in frustration and went looking for easier targets. He never hit me, but the bush took quite a beating.

The battle raged for more than an hour. When the cops fell back to reorganize, the students pressed forward. When the cops moved out again, the students retreated, some picking up tear gas canisters and tossing them back. At one point, I made my way to the nearby university hospital emergency room to check on casualties. Blood drops and vomit were near the entrance. Shortly after I arrived, three white male students straggled in, all with bloodied heads.

"They're hitting everybody," one said.

At about 7:15, police withdrew inside the Allen Building. Exultant students surged around outside, shouting triumphantly. Doug Jenson, the coordinator of student activities, entered through the main entrance to talk with the officers. He came out shortly and was handed a megaphone by a student protester.

"The situation is extremely awkward at this point," he said.

If the students would disperse, Jensen told them, the police could leave.

The students jeered, making it clear they would not fulfill his request. Jenson retreated into the building. Half an hour later, he came out again.

"All we ask is that you back away from the building," he said, "and all the police will leave the campus immediately."

With urging, the students began moving back, but not far. They formed a gauntlet.

"They're not going to run this gauntlet," a male student said. "Cops are basically chicken."

"Don't touch them," a female student responded. "Let them leave."

When nothing happened, students closed in again around the main entrance. Not far from the rear entrance, the heavily damaged lead patrol car that had been instrumental in starting the melee had been abandoned. A laughing student now sat in it, turning the siren off and on as the wait continued.

At a little after 8, police began quietly slipping out through the basement door by which they first had entered. They were carrying their clubs, shotguns, fogging machines, tear gas launchers, and even combat stretchers, still folded. When students got word of the departure, cheers erupted, and exultant groups began heading to Page Auditorium near the chapel to discuss the day's activities. Five officers had been hurt by thrown objects and taken to the hospital. More than 20 students and been injured enough to require treatment, none seriously.

I hurried back to the hospital emergency room, because I had spotted a pay telephone there from which I could call in my story. For the next hour, I sat in the waiting area, furiously scribbling a lengthy narrative of the day's events. Never had I written anything that long in so little time. I hurried to the phone booth, immensely relieved to be making the final deadline. I dialed the long-distance operator and placed a collect call.

I heard an unfamiliar voice answer, "Greensboro News Company," a switchboard fill-in, I feared.

"I have a collect call from Jerry Bledsoe," the operator said.

"I'm sorry, we don't accept collect calls," the switchboard operator replied.

It had been an intensely stressful day and I blew up. "You'd better accept this call," I screamed, "or your ass is going to be in deep trouble."

"Let's watch our language, please," said the long-distance operator.

"One moment," the switchboard operator snipped with more than a hint of indignation. A short time later, she came back on line.

"We accept the call," she said resentfully, and connected me to Henry Coble, the night editor.

"What did you say to that operator?" Coble asked. "She said some crazy person named Bledsoe was threatening her because she wouldn't accept a collect call."

"She could be right on all counts," I said.

He chuckled and switched me to a copy desk editor who took my dictation. The story appeared on the front page in the final edition under the headline, "Battle In A Gothic Setting," with a long jump inside.

I left the emergency room exhausted but relieved. It suddenly struck me that not only hadn't I eaten since a doughnut that morning, I also couldn't remember where I'd parked my car. It took me half an hour to find it, and I still had nearly an 80-mile drive home.

On Friday, about a third of Duke's students didn't show up for classes. I didn't return that day. I was slow in recovering and had a column to write. But I did go back Saturday. Knight was supposed to address the student body at Page Auditorium that afternoon, Governor Bob Scott had called out the National Guard after Friday night's violence, and the troops were on standby. State officials were concerned that Knight's appearance might prompt more violence. The Guard's adjutant general requested that Knight cancel the session, which he did.

More than a thousand students turned out anyway. They booed, hissed and shouted insults when Bill Griffith informed them that Knight would be making a statement on university radio that evening. A faculty member from the history department who supported the black students, condemned the faculty majority that stood behind Knight's decision to call in police.

"I submit that the faculty of Duke University is both intellectually and morally corrupt," he declared.

He was interrupted by an angry faculty member who yelled that he was "a bald-faced liar" and stood screaming obscenities at him.

Mike McBride, president of Duke's Afro-America Society, defended the takeover, for which he and Chuck Hopkins, the group's previous president, had been leaders.

"We had a right to do what we did, because we're fighting for our humanity," McBride said before turning his attention to white students.

"You're getting messed over," he told them, "you better start bucking..."

The audience was ready to buck. They had expected a meeting with Knight and they wanted it now, face-to-face. They marched more than a thousand strong on his swank, modern university-owned home. Howard Fuller, who also had spoken at the gathering, was at the front of the group.

Knight was waiting for them, standing on a high wall. The students closed in, surrounding him, filling his driveway and spreading into surrounding woods. Some clambered onto the roof of the house. I worked my way within a few feet so I could hear the interchange.

Knight was a genteel man, 47 years old, father of four, a former literature professor at Yale, a person with an aversion to conflict and rudeness and little experience with it. I noticed that his hands were trembling, and I felt sorry for him. Yet he held his own as network TV cameras whirred and reporters gouged microphones at his face.

It was to his great regret that he had to call in the police, Knight said, but he was left with no other choice. Despite loud and nasty protestations, he was adamant that amnesty would not be granted. The suspended black students would have to face hearings. After an hour of fruitless back-and-forth, Knight agreed to meet in his home later that evening with representatives of the black students, key administrators, and members of a faculty committee that had been created to look into a black studies program. Howard Fuller also was included. He would become the primary negotiator for the black students.

That often heated meeting went on until midnight, but by the end an agreement had been reached that Duke would create a black studies program, the first for a southern university.

EARLY IN THE OCCUPATION of the Allen Building, the students inside created a hand-made sign and hung it out a window: "Malcolm X Liberation School."

Howard Fuller became obsessed with that sign. It started him thinking that such an institution should exist, a university where black students had authority over their own educations. He talked to his boss about it, and not only did he get his permission to develop the idea on the job, the board of the foundation, which received public funds, gave him $14,300 to finance the project.

Three weeks after Duke had agreed to the black studies program, a problem developed. Black students were outraged because they had not been given a big enough role in planning it. About 40 black students coached by Fuller announced that they were going to withdraw from Duke and create their own university.

On Monday March 10, black students and many of their white campus supporters, including some faculty, held a torch-light march on downtown Durham. At the front of the procession they carried the sign that had hung outside the window of the Allen Building. At a spot called Five Points, they joined community groups organized by Fuller for a rally. Some of Durham's prominent black leaders, who ordinarily didn't involve themselves in matters at Duke, made it clear that they would support the black students.

The following night, after the university failed to appease them, black students staged another protest downtown. Some participants began smashing store windows and attacking vehicles. Mayhem ensued. Students using bricks, clubs and other weapons fought with police. The mayor requested that the governor call out the National Guard again and put the city under a dusk-to-dawn curfew for two days.

Eight days later, Duke held a hearing for students who had seized the Allen Building. They were found guilty of violating university rules and placed on probation. University officials moved swiftly to institute the black students' demands. And one by one, the students who had threatened to leave and create their own university decided to remain at Duke.

That would not be a choice for Douglas Knight, however. He was under attack from all sides: students, faculty, trustees, alumni and community leaders. Threats were made against his life. Guards were assigned to his home at night. He and his wife no longer would allow their children to sleep there. "Dump Doug" bumper stickers abounded on campus. At the end of March, trustees forced his resignation. He would leave academia for the corporate world and never again return to Duke.

The trustees chose as Duke's new president former Governor Terry Sanford, the man who created the North Carolina Fund whose employee, Howard Fuller, had played a leading role in creating the crises and resulting violence that forced Knight out and would change and haunt Duke forever.

Losing the Duke students didn't keep Fuller from moving forward with Malcolm X Liberation University. Using $45,000 from the Episcopal Church, along with other donations, he opened it at the end of October in an old warehouse building in the same rundown neighborhood in which he had started working in Durham. Fifty-one students from 17 states signed up for classes, some of whom had been expelled from other schools. By spring the number had dropped to 20. That summer the Council of Elders decided to move the school to Greensboro. In October it opened with 65 students in the education building of a Baptist Church on Asheboro Street that had moved to new quarters

By this time Fuller had grown a beard, let his hair get even bushier, started wearing dashikis and adopted an African name, Owusu Sadaukai. He also had become an ardent Pan-Africanist, a movement promoting worldwide solidarity for people of African descent.

In August, 1971, Fuller went to Tanzania and embarked on a 400-mile trek with freedom fighters into Mozambique, where he was fired upon from the air by Portuguese soldiers. He returned to Greensboro in October just after Malcolm X University began its second year in the city. By the end of its third year in Greensboro, the school had only 24 students and closed in June, 1973, for lack of funding.

Fuller had no problem keeping busy. He had become an ardent proponent of Pan-Africanism, speaking around the country and planning national and international conferences. He also had become a devout member of the Revolutionary Workers' League, a black power communist group that had no qualms about violence. But both of these movements would disintegrate due to internal bickering, turmoil and even physical conflict, leaving Fuller temporarily without a cause. His marriage ended, and in late summer, 1976, he returned to Milwaukee broke and dispirited. For a while he sold insurance, but he quickly became engaged in local educational issues and landed a job at the Equal Opportunity Program at Marquette University, where he later earned a PhD in education.

I was unaware of most of this. I had lost touch with Fuller after the events at Duke and considered Malcolm X University to be a hopeless, racially exclusive venture that likely only would lead to more divisiveness. The next thing I heard about him came as a surprise. In 1991, he was appointed superintendent of public schools in Milwaukee, a job that lasted only four years, ironically, considering his past, because of his constant battles with the teachers union. He returned to Marquette as a professor.

Fuller, a campaigner for educational reform, came to believe that charter schools were the best hope for educating children of all colors and backgrounds, especially black children. After George W. Bush was declared victor in the 2000 presidential election, he summoned Fuller to Austin and invited him to come to Washington with the Department of Education. Fuller declined. He had too many other things going on.

In addition to teaching, he founded and directed the Institution for the Transformation of Learning at Marquette and the Black Alliance for Educational Options, which promotes charter schools and has chapters in 22 states. Contributors to these non-profits included foundations of the Wal-Mart Waltons, Bill and Melinda Gates and others.

In 2011, *Forbes* magazine named Fuller one of the seven best educators in the world.

As I write this, Fuller has a wall of honorary doctorates, serves on boards of numerous prestigious institutions and travels the country preaching the virtues of charter schools. In 2014, he published an autobiography, *No Struggle, No Progress*, written with former *Washington Post* reporter and civil rights author Lisa Frazier Page.

Based on photos and TV news segments I have seen, Fuller no longer wears dashikis or other African garb, and long ago abandoned his bushman do. What hair he has left is nearly as white as mine.

It would be interesting to see how he might react if at one of his appearances some brash, young upstart dared have the audacity to tell him he was among the most conservative people in the country, "in the same boat as whitey," and thinking he no longer is black, even though, brother, he is.

21

THE FINAL YEAR OF this tumultuous decade got off to a good start for me. In January I won the Ernie Pyle Memorial Award for human interest writing. I didn't even know I'd been nominated. The entry Irwin Smallwood submitted was made up of columns I had written about interesting folks and the piece about my visit with Mrs. Sandburg.

Scripps Howard Newspapers, for whom Pyle had been a columnist, first traveling the country writing about people he encountered, then from the war zones, had started the award in 1953. This recognition happily put me in the company of two of my heroes who were early winners of the award: Kays Gary, columnist for *The Charlotte Observer* in 1955, and Charles Kuralt of *The Charlotte News* the following year. Although I never had read any of Kuralt's newspaper columns, I loved his "On the Road" features on CBS (a TV version of Ernie's early columns), and later in the year I'd get to meet him.

A news story about the award appeared on the *Daily News* front page on January 17. This is what the three judges, all editors of Scripps-Howard newspapers, wrote about me: "He is one of the freshest young writers we have encountered in years. His columns are reminiscent of Ernie's *Home Country* stories written prior to World War II. They are moving little glimpses into the lives of people about whom he writes, often touched with humor and sentiment. He is capable of painting a word portrait of an individual in very little space, yet he can also create and sustain a mood over the course of a lengthy feature article."

As hard as it was to believe such glowing words, they meant a lot to me because I had become a great admirer of Pyle's reporting and writing. Tom Wingate loved his work and talked with me about it while I was at the *Independent*. I had scrounged around in second-hand book stores and found frayed copies of Pyle's books of war columns, which had been bestsellers, *Here is Your War* and *Brave Men*. Later, I came upon a copy of *Home Country*, published after his death.

Another aspect of the award was that it came with a check for a thousand bucks, nearly a fifth of my annual salary. But there were other benefits as well. An article in *Editor and Publisher*, as well as a full-page ad by Scripps Howard, spread my name nationally.

THE AWARD BROUGHT ME a request to speak at a conference of student journalists at Southern Illinois University. I, of course, was reluctant to accept. I hadn't spoken before any group since my debacle before the English Speaking Society at Doshisha University nearly seven years earlier. I'd had requests from civic and church groups, but I made excuses avoiding all.

The journalism professor who called was a former newspaper man.

"I need to let you know a few things up front," I told him. "I'm scared to death of speaking in public, won't be good at it, and I don't have a college degree. I only went to college for one semester and barely managed that."

"Oh, that makes it all the better," he said with a laugh.

The convention was a couple of months off, in late April.

"I need to think about this before I give you an answer," I told him.

This opportunity had an appeal strong enough to encourage me to confront my fear.

I wanted to go to Dana, Indiana, where Ernie Pyle had been born and reared, to see what the town and countryside were like, maybe find the farm house where he had grown up, if it still existed, perhaps even meet some people who knew him.

I got out my highway atlas and saw that Dana was near the Illinois border, west of Indianapolis. I knew it was just off U.S. Highway 36, called the Lincoln Highway, because Pyle had written about that. The university was at Carbondale on the western border of Illinois, well to the south, but it was only a couple hundred miles from Dana. If I made the trip by car I could shoot up there on my way back.

When I told Smallwood about this opportunity, he thought I should do it. The *Daily News* had bought two new Nash Ramblers as staff cars. I could take one, he said, and Linda and Erik could go with me. Unlike our old staff cars, it even had a functioning radio for news and entertainment.

My speech at the awards luncheon went better than I expected. That was because I had written it and typed it in all capital letters to make it easier to read. The third paragraph began this way: "You may be able to tell by now that I am reading this. I am reading it because I am scared." To my immense relief that got a laugh, and the rest went well.

After the event ended many students gathered around to ask questions, chat and seek advice. It was clear that some were dreaming of working for a newspaper and maybe even winning a national award someday, and my story, I thought, made them think it could be possible.

The day after the speech, we went to Springfield, where Lincoln lived when he was elected President, and where the only house he ever owned was open to the public. We drove the Lincoln Highway to Dana on Saturday. Before the war, Pyle had written a column about all the famous people who had been born along that highway and speculated what a marker about himself might say near Dana.

"Three miles south is the house in which E. Pyle, Indiana's great skunk-trapper, jelly-eater, horse-hater, and snake-afraider-of, was born. In his later years, Mr. Pyle rose to a state of national mediocrity as a letter-writer, a stayer in hotels, a talker to obscure people, and a driver from town to town. The old house is in a good state of preservation, although the same cannot be said for Mr. Pyle. Historians say he has been falling to pieces for years."

That marker never got erected, but the Ernie Pyle Rest Park did, a small shady square carved from a farm field. It offered picnic tables for travelers. A monument stood near the highway. It was an exact replica of the permanent marker that the 1118 Engineer Combat Group erected in 1946 at the site of his death. It bore a bronze relief of the Statue of Liberty and a metal plaque with the inscription: "At This Spot the 77th Infantry Lost a Buddy ERNIE PYLE 18 April, 1945."

I took a photo of Erik standing at the base of the monument looking up at it. I was trying to make up for my failure to pay homage at the actual spot of Pyle's death on Ie Shima while I was in Okinawa.

Dana was not on the Lincoln Highway. It was a half mile north on Indiana Highway 71, the town's Main Street. It wasn't much of a town, just 185 acres filled with modest houses and surrounded by flat farm fields. Only a few hundred people lived there. The skyline was dominated by a huge grain elevator and a water tower alongside a single straight stretch of railroad tracks. The business district was a block of old brick stores, several empty. First National Bank with its granite facade and two big columns was most prominent. In early afternoon a few people still were eating at Mag's Cafe. Two farmers in overalls stood talking in front of the farm implement place. The IGA Food Store was the busiest spot in town. The office of *The Dana News* had been shut down and deserted. Ed Columbo's Soda Shop was next door. He was standing at the fountain.

"Paper moved up to Cayuga," he said. "Been about a year ago, hadn't it?" he asked his wife, who nodded agreement.

I was hoping to meet some people who might have known Ernie Pyle, I told him.

"I saw Ernie Pyle and I was well acquainted with his dad and Aunt Mary," he said. "They don't have no more relatives here. The house is still out here south of town. You seen it?"

"Not yet."

"Widow woman lives in the house. Mrs. Hasely...what is her name?"

"Mrs. Hazen," his wife corrected.

Columbo dug around underneath the counter and found a folder the Dames Club of Dana had put out a few years earlier about Pyle and the town.

"You can get about all the information out of that," he said, then gave me directions to the house.

"You go down this road about three miles and take a left, it's the fourth house on the left, just before you get to this hill. We call it the mountain."

"The house sets way back," his wife said.

"Oh, it don't set too far back," he said.

A young woman who was sitting at the counter with two children, all sipping fountain drinks, spoke up.

"What about that Mrs. Bales that lives out there? Wasn't she some kin to the Pyles? Aunt Mary was a Bales."

Aunt Mary was Pyle's favorite aunt, a real character. He wrote about her in his columns. Aunt Mary to Pyle was what Aunt Vivianne would become for me—a constant supply of good material.

Nobody was sure of this woman's relationship, but they knew where she lived and I stopped to see if she was indeed related to Aunt Mary. I knocked and knocked before she responded. A tiny woman with frightened, watery eyes peeked up at me between glass louvers she opened. I told her I'd been informed that she might be related to Ernie Pyle's Aunt Mary.

"She was my step-mother," she said.

Would she be willing to talk with me?

"I couldn't tell you any more than's in those books," she said. "It's all in those books."

Before closing the louvers, she told me the Pyle house was just up the road. It was set back but not too far, a typical farm house for the area, painted white with a green asphalt shingle roof, surrounded by tall maples. The main portion of the roof had a high beam, creating two small rooms with slanted ceilings upstairs. A long narrow porch stretched across the front of the house, and brick chimneys stood at the kitchen on the back and the living room on the west side.

Carmen Hazen was quick to answer my knock. She would be delighted to talk, she said, and happy to have company. She saw Linda and Erik in the car and went out to bring them in. She made a big to-do about Erik. She soon was to become a great-grandmother and was anticipating it with obvious joy. She had lived in the house for six years, she said, the last three by herself. She and her husband Clyde were on a fishing trip in Michigan when she lost him.

"Just died sudden," she said. "Never said a word. Just died."

She rented the house from Ed Goforth, who lived on the next farm over. He bought the Pyle farm after Ernie's father died in 1950.

"It's a restful little place out here," she said. "Nobody bothers you."

She took us on a full tour of the house. She had filled it with sturdy furniture and pictures of her grandchildren. She called it "just a simple old farmhouse," but it had a lot of fancy porcelain light fixtures decorated with images of colorful flowers.

"Aunt Mary bought those and put them here," she said. "After Ernie started writing about her, people would send her money sometimes. She took it and bought those. Now there was a good old soul. She lived by me in Dana. Witty. A good old soul."

She wished she'd known Ernie, she said, but never got to meet him, although she'd heard much about him.

"He used to get up there by that old barn, where it's half painted," she said.

The barn was one of several outbuildings on the hill near the house that everybody called the mountain, the only hill anywhere around, actually an ancient Indian burial ground.

"He used to sit up there and shoot groundhogs and then he'd come down here and grieve about it. I read that somewhere. I used to read his columns in *The Indianapolis Times*. Never did dream I'd ever live in his home."

While we were talking, Ed Goforth pulled into the driveway in his old pickup truck. He had come to feed the cattle fenced behind the house.

"Now, there's somebody who can tell you about Ernie," Mrs Hazen said.

Goforth was tall, lean and hard-jawed, his face darkened and wizened from countless hours in open fields. He wore dull green work clothes and a billed cap that matched. He had been born on the adjoining farm but had left to teach school in Gary for 40 years, all the while acquiring farm land. He now owned several big farms in the area. He pulled off a work glove to shake my hand.

"Oh, yes," he said. "I knew Ernie. Went to school with him. He was a little older than me. He'd have been 69 this summer. I'm only 66.

"We threshed together, ate threshing dinners together. He hated the farm, though. He had to do the plowing, had to do it by horses then."

Pyle, he noted, was an only child.

"He'd get out here in these fields behind the house and he'd get lonesome, you know. So he went off down to the University of Indiana—I don't know that he finished there—and got into the newspaper business. He'd travel around the country writing stories, just like you're doing.

"He'd put people's names in his columns. That's what the people liked, you know. He'd write where people could understand it. He was a very common man. His mother and dad were fine folks."

He pointed to a small car shed at the back of the house.

"His dad built that for him for his model T Ford," he said.

While Goforth went about feeding his cattle, I took photos of everything in sight, including several shots of him, one a close-up. He wished us a safe trip home before he left.

Carmen Hazen had been entertaining Linda and Erik while I was talking with Goforth. She declined sharply when I asked if I could take a photo.

"Oh, god, no," she said, attempting to smooth her windblown hair. "I look like holy hell today."

Before we left, she asked for our address in case she came across something interesting that I might be able to use. For several years afterward we received Christmas cards from her, the first including a snapshot of her holding her great grandchild.

We got one more glimpse of the Ernie Pyle monument as we headed east on U.S. 36 toward Indianapolis and home. In two days, we'd visited the homes of two great Americans, and I left feeling as if I'd just read an Ernie Pyle column.

THE BEST PLACE TO watch one of the greatest events in human history, I decided, was my living room in Randolph County in the company of Walter Cronkite on our black-and-white TV. This was Sunday afternoon, July 20, and Neil Armstrong and Edwin "Buzz" Aldrin were attempting to fulfill John F. Kennedy's promise to set humans on the moon before the end of this incredible decade. The landing craft had begun to descend and the tension was nearly heart stopping.

Viewers couldn't see what was happening, only hear the technical talk back and forth between Houston and the astronauts, as a depiction of a moon ship skimming the surface appeared on the TV screen. The tension was incredible, and in the midst of it, Erik, who would turn four in two weeks, asked if he could go play in the sand box.

"Son, men are about to land on the moon," I said. "Don't you want to stay and watch that?"

He reluctantly took his chin-in-hand cartoon-watching position on the carpet, close to the screen, a look of disappointment on his face. As seconds ticked by and the elevation readings lessened dramatically, I found myself on the floor, too, practically crawling toward the screen in high anxiety.

Then came those incredibly wondrous words from Neil Armstrong: "Houston, Tranquility Base here. The Eagle has landed."

I wanted to whoop and holler, but that didn't seem appropriate in my living room on a quiet Sunday afternoon.

Instead, I started laughing joyously.

"The Eagle has landed," I said. "The Eagle has landed. We're on the moon. Erik, we're on the moon!"

"Can I go play in the sand pile now?" he asked.

The astronauts had their own big sand pile to play in, but it would be hours before they did that. My buddy Darrell Hall and his wife Georgeanne came to watch it with us. It was almost midnight when the hatch opened and Armstrong began his climb down, but the picture on the TV screen was upside-down. Darrell and I immediately got in the floor in football center positions so we could look back through our legs and see it correctly. The picture had turned upright by the time Armstrong set his foot on the surface and pronounced his famous prepared line: "That's one small step for (a) man, one giant leap for mankind."

We were left saying such profound things as, "Boy, ain't that something!"

Shortly, Aldrin joined his commander on the surface. They erected a U.S. flag, and Armstrong began hopping around like the Abominable Snowman.

When we began to feel comfortable with their presence there, the jokes started.

"You got the key, Neil?"

"No, I don't have the key. I thought you had the key."

Not until early Monday afternoon did Armstrong and Aldrin blast away from the moon's surface. I still was in the living room watching. As soon as I knew they were back in orbit, I began writing my Tuesday column on a legal pad.

"Making history is all right," I wrote about the astronauts. "But when they make it so that guys like me—who don't have the brains, initiative or guts to make it—can sit in their living rooms and watch it happening, that's too much. It not only boggles the mind, it churns the stomach.

"Take just a few minutes ago, when those guys were getting ready to blast off from the moon. I was sitting in the living room with my stomach shriveled and knotted, hanging onto my chair as if I were in the backseat of the moon ship. If somebody had shouted boo, I'd have been hanging from the light fixture.

"And there was Walter Cronkite, calmly reassuring me, in his fatherly way, that everything was going fine, looking great. Man, you just don't go to the moon, walk around as if you were visiting a state park, and drive safely away.

"But they did."

CHARLES KURALT CAME TO Greensboro in October to be the featured speaker at an awards luncheon at the Hilton Hotel for a regional student art contest held by WFMY-TV. (Erik would be a winner in the photography division 13 years later, proud father notes.) WFMY was a CBS affiliate and Kuralt was a pleasing choice for family members and others attending the event. His often touching *On the Road* stories on the evening news, which had begun two years earlier, not only made him famous but beloved.

Chuck Whitehurst, the station's news and public relations director, arranged for me to have a private interview with Kuralt prior to the luncheon. A North Carolina native, Kuralt had been a history major at the University of North Carolina, where he worked on *The Daily Tar Heel* with Chuck Hauser and others I would come to know. In the spring of 1954, he was elected editor for his senior year and became so wrapped up in running the paper that he kept dropping courses and failed to get his degree. He was as warm and jovial in person as he appeared on TV. He knew I had won the Ernie Pyle Award. After offering his congratulations, he told me that award had gotten him his job at CBS. A news editor there sent him a complimentary note, he recalled.

"I wrote back and told him if he meant it, offer me a job. They did."

He started as a news writer for radio, and three years later became a TV correspondent. That got him sent to "all the Hell holes of Asia" and even the North Pole, he said, but never to London, Rome, or any posh spots.

"When a really good assignment comes along, like the presidential trip to Paris," he said, "they just send Harry Reasoner again."

My award hadn't brought results as rewarding as his, I noted.

"Don't worry," he said. "They'll come."

Kuralt began his speech by telling the audience that he felt a little irreverent coming to Edward R. Murrow's home county to talk about CBS News.

"It's sort of like talking theology at the Vatican," he said, "or maybe giving a sex education lecture beneath Juliet's balcony."

That got a big laugh, and he was off and rolling about CBS, his job, America, its amazing people and the bright future they promised. It got him a standing ovation. After the event ended, Kuralt had to sign a lot of autographs and pose for photos with many groups, including executives of the TV station, before heading downstairs for a press conference, which included high school journalists.

He propped himself on the edge of a table and a student asked the first question, which had been prepared by her journalism class. It was about Judge Clement Haynsworth's doomed nomination to the Supreme Court.

"Oh, good heavens," Kuralt said, "I really don't have an opinion on that. That's not my bag...."

Nothing but serious questions followed. The Vietnam War. Censorship. Other depressing matters. Then a female newspaper reporter from a nearby town asked a question about the press and the war that was so long and complicated neither Kuralt nor anybody else understood it, including, it seemed, herself. She tried to recover by asking what he thought about female TV reporters.

Kuralt grimaced at that question, too.

"I've never met a woman in TV who was very good, except for Pauline Frederick of NBC," he responded. "They tend to be show-offy. That's really going to make people mad, isn't it?"

"Why aren't there more female reporters at CBS?" the reporter asked, pressing her theme.

"Because of the wisdom of the management?" Kuralt said, his frustration about the line of questioning becoming apparent.

"Are they bad because they're women?" she persisted.

"Yeah..." Kuralt said slowly, giving her the gift of the answer she was digging for, "just ab-so-lute-ly awful."

She scribbled his response with an expression of smug satisfaction. She had the derogatory story she wanted.

The final question came from a student. "Have you considered going into politics?"

"Oh, no," Kuralt said, perhaps considering his previous responses, "I can't sell anything, especially myself. All I want to be is just a reporter."

That final line would be the headline for the column I wrote for the following day's edition. In that column I described Kuralt as "looking for all the world like my Uncle Ray. Hair slicked back over the bald spot. Double chin. Nice smile. Shorter than you'd think from seeing him on TV."

A week later, I went to the newsroom mail rack and pulled out a stack of letters. One had a return address of CBS News, New York, and scribbled above it in ink was "Uncle Ray Kuralt."

He wrote that he enjoyed the column and meeting me as well. He hoped we could keep in touch. We did keep in touch. I occasionally sent notes about subjects for his series. A couple of times we got together covering the same events, the National Hollerin' Contest in Spivey's Corner, and the International Whistlers Convention in Louisburg. It was at these that I got to know Kuralt's longtime cameraman and traveling companion Isadore Bleckman, known as Issy. Kuralt and I would come to have close mutual friends in North Carolina artist Bob Timberlake and Charlotte's beloved jazz pianist and composer Loonis McGlohon. I also came to know his brother, Wallace, who operated the Intimate Book Shop in Chapel Hill.

Kuralt surprised me with a heartening blurb for my book *Just Folks*, published in 1980. "Jerry Bledsoe is Carolina's Listener Laureate," he wrote. "Nobody beats him at listening to the human voice and to the human heart...."

A few times we got together for a beer when he happened to be passing through. I didn't get to see him after he gave up the *On the Road* series, but I tried to watch him as often as possible on the *Sunday Morning* show he hosted.

I was shocked and saddened by Kuralt's death from lupus in 1997 at 62. He had requested to be buried at the Old Chapel Hill Cemetery on the campus of the University of North Carolina. I attended his service at Memorial Hall with my friend and former co-columnist Jim Jenkins, who had become an editorial writer at *The News & Observer* in Raleigh. The service already had begun when *CBS Evening News* anchor Dan Rather hurried down the aisle with an assistant and took seats directly in front of us.

After the service ended and the assemblage rose for the family to depart, I heard loud sobbing. It was coming from Issy, as he was emerging into the aisle with the family. Suddenly Rather strode down the aisle. He grasped Issy in a tight embrace and held him as the sobbing subsided. That single moving moment changed the way I thought about Rather.

ONE SATURDAY THAT FALL, I had to go back to the office to finish my Sunday column because I had gone out the night before with fellow newshounds to enjoy a nip or two at Richard's City Club, where news folks and lawyers liked to gather. Unfortunately, I had stayed a bit longer than I anticipated, thus mandating my Saturday morning trip back to Greensboro. I was approaching the front door of the building when I heard strange sounds coming from the dumpster in a deep depression close by the entrance. I stepped back and saw the head of my friend Buck Paysour, the business editor, rise in the dumpster. He was a gentle and sweet man, rarely angry, but he was muttering something I couldn't understand.

"Buck!" I yelled. "What in hell are you doing in the dumpster?"

"That blankety-blank blankety-blank went through the newsroom early this morning wiping everything off everybody's desks and throwing it in the blankety-blank dumpster," he yelled.

For the record, it should be noted that the "blankety-blanks" were not his actual words.

Unfortunately, the blankety-blank he was referring to was our executive editor. When Chuck Hauser left to go to Norfolk, I had hoped that Irwin Smallwood would replace him, but that didn't happen. The managing editor of the afternoon paper got that position. He was far from being in the class of Hauser or Smallwood, and time would prove that he never should have been an editor at all. I tried to steer clear of him, but hadn't fully succeeded.

When U.S. Senator Sam Erwin came to speak at a dinner at Sedgefield Country Club, I arranged a private interview after his talk. The staff member who worked it out said I could have 20 minutes. Senator Sam, who would become internationally famous a few years hence at the Watergate hearings, was a great storyteller. I just was beginning to get him warmed up in that direction, hoping that he might extend the time I was allotted, when the door to the room burst open. Through it came my executive editor, a huge smile on his face, glad-handing, brown-nosing, telling the senator what a great speech he had made and how wonderful it was to have him in Greensboro, as if he were the mayor or the head of the Chamber of Commerce. Others, seeing the open door and what appeared to be a reception, flooded in, ending my interview and forcing the staff member to rescue Erwin and get him to his car. So much for that column.

Buck was a great practical joker, but I'd never seen him go quite to this extent to pull one.

"You're kidding me, right?"

"Hell, no!"

"My desk, too?"

"Yours and everybody else's."

That had to be a heck of a job for that blankety-blank considering all the stuff that was piled on my desk and Jim McAllister's. I rushed upstairs and was stunned by all the cleared desktops.

Apparently, at some earlier point this blankety-blank had issued a directive that every desk had to be left clear and immaculate when the occupant left at the end of the day. Only the telephone would be allowed, and it had to be in a certain spot. That directive obviously had been ignored, and this outrageous tantrum was his means of directing attention to it.

I was in a fury. Gone were the pages of the column I was writing, as well as all my notes and research materials, not to mention a hoard of other stuff, including the buckeye that Mrs. Sandburg had given me. I called Smallwood, told him what had happened and that I was not climbing into a dumpster, wouldn't have a column for Sunday and maybe not for days to come because my material was gone. He hurried to the office to begin attempting to repair the damage.

The problems that I foresaw were far greater than the loss of material. It suddenly became apparent that I was facing a future with another Blubberbutt, an anal-retentive incompetent, having control of me and my work. I would come to refer to this nincompoop as Bug Eyes, due to his protruding eyes and lack of chin.

I didn't return to the office for a few days out of fear that I might snap and attempt to throw Bug Eyes into the dumpster, leaving me jobless and perhaps in jail. Smallwood did his best to smooth things over and worked hard in the future to protect me. I did have one advantage with Bug Eyes, though, that I didn't have with Blubberbutt. I was free to leave at any time, and eventually Bug Eyes would cause me to do just that.

NOT LONG AFTER I started working in Kannapolis, I became enraptured by the "new journalism" that was flowing out of New York in magazines such as *Esquire*, which was edited by Harold Hayes, a Baptist preacher's son from North Carolina, and *Harper's*, edited by Mississippian Willie Morris, who was a friend of *Daily News* editorial page editor Ed Yoder (the two had been Rhodes Scholars together). I couldn't wait for the next narrative piece by Tom Wolfe, Gay Talese, Gary Wills, Rex Reed, Dan Wakefield, Larry L. King, Marshall Frady, and later Nora Ephron and others. I devoured them all, wishing I could be as good as they were.

The October, 1966, issue of *Esquire* really caught my attention. The black cover had only a single quote in big white letters, "Oh my God—we hit a little girl." At the bottom of the page in smaller white letters was: "The true story of M Company. From Fort Dix to Vietnam." I was surprised to see that it had been written by John Sack.

Sack had been drafted during the Korean War, and covered its closing months as a PFC correspondent for PIO and *Stars & Stripes*. When the war ended, he was reassigned to the 1st RB&L Battalion headquarters (predecessor of B&VA) in Tokyo as a psychological warfare writer, the same job I'd hold eight years later. My former editor in Tokyo, Bernard Dekle, got to know him and held him in high regard. He gave me a copy of a humorous book Sack had written about his time in the Army, *From Here to Shimbashi*, which came out in 1955, and was compared to Mac Hyman's bestseller *No Time for Sergeants*.

Sack's piece may be the longest that ever appeared in *Esquire* and was an incredible job of reporting and writing. It pulled readers right into M Company as it was training at Fort Dix to go to Vietnam. They got to know some of its soldiers, experience their feelings as they headed to war, and see how combat dehumanized them.

From the time I first read *Esquire*, I wanted to write for it, see my name in it. Reading such an amazing cover story written by somebody who had been a psywar writer in Tokyo and worked with Deke, just as I had done, both of us PFCs, made me wonder if I couldn't finagle my way into *Esquire*, too, although I didn't have a clue how to go about it. Neither did I have the credentials and connections that Sack had, although I wasn't aware of that wide variance at the time. Even before he was drafted, I later would learn, Sack had a degree from Harvard, where he had served as editor of both *The Harvard Crimson* and *The Harvard Lampoon*, already had written two books, and was turning out pieces for *New Yorker* and other magazines.

Nonetheless, I began trying to come up with a subject that might interest *Esquire*. By the summer of 1969, I thought I might have found it.

That was Charley Pride, a true phenomenon, a black sharecropper's son from Sledge, Mississippi, who wanted to be a professional baseball player, but became a country music singer who sounded a hell of a lot like Hank Williams, the ultimate country music singer. The national media image of country music fans was lower to middle-class white Southerners, so-called rednecks, who therefore had to be racists. Yet they loved Charley Pride, listened to him on country stations, bought his records, flocked to his concerts. Somehow that image didn't seem to fit. I wanted to find out if it did, and how and why it had happened.

I learned from my friend Tom Miller that Pride was coming to Greensboro for the big Country Shindig at the coliseum in October. Miller was a half-crazed, hilarious, often drunk local country music DJ, called the Country Colonel when he served as Emcee for country music shows at the coliseum. He was a friend of the promoter, Keith Fowler, and gave me his number. I called and told Fowler I wanted to spend some time with Pride while he was in Greensboro so I could write a piece to submit to *Esquire*.

He called back the following day and said it was fine with Charley, who was to be the star of the show, which also would feature Tex Ritter; Billy Walker and the Tennessee Walkers; and Porter Wagoner and the Wagonmasters, with his female partner for the past two years, Dolly Parton. I was waiting with Fowler at the Greensboro airport when Pride arrived on a chartered jet. He bounded down the steps from the plane, and Fowler introduced me.

"Oh, you're the guy from *Esquire*," Pride said.

"Well, uh…" I said.

"Yeah, he's going to be writing the story," Fowler interjected.

I spent the rest of the day with Pride, interviewing him in depth. He was friendly, open, forthright, a nice guy, a genuine lover of country music, not a gimmick.

He seemed to love and respect his fans as much as they cared for him. He said he grew up like every country singer, listening to the music and loving it from childhood.

"I came up the same as Hank Williams, Jim Reeves, Johnny Cash, and all the rest," he said. "There's only one difference: I have a permanent tan."

The show was sold out, more than 7,000 people present. Tex Ritter opened, followed by Porter and Dolly with her ample bosom. I went out front to watch Dolly perform.

"Lord," I heard one good ol' boy say to his buddy, "I wonder what she can do besides sing?"

"I hear she can sit up with help," he said.

When Billy Walker came on, I went back to the dressing room where Pride was getting ready for his performance. He was wearing a green wrinkle-proof suit and glittering black patent leather shoes when he stepped out to join me. We were standing outside another dressing room door chatting when that door swung open as a woman was leaving. She paused when somebody in the room said something to her, leaving the door open. That person was Dolly and she was wearing only her bra and panties, minus her blonde wig. Seeing us, she suddenly squealed, "Charr-leee, you're not supposed to be standing there!" and rushed to slam the door.

Pride laughed. I, for one, was glad he was standing there, and even happier that I was standing with him.

It was 10:45 before Pride went on and the crowd went wild. He was supposed to perform for only 30 minutes including encores, but the crowd wouldn't let him stop. It was almost midnight before he was able to make it off the stage.

I spent weeks working on the piece I intended to send to *Esquire* on nothing more than hope. I had become convinced that the Charley Pride phenomenon—his audience's love and admiration for him, and his for them—was real and thought it might be an indication of a change in racial attitudes and relations, particularly in the South.

The piece was 26 double-spaced pages long when I finished. I put it in a *Daily News* manila envelope and inserted a folded envelope with return address and postage. In the past I had sent unsolicited articles to other, far lesser magazines, only to have them come back with printed rejection slips. I expected the same for this one. But that wouldn't be the case.

In just a couple of weeks, the return envelope I had enclosed came back. But there was no standard rejection slip inside. Instead I found a letter from an *Esquire* editor, Bob Sherrill. He said that he had enjoyed the piece and thought it was well written, but Charley Pride wasn't an appropriate subject for *Esquire*. He went on to explain why but I later misplaced the letter and those details escaped me.

As dejected as I was about the rejection, I was heartened that an editor had taken notice of it. He now knew my name and I knew his. All I needed to do was find another subject that fit his view of appropriateness and send the piece directly to him. But what could that be?

As oddly as things sometimes turn out, all the time that I was working on my Charley Pride piece, I had another subject underhand that might well have been acceptable to *Esquire*, although that never crossed my mind. I soon was to discover, however, that it was appealing to *Harper's*, which sent one of its finest writers to cover it.

FRED KOURY WAS ONE of my favorite people in Greensboro. He owned the Plantation Supper Club on High Point Road. In the '50s, the Plantation had been proclaimed to be the best and most beautiful supper club in the South, and one of the top 10 in the nation. People came to the Plantation from several nearby states, especially when the big bands were playing—Tommy and Jimmy Dorsey, Guy Lombardo, Harry James, Les Brown and others.

Koury had a mail-order hosiery business when World War II began. Shortly after the United States entered the war, the Army built a base to train new recruits in northeast Greensboro, just a short distance from downtown. In 1944, that base became the Overseas Replacement Depot, called ORD, where soldiers came to be dispatched to battlefronts. Koury realized those soldiers needed entertainment. He and partners opened a club in a building at the fairgrounds where the Coliseum later would be built. It offered green beer and bad live music for rowdy crowds but it was a big hit.

The profits made Koury want to build a classier club. He found an empty furniture store farther out High Point Road and opened the Plantation. After two fires, he built an even bigger and fancier club with plush furnishings, a stage, a large dance floor, and began bringing in big bands and top acts.

Andy Williams made his first solo night club appearance at the Plantation. Doris Day and the Clooney Sisters performed on that stage. Andy Griffith started his comedy career there. Jayne Mansfield was a sensation with her delightful nightclub act and 43-inch bust line. Fred said he never could determine which was the main attraction.

People dressed in their very best when they went to the Plantation, and so many came from other cities and states that Koury built a motel next to the club to accommodate them.

By the late '60s the Plantation had fallen into decline, which turned out to be a benefit for me. The big acts were performing in coliseums then and Koury no longer could afford their high fees. Tastes in music and dance also had changed. Koury was trying a lot of things to keep the club going, including bringing in one-time big names who were not so hot anymore, but were good column subjects for me.

In August, 1969, he brought in rocker Jerry Lee Lewis, whose fortunes had fallen so far that he was performing country. Not only was he crabby and insulting with customers, he threatened me with a Jack Daniels bottle which he nearly had emptied while I was interviewing him. For some reason he took offense to my bringing up his marriage to his 13-year-old cousin.

In November, Koury called to tell me that he was bringing back Brother Dave Gardner who once had been a nationally hot comedian and had packed the Plantation in earlier years.

Gardner had been born into a Baptist family in Jackson, Tennessee, and spent a semester in seminary before becoming a drummer and singer. Chet Atkins discovered him and gave him a hit record, "White Silver Sands," in 1957, which got him a spot on *The Tonight Show* with Jack Paar.

Gardner's quick wit and quirky brain convinced Paar to give him a shot at a comedy routine, and he became a regular on the show, also appearing on *The Ed Sullivan Show*. It was Paar who started calling him Brother Dave because of his stories about southern preachers. The TV appearances led to a series of top-selling comedy albums in the early '60s. Brother Dave and his wife Mildred—Miss Millie, as he called her—were living high. They had a 23-room mansion in Los Angeles, a yacht, and two Cadillacs.

Unfortunately, Brother Dave had become involved in a close friendship that would bring about his downfall. That friend was H.L. Hunt, a Dallas oil tycoon and one of the richest men on Earth. Hunt was a radical right-winger, strongly opposed to President John F. Kennedy. He also had connections to Lyndon Baines Johnson. Specious tales attempted to connect Hunt to JFK's assassination. Hunt also believed that federal income tax was a violation of the constitution and convinced Brother Dave of that.

Brother Dave quit paying taxes. The consequences would have been expected by a normal person. But not only had Brother Dave never been normal, he had become out of touch with reality. In 1966, Brother Dave, Miss Millie and their daughter were seriously injured when a private jet in which they were flying crashed on takeoff in Biloxi, Mississippi. During their year-long recovery, Brother Dave and Miss Millie became addicted to prescription drugs. But those weren't the only drugs Brother Dave was using.

By the time I met him, Brother Dave had fallen on hard times indeed. The IRS had seized his mansion and yacht, and was attempting to take any income. H.L. Hunt apparently had not come to his aid. Brother Dave, who was only 43 at the time, was depending on owners of Southern clubs where he once had appeared to help him try to make a comeback.

Although Brother Dave hadn't drawn large audiences, Koury let him and Miss Millie live temporarily in a small cottage behind the club next to the motel while their son scoured the region for new gigs. I spent an afternoon there with them and came away thinking that both were completely looney, still dedicated to H.L. Hunt, filled with conspiracy theories and convinced that assassins were after them.

While I was talking with them, Brother Dave lit one joint after another and brought up the subject of another drug—LSD. He'd used it more than 150 times, he told me, and had accompanied the LSD guru Timothy Leary on his first 23 trips.

I had met Leary a couple of months earlier when he spoke at Wait Chapel at Wake Forest University in Winston-Salem, where he was being paid a hefty fee. He told students that the only purpose of life was the religious quest, and he believed that consciousness-altering drugs would be the religion of the future. He didn't recommend that students use LSD but implied that to him LSD was God. I thought he was a con artist, I told Brother Dave, little different from TV evangelists.

Brother Dave, who had listened intently to this, nodded.

"I know Tim Leary very well," he said.

He told me that he thought LSD was dangerous unless a person was prepared for the trip, but he didn't dispute Leary's contention that it might be a connection to God.

"Let me put a thought on you," he said. "I got under the influence of that jive. I was just sitting around talking to myself. I said, 'Well this stuff ain't much.' Then I said, 'Yeah, it is, too.' Sometimes you have to talk to yourself, you know, just 'cause you like to talk to somebody that's got some sense. Here was my thought: Now who is God responsible to? Now you can play with that."

Later, I took Brother Dave and Miss Millie to Guilford College, a liberal Quaker school, so he could speak to a religion class taught by Dr. J. Floyd Moore, whom I'd gotten to know and liked. Miss Millie rode in the passenger seat of my Mustang, while Brother Dave lay in the backseat so he couldn't be an assassin's target, puffing a joint all the way, the smoke roiling around my head.

He wasn't able to connect with the students.

"I'm white trash," he told them, "so I ain't got no heritage. It ain't easy being Southern and white. Talk about toting a cross."

I felt sorry for Brother Dave and Miss Millie and never wrote anything about their looniness or troubles. But a few weeks after they finally left Koury's cottage for a gig at the Pecan Grove Supper Club near Charlotte, Larry L. King, a Texas writer I admired and later would get to know, showed up to smoke pot with Brother Dave (something I didn't do as an affirmed non-smoker) and reveal in *Harper's* all the sad details of his situation, including Klansmen standing guard against assassins, something that didn't happen in Greensboro to my knowledge.

A few months after I learned about this, while I still was kicking myself for failing to see a story that *Harper's* would give great attention, I was sitting at my desk one morning, going through the mail, struggling to come up with a column idea, when the phone rang. I answered and heard, "This is Bob Sherrill at *Esquire*."

"Oh, hey," I said, my senses sharpening.

"I'm just calling to tell you that *Esquire* is going to be running a story about Charley Pride," he said. "I argued against it until I was blue in the face, but they're going to do it anyway. I told them that I had a much better story several months ago but that didn't matter. I just wanted to let you know what's happening so you wouldn't think that we had stolen your idea and got somebody else to write it."

"Well, I appreciate that," I said.

I wondered how he had come to read my article in the first place and asked about it.

He was chatting one morning with the slush-pile editor, he told me, when a mailbag was dumped upon her desk. He noticed a manila envelope with *The Greensboro Daily News* return address on it, picked it up and took it back to his desk. He was from North Carolina, born in the mountains near Asheville, had gone to Wake Forest College, where he became a friend of Harold Hayes. Later, he worked on the copy desk at the *Daily News*. Those connections had led him to pick up the envelope out of curiosity.

I was marveling at how all of these coincidences had come together at that precise moment, when Sherrill stunned me with a question.

"Would you be interested in doing some other stuff for *Esquire*?"

I couldn't believe what I was hearing.

"Well, uh, yes," I said.

"There's a situation I've been following down in Alabama," he told me.

That weekend I was on my way to Pell City, Alabama, to deal with Black Muslims, Baptist preachers, the Klan, suspicious sheriff's deputies, and two feuding brothers.

A new decade was dawning, and my life was taking a different direction. Within two years, not only would I be receiving assignments from *Esquire*, but from *New York* and *Rolling Stone* magazines as well. This would prompt *Esquire* to make me a contributing editor and allow me to see my name on the masthead alongside those of Tom Wolfe, Gay Talese, John Berendt, Nora Ephron and others I envied. Agents and book publishers would come calling too. I would write six books before one called *Bitter Blood* hit number one on *The New York Times* bestseller list and turned me into a crime writer for a decade. But that's a story for another time.

www.ingramcontent.com/pod-product-compliance
Lightning Source LLC
Chambersburg PA
CBHW030433010526
44118CB00011B/616